PUBLIC CITIZENS

OTHER BOOKS BY PAUL SABIN

The Bet:
Paul Ehrlich, Julian Simon, and Our Gamble
over Earth's Future

Crude Politics:
The California Oil Market, 1900-1940

PUBLIC CITIZENS

*The Attack on Big Government and
the Remaking of American Liberalism*

PAUL SABIN

W. W. NORTON & COMPANY
Independent Publishers Since 1923

For information about permission to reproduce selections from
this book, write to Permissions, W. W. Norton & Company, Inc.,
500 Fifth Avenue, New York, NY 10110

For information about special discounts for bulk purchases, please contact
W. W. Norton Special Sales at specialsales@wwnorton.com or 800-233-4830

Manufacturing by Lakeside Book Company
Book design by Lovedog Studio
Production manager: Lauren Abbate

Library of Congress Cataloging-in-Publication Data

Names: Sabin, Paul, 1970– author.
Title: Public citizens : the attack on big government and the remaking of
    American liberalism / Paul Sabin.
Description: First edition. | New York, N.Y. : W. W. Norton & Company,
    [2021] | Includes bibliographical references and index.
Identifiers: LCCN 2021007966 | ISBN 9780393634044 (hardcover) |
    ISBN 9780393634051 (epub)
Subjects: LCSH: Liberalism—United States—History—20th century. |
    Bureaucracy—United States—History—20th century. | Public interest
    groups—United States—History—20th century. | Pressure groups—
    United States—History—20th century. | United States—Politics and
    government—1945–1989.
Classification: LCC JC574.2.U6 S24 2021 | DDC 320.5/13097309046—dc23
LC record available at https://lccn.loc.gov/2021007966

ISBN 978-1-324-08916-2 pbk.

W. W. Norton & Company, Inc., 500 Fifth Avenue, New York, N.Y. 10110
www.wwnorton.com

W. W. Norton & Company Ltd., 15 Carlisle Street, London W1D 3BS

10 9 8 7 6 5 4 3 2 1

For Eli and Simon, who are charting their own paths

Contents

Part III
"GOVERNMENT IS THE PROBLEM"

Introduction

IN THE FALL OF 1965, A THIRTY-ONE-YEAR-OLD
Harvard Law School graduate named Ralph Nader published a blistering attack on the poor safety record of the American automobile.
Tens of thousands of Americans were dying needlessly every year on
the nation's highways, Nader wrote in his first book, *Unsafe at Any
Speed*. The cause? The federal government's failure to force American
automakers to build safer cars. In the outcry that followed, Nader's
book became a bestseller, and he became a national celebrity. Nader
also won a landmark regulatory victory: just one year after his book
was published, Congress passed the Traffic Safety Act and the Highway Safety Act, wresting power away from industry to create a new
and independent Highway Safety Bureau.

In a testament to Nader's soaring public profile, the *New York Times*
published side-by-side, full-length public statements from Nader and
President Lyndon Johnson on the new safety laws. Both men praised
the legislation. Yet by placing Nader on an equal footing with the
president, the *Times* invited a question: How did a young muckraker
such as Nader fit into the big-government world of 1960s liberalism?
Was Nader a supporter of government, an antagonist, or something
in between? Nader's savage indictment of the government's collusion
with big business and its failure to protect the public had made the case
for the new legislation. In light of Nader's critique, President Johnson's

moral authority vouching for the safety laws seemed insufficient for the *Times*. In search of the most credible judge, the newspaper turned to Nader. It was a vivid example of how Nader was becoming the activist who would force liberals to rethink their trusting embrace of federal regulatory agencies.[1]

✦

WHEN MOST AMERICANS HEAR the name Ralph Nader today, they tend to think of his divisive role in the 2000 election. Nader ran for president on the Green Party ticket that year and contributed—a lot or a little, depending on whom you ask—to tipping the election to Republican George W. Bush. In the November election that year, Vice President Al Gore won the national popular vote but lost the electoral college with a razor-thin defeat by just hundreds of contested votes in the crucial state of Florida. Nader had campaigned actively in Florida, where he received more than ninety-seven thousand votes.

But decades earlier, Ralph Nader was key to a much larger and more complex attack on traditional liberalism, one that has largely been forgotten, and that helps explain much more than his quixotic campaign. Beginning in the 1960s and through the end of the 1970s, Nader and other public interest advocates, including many in the burgeoning environmental movement, crusaded against what they saw as a misguided and often corrupted federal government. They targeted for reform the cozy post–World War II alliance between government, business, and labor. In the process, Nader and his allies changed how American public policy is made, while raising many still unresolved questions. Is government the solution to, or an important cause of, societal problems? How do we balance collective action and the exercise of institutional power with individual needs and citizen participation? In our present time of significant antigovernment sentiment, with a regular onslaught of attacks on the regulatory state from the conservative political right, it's important to study more closely the ways that Nader and his allies contributed—from the left—to the crucial political shift in attitudes toward government during the 1960s and 1970s. It's also worth revisiting these critiques of government as the country debates renewed appeals for increased federal investment and regulation, harking back to the New Deal, to address the pressing challenges of climate change, economic inequality, and lack of opportunity.

The heyday of Nader's influence coincided with the fifteen years during which the United States turned from Great Society liberalism to Ronald Reagan's conservative revolution. In the mid-1960s, Lyndon Johnson was at the height of his power, laying the foundation for Medicare and Medicaid and for civil and voting rights. During that period stretching from Johnson to Reagan, the United States established an extensive new regulatory regime to protect health, safety, and the environment. During those same years, Nader and other advocates created a robust nonprofit sector to protect a "public interest" that the government, they argued, did not reliably serve. Under pressure from both the left and the right, the traditional liberal establishment fell into disarray. By 1980, the Reagan Revolution was whipping the country in a different direction, touting so-called free markets and questioning whether the government had any productive role to play. Reagan declared the end of the liberal state and set his sights on curtailing the role of the federal government.

In the decades following Reagan's election, American politics have grown ever more starkly polarized along partisan lines around the role of government in American life. Popular narratives emphasize the standoff between left and right: conservative critics of "big government" clashing with the federal government's liberal defenders. On environmental policy, a bitter stalemate ensued after 1980. Conservatives sought to cut environmental enforcement and limit federal regulation. Liberals struggled to protect the foundational environmental laws of the 1970s, including laws protecting clean air and clean water. During these recent decades of strife, federal environmental protections largely endured against conservative attack. At the same time, relatively little new environmental legislation passed through Congress. Notable exceptions include clean air legislation in 1990 and a 2016 chemical safety bill.

As this partisan conflict over governance has deepened, Nader and the broader left-wing critique of government—so vital to 1970s political reforms and environmental legislation—have slipped from historical accounts. We have lost touch with how the struggles of the late 1960s and 1970s destabilized the old framework for business and government, predating many conservative attacks, yet failed to provide a coherent and politically viable replacement. Historians of conservatism have recently portrayed the political battles of the 1970s in terms of a clash between proregulation liberals and antigovernment, market-oriented businessmen, suburbanites, and religious conservatives. Conservative antigovernment sentiment, according to this interpretation, culminated in Ronald Reagan's famous 1981 declaration that "government is not the solution to our problem; government is the problem." In this historical narrative, the environmental, health, and safety regulation of the early 1970s fits easily into modern liberalism. The environmental movement, with its wave of 1970s legislative victories, represents a final extension of the "modern activist state," which conservatives and Reaganism rejected.[2]

These interpretations fail to explain why the New Deal regulatory state became so vulnerable to conservative critique, what part liberals and the left played in its demise, and why liberals struggled to create a coherent alternative to market-oriented conservatism. My goal in this book is to address this gap by mapping the more complex and bipartisan origins of American assaults on government power. During this era, *how* did government go from being the solution for society's ills to being the cause of its problems? Understanding why and how public confidence in government declined requires a closer analysis of the rise of citizen activists like Nader and the nonprofit sector as an *alternative* to government. Undermining government's role surely was not the intent of the new watchdog organizations that Nader and other critics established. They believed passionately in collective, societal action. They focused their energy on government reform because they believed that laws and regulation were essential to creating a good society. Yet the political right ran with their critique, even if that was never their desire or intention.

By tying the public interest movement so closely to traditional liberalism, historians have obscured tensions within liberalism and the political left around post–World War II economic development strategies. Nader and other critics challenged traditional liberalism and its emphasis on federal agency discretion and its ambitious deployments of technology, private investment, and public infrastructure. The attack on federal agencies, usually credited to the political right, came from across the political spectrum and was an important factor in the fragmentation of the Democratic Party after 1968. The history of these attacks on government policies shows how the left grew suspicious of the grand projects, social engineering, and progrowth policies of the postwar period. "A great problem of contemporary life," Nader explained in his 1965 book on automobile safety, was "how to control the power of economic interests which ignore the harmful effects of their applied science and technology." Nader and other prominent critics, including Rachel Carson, author of the legendary book *Silent Spring*, questioned government-led efforts to deploy science and engineering, and disputed the legitimacy and trustworthiness of agency decision-making.[3]

The public interest movement flourished on the idea that *flawed* government failed to meet society's needs. "There is administrative arrogance at every level," the lawyer Frederick Sutherland, of the Los Angeles–based Center for Law in the Public Interest, explained in 1975. Government agencies "need to have their butts kicked once in a while." David Zwick, one of Nader's young associates, captured their complex attitude toward government in his 1971 testimony on water pollution legislation. Zwick declared, "We need laws which are essentially 'government-proof.'" Left to its own devices, Sutherland, Zwick, and other activists argued, government would not serve the public interest, because of both bureaucratic ineffectiveness and industry influence.[4]

Public interest advocates and government agencies differed in how they understood the public interest. With lawsuits, investigations, and lobbying, the environmental movement disrupted plans for new infrastructure and technology, from the supersonic transport plane to DDT and the Trans-Alaska pipeline. The public interest movement's lawsuits targeted infrastructure triumphs celebrated by many post–World War II liberal leaders: dams, power plants, highways, airports, and urban redevelopment. In the process of "kicking butt," Nader and the public interest movement framed a new conceptual challenge, particularly for liberals: How could they reconcile their long-standing critique of market failures with their new understanding of the limits and pitfalls of government power? The post–New Deal partnership between business, labor, and government became increasingly untenable in the face of savage attacks by Nader and other liberal activists. Their assault on this power structure helped to break apart the New Deal coalition that supported—and relied on—a strong and active federal government, and made it harder for the government to do big things.

For believers in traditional New Deal liberalism, Nader and his fellow activists helped destroy a political economic system that served the working class. According to this view, a dominant Democratic Party, robust labor unions, and empowered government agencies delivered a broadly shared prosperity in the postwar years. Nader's attack on the failings of all three of these institutions "undermined popular support for social democratic solutions" and helped fuel a corrosive antigovernment legacy. This school of thought downgrades Nader's emphasis on health, safety, and the environment, and his demands for transparency and accountability, as a distraction from more fundamental economic concerns, such as wages and growth and the need for housing and transportation. But it's a nostalgic perspective on pre-1970s liberalism, which does not adequately address the profound problems inherent in the liberal establishment's embrace of applied science and technology. The tight alliances between industry, labor, and government questioned by Nader and his allies were deeply problematic. The government, often in partnership with industry and labor, *was* testing nuclear weapons in the atmosphere, spraying millions of tons of pesticides across the land, and plowing highways through urban neighborhoods. The government *was* allowing strip mines to ravage the Appalachian Mountains and leaving coal miners to suffer from black lung disease with little compensation. Government policies *were* permitting oil refineries to freely dump toxic emissions into low-income communities of color, and letting oil spills pollute the nation's waterways and coasts. The enduring failure of 1970s liberalism was not that liberals failed to blindly defend traditional New Deal institutions and political coalitions, but rather that liberals failed to adapt and respond effectively to their own substantive critique of the ways that the postwar administrative state threatened nature, community, and individual well-being.[5]

The public interest critique by Nader and his allies highlights a tension in the liberal approach to governance that remains unresolved to this day. It was as if liberals took a bicycle apart to fix it but never quite figured out how to get it running properly again. Every Democratic president since Lyndon Johnson has struggled to balance support for public action with an increasingly sophisticated awareness of the limitations and flaws of government. Each has attempted to pair "reinventing" or "reforming" government with an ambitious agenda to expand the federal government's commitment to the health and welfare of American citizens. Under Presidents Carter, Clinton, and Obama, each administration in its own way embraced this complex view of government, yet struggled to "sell" it politically to the nation. Often they especially found it difficult to persuade the very liberal critics of government who had helped lay the groundwork for this more complex and critical view of government. These critics continued to denounce the failures of government and the insanity of various bureaucratic practices and proposals, but they also resisted the reforms, including more cost-effective approaches to regulation and public administration, that liberal policy makers sought to institute to improve agency performance and build trust in the government.

Revisiting an earlier time, when liberals attacked the government and established citizen advocacy groups to watch over bureaucratic agencies and counter corporate power, helps clarify America's fraught relationship with government. New Deal big-government liberalism contained within it the seeds of its own decline. It fell apart not just because of the rise of the right, but rather because of broad opposition from the left, the right, and even the liberal mainstream itself. To imagine new, pragmatic governing strategies, it's necessary to fully grasp government's strengths and weaknesses, rather than see only a demonized conservative or idealized liberal past.

Part I

"A GREAT POWER WITH NO CHALLENGERS"

Chapter One

The Postwar Partnership of Business, Labor, and Government

"LET THE PUBLIC SERVICE BE A PROUD AND LIVELY career," President John F. Kennedy proclaimed in his January 1961 message to Congress. As eager young Democrats rushed to fill the offices of the nation's executive agencies, Kennedy equated government with the public interest. Kennedy declared, "And let every man and woman who works in any area of our national government, in any branch, at any level, be able to say with pride and with honor in future years: 'I served the United States government in that hour of our nation's need.'"[1]

Kennedy's celebration of public service reflected the federal government's role in shaping the broadly shared prosperity of the post–World War II period. The New Deal and the war had created a kind of managed capitalism in the United States that generated rising wages and strong economic growth. Historians sometimes call this period of time the "New Deal Order" after the productive partnership between government, business, and labor established during the 1930s. In the decades that followed, the federal government, working closely with large business and labor organizations, greatly expanded its regulation of the national economy and individual industries, as well as its development of natural resources and public infrastructure projects.[2]

The New Deal and its aftermath represented a high point in Americans' faith in government's capacity to shape society and the economy. The New Deal, of course, was not a single unified endeavor, and historians have highlighted the era's complexities and its contested and inequitable outcomes. Yet for many liberals in the 1930s, confidence in government as a tool for social reform inspired them to go to Washington, where they hoped to use specialized federal agencies to address societal problems. For President Franklin D. Roosevelt, the government stood as the sole guarantor of democracy and freedom against corporate power and a "new industrial dictatorship." Against "economic tyranny," Roosevelt declared in his 1936 speech to the Democratic National Convention, "the American citizen could appeal only to the organized power of government." The government's efforts to create employment and turn around the economy were nothing less than a "war for the survival of democracy." FDR rewove the individualistic myth of the American frontier into a story about "frontiersmen" who "naturally reached out to government." White settlers in the Northwest Territories, Roosevelt said in a 1938 address in Marietta, Ohio, "looked on government not as a thing apart—as a power over our people. They regarded it as a power of the people, as a democratic expression of organized self-help." So, too, should Americans in the 1930s, Roosevelt argued. "Let us not be afraid to help each other," he said. "Let us never forget that government is ourselves and not an alien power over us."[3]

Belief in government's ability to represent the public interest underlay many of the period's economy-wide planning efforts and its large-scale public works. The United States, of course, rejected the kind of five-year plans undertaken by the Soviet Union. But many Americans were attracted to the idea that experts could wield government power to structure the economy and society as a whole. The lawyer and scholar James M. Landis embodied this 1930s celebration of administrative power in the public interest. Landis served on both the Federal Trade Commission and the Securities and Exchange Commission, before becoming dean of Harvard Law School. In his landmark 1938 book *The Administrative Process*, Landis dismissed judicial review and congressional legislation as insufficient tools for addressing "modern problems." Technical experts in the executive branch also had a critical role to play. Landis spoke for a generation of federal institution builders when he contrasted the "overheated atmosphere of litigation" with the "calm of scientific inquiry" represented by expert-led agencies. Separated from politics, and able to act effectively and impartially, federal agencies, Landis believed, could best serve the public interest. Landis's views, widely shared among New Deal regulators, reflected an enduring Progressive Era belief in scientific expertise. His enthusiasm for executive agencies also expressed liberal frustration with conservative courts that blocked workers' rights legislation and New Deal economic controls.[4]

The Tennessee Valley Authority (TVA) perhaps best symbolized the New Deal faith in federal administrative agencies and the government's embrace of grand schemes to encourage economic development by controlling nature. TVA's broad mandate for regional improvement sought to benefit the people of seven states. The agency's leaders were "dreamers with shovels in their hands," wrote TVA chairman David Lilienthal in *TVA: Democracy on the March*, a triumphant 1944 account of the agency that he headed. Their dreams were plans made by experts to use federal money to physically transform the region. TVA controlled the Tennessee River system and "put [it] to work" for the people. "What God had made one," Lilienthal said of the river valley, "man was to develop as one," through coordinated planning. While TVA's specific regional planning model was never replicated around the country, in the post–World War II period the agency showed the possibilities for government planning and transformative development projects, at home and abroad. Writing in 1950, the historian and leading liberal Henry Steele Commager celebrated TVA as "the greatest peacetime achievement of twentieth-century America." TVA, Commager said, "triumphantly allied science and politics . . . in an integrated and coordinated plan for the whole life of the region." In celebrating TVA, Commager portrayed government action as superior to private initiative. The agency, Commager wrote, showed that "pub-

Hydroelectric turbines at Wilson Dam in Alabama in the 1930s. The Tennessee Valley Authority brought hydroelectric power and flood control to the American South, demonstrating the transformative possibilities of government planning and intervention. U.S. National Archives and Records Administration.

lic intelligence can operate most effectively through government and that government can be more efficient than business." Sweeping public development projects occurred not just at the federal level, but also through state and local governments. In New York, for example, urban developer Robert Moses followed this agency-led development model to dramatically alter the region's infrastructure. Moses used independent public authorities, federal funding, and other bureaucratic levers to marshal the necessary resources.[5]

✦

To be sure, not everyone enthused, as Commager did, over this expansion of government activity. Roosevelt's conservative opponents in the 1930s denounced the New Deal program as a form of social-ism. In the postwar period, many business leaders continued to criti-cize government action and the growing power of labor unions. One fear about the expansion of executive power was that agencies would act in arbitrary and capricious ways, and that regulated entities, par-ticularly companies, would have no recourse or ability to appeal. The 1946 Administrative Procedure Act sought to protect the ability of regulated entities to participate in administrative proceedings. Senator Pat McCarran, a Nevada Republican, called the act "a bill of rights" for those Americans "whose affairs are controlled or regulated in one way or another by agencies of the Federal Government." Among its provisions, the Administrative Procedure Act mandated that agencies inform the public about their operations; required public participation in agency rule-making; set uniform standards for rule-making and adjudication; and established procedures for judicial review.[6]

The Administrative Procedure Act's enumeration of rights also served as a kind of truce in the struggle over the legitimacy of federal regulation. According to one historian's account of the bill's passage, the measure represented a "cease-fire agreement of exhausted combatants in the battle for control of administrative agencies." Yet the cease-fire was only between private power (rep-resented by corporations) and public power (embodied by the agen-cies). The Administrative Procedure Act created rights principally for regulated businesses and other economic actors. In order to par-ticipate in procedural litigation, a plaintiff had to demonstrate an economic interest in the legal proceedings. Unorganized groups and noneconomic interests did not have a clear role in the government's administrative proceedings under the act. The procedural "bill of rights" did not apply to them.[7]

In the Cold War politics of the 1950s, the Administrative Proce-dure Act reflected a liberal conception of American capitalism that imagined a set of "countervailing powers" held in balance by the regulatory state. Large businesses would check each other's excesses through competition, and powerful unions would represent the interests of workers. Government would play a crucial role, ensuring that the system did not tilt too far in one direction or the other. The National Labor Relations Act of 1935 facilitated union organizing, and minimum-wage legislation looked after unorganized workers. Federal price supports boosted the market power of farmers. Investors gained protection through the Securities Exchange Commission. In his 1952 book *American Capitalism: The Concept of Countervailing Power*, the economist John Kenneth Galbraith called this balancing role "perhaps the major peacetime function of the federal government." Importantly, in all of these instances, the federal government intervened to structure the *economic* interactions of market participants. Competitive prices, reasonable wages, and the containment of monopoly power, all in the service of economic growth and expanding production—these were the paramount concerns of this postwar regulatory system. Only later, in the 1960s, would liberal theorists, including Galbraith himself, concede that the concept of "countervailing powers" might not adequately represent all the interests whose voices needed to be heard in the policy-making process.[8]

In this economic system of the 1950s, the federal government was not just an arbiter between private parties; it also was an active partner and frequent initiator. Major hydroelectric dam construction, building on the triumphant completion of Hoover Dam and Grand Coulee Dam, accelerated in the 1940s and 1950s, spurred on by the Bureau of Reclamation. Leading engineering and construction companies, including Kaiser, Bechtel, and others, used government dam contracts to expand their operations domestically and overseas. The US nuclear production system also continued to expand for both military weapons and atomic energy. The Atomic Energy Commission worked with private utility and engineering companies to launch an atomic power industry, starting with the Shippingport Atomic Power Station, completed in western Pennsylvania in 1957. The 1956 interstate highway bill (the Federal-Aid Highway Act) expanded a postwar state-level construction boom to establish toll-free highways linking major US

*New York's Cross Bronx Expressway under construction in the early
1960s. In many postwar cities, government planners pushed new
highways through existing neighborhoods, helping to remake the urban
landscape around motor vehicles.* Courtesy of MTA Bridges and Tunnels
Special Archive.

cities. President Dwight Eisenhower declared that highways were "an
obligation of Government at every level. The highway system is a public enterprise." Labor, capital, and government worked in tandem to
fuel the postwar economic boom, remaking the American landscape
with complex infrastructure to manage water, energy, transportation,
and housing.[9]

✦

When John F. Kennedy, in his January 1961 inaugural address,
implored idealistic young people to "ask what you can do for your country" and to join him in Washington, the president embraced this liberal and broadly shared postwar celebration of government action and

public service. Yet Kennedy's inspiring rhetoric masked an unsettling countertrend that would accelerate during the 1960s. Even as Kennedy called young people to government service, the ideological and political foundations of progovernment liberalism were cracking. A generation after the New Deal, the liberal embrace of federal executive agencies had started to falter. The postwar American faith in government crashed against the realities of how that government was working, and what it was doing to the American people and to the land itself.

James Landis, the earlier champion and theoretician of administrative governance, demonstrated the ideological turn underway, even at the very heart of the new administration. In an influential 1960 report that Landis prepared for president-elect Kennedy, Landis highlighted pervasive problems with federal regulation. Now in his early sixties, Landis reported that federal agencies faced a crisis of legitimacy. One key issue was that public agencies had gotten too close to private industry, and had ended up serving private purposes. While sometimes a government official's industry orientation reflected their business background, more troublesome from the perspective of the system's integrity, Landis wrote, were those regulators "originally oriented towards the public interest but who gradually and honestly begin to view that interest more in terms of the private interest." The problem was particularly acute in agencies that combined industry promotion with industry regulation.[10]

Landis had seen this problem up close when he served for one year as chairman of the Civil Aeronautics Board, starting in 1946. Landis favored increased airline competition rather than monopolistic control, and he clashed with the airline lobbyists and other commissioners over whether the government should favor a small set of dominant players. Pushed out of his board position by President Harry Truman under pressure from the airline industry, Landis later commented on how the experience changed the views he had expressed in *The Administrative Process*. "Some years ago I wrote a fairly popular book defending the administrative process on the ground that it would be expeditious and less costly than going to court," Landis wrote to a colleague in 1951.

But after his tangles with the Civil Aeronautics Board, Landis said, "I almost feel it a moral duty to revise my estimate of that process made before my acquaintance with the organization." Regulatory commissions, he now saw, were too susceptible to political pressure, overly rigid, and suffering from inertia and a lack of administrative capacity.[11]

In his 1960 report to President Kennedy, Landis described a subtle shift toward "industry orientation" that resulted from frequent and productive contacts with industry representatives. In a frequently quoted passage, Landis wrote, "It is the daily machine-gun-like impact on both agency and its staff of industry representation that makes for industry orientation on the part of many honest and capable agency members as well as agency staffs." Landis no longer believed that agencies could be separated from external pressures and operate only according to scientific expertise.[12]

Did federal agencies adequately represent the American citizen and consumer? In his 1962 congressional message on consumer rights, President Kennedy himself framed a dilemma that would help split liberalism by the end of the decade, and that would pit advocates like Ralph Nader against the liberal establishment. On the one hand, Kennedy said in his 1962 speech, the federal government was "by nature the highest spokesman for all the people." On the other hand, consumers, who "by definition, include us all," were "the only important group in the economy who are not effectively organized, whose views are often not heard." Read carefully, Kennedy's special message on consumer rights suggested that the federal government wasn't speaking effectively for the people it was supposed to represent. If the government was not fulfilling that role, then who would?[13]

Kennedy called for a new set of rights for consumers: rights to safety, to information, to choice, and to be heard. These rights had grown in importance in the postwar period, and he thought that the government could do a better job securing these protections. The "march of technology," Kennedy noted, left "outmoded" many regulations. New kinds of food, medicine, and appliances that could be "hazardous to health or life" were being marketed misleadingly or even deceitfully to consumers. As Kennedy explained in the period's gendered framing of concern for homemaking and health and safety, "the housewife is called upon to be an amateur electrician, mechanic, chemist, toxicologist, dietitian, and mathematician—but she is rarely furnished the information she needs to perform these tasks proficiently." Americans enjoyed the highest standard of living in the world, Kennedy said, but the federal government needed to do more to "protect the common interest in every decision we make." Lyndon Johnson affirmed Kennedy's declaration of consumer rights in a February 1964 message to Congress, and he appointed the first special assistant for consumer affairs in the federal government.[14]

Kennedy's questioning of the effectiveness of federal regulation reflected a growing theoretical understanding of the ways in which federal regulators risked going astray. An emerging social science literature explained the "regulatory capture" described by Landis, and the growing consolidation of corporate power in American democracy. While some scholars argued that political pluralism resulted in an evenhanded balance among societal forces, others writing in the late 1950s and early 1960s described a historical pattern of private dominance of the government that increasingly controlled many aspects of American society. They showed how earlier government reform efforts, including Progressive Era railroad regulation, served the narrow interests of business, not the general public. Industry used regulation to exclude competitors, boost prices, and gain market power.[15]

Even as government increasingly seemed controlled by "narrowly based and largely autonomous elites," in the words of Grant McConnell's 1966 book *Private Power & American Democracy*, public institutions in the United States had gained more control over people's daily lives. The individual, scholars argued, needed protection against arbitrary and oppressive power exercised by government. In a landmark 1964 article, Yale law professor Charles Reich called for a new kind of "property right" that would provide due process rights for public benefits, such as unemployment compensation, veterans' pensions, and occupational licenses, instead of leaving them at the whim of bureaucrats and agencies. "We cannot permit any official or agency to pretend to sole knowledge of the public good," Reich wrote, as he questioned many traditional liberal responses to social problems. Reich's best-selling 1970 book, *The Greening of America*, would reject the "consciousness" and structures of the "Corporate State" that had dominated American society since the New Deal and that had become, in his words, a "mindless juggernaut."[16]

Student activists influenced by these ideas in the early 1960s joined calls for a "New Left" in which students and the universities would generate social change. The New Left feared the concentration of power in large, centralized institutions that could crush the common citizen. At a 1962 meeting in Port Huron, Michigan, Students for a Democratic Society called for "participatory democracy." Americans had grown "structurally remote and psychologically hesitant with respect to democratic institutions," the student activists argued. The growing power of corporate and government institutions had isolated the individual and given birth to a "democracy without publics." As democratic institutions grew "progressively less accessible," the "democratic connection" had become "so wrenched and perverted that disastrous policies go unchallenged time and again." The Port Huron Statement, as the Students for a Democratic Society manifesto became known, called for new forms of "voluntary association," separate from the two-party political system. "Private in nature, these should be organized around single issues (medical care, transportation systems reform, etc.), concrete interest (labor and minority group organizations), multiple issues or general issues. These do not exist in America in quantity today." In imagining issue-based advocacy groups separate from the political parties and the government, the Students for a Democratic Society statement anticipated the nongovernmental organizations that would proliferate in the late 1960s and early 1970s. The public interest, the Port Huron Statement suggested, might best be expressed and pursued through smaller, independent groups separate from the government and from other traditional institutions.[17]

✦

LANDIS'S 1960 REPORT, Kennedy's consumer message, and the
Port Huron Statement illustrate how concern about the nonrespon-
siveness of government institutions, including problems with regulatory capture and agency ineffectiveness, had started to spread widely
by the early 1960s, even within the liberal establishment. Ideas, of
course, differed from substantial action. The Kennedy administration's expressions of concern and calls for change did relatively little to change the behavior of federal agencies themselves. Kennedy
sought to improve the performance of regulatory agencies by creating the Administrative Conference, which would promote model
administrative procedures and make them more uniform across
agencies. Yet most federal agencies still remained concentrated centers of power, with their own internal logic and rules. They responded
primarily to a constituency of powerful congressional patrons and to
regulated industries. Even as Landis raised concerns about agency
practices, and Kennedy called for protecting and empowering the
consumer, federal agencies continued to run roughshod over local
communities and the environment in the early 1960s.[18]

Administrative power, coupled with new advances in science and
technology, generated grand plans for reshaping the nation. Highway planners envisioned blasting freeways through urban neighborhoods. Technologists proposed using atomic explosions to create a
harbor in Alaska and to free up oil and gas resources in Colorado
and Wyoming. Agricultural scientists saw mass spraying of chemical
insecticides across the countryside and in residential neighborhoods
as the best way to combat pest infestations. Land managers proposed
massive hydropower projects, even within the Grand Canyon, to fuel
urban growth in the Southwest and to irrigate corporate farms. It
was against this conjunction of administrative power—the New Deal
postwar alliance of big government, big business, and big labor—that
Ralph Nader, Jane Jacobs, Rachel Carson, and other best-selling writers rose up in full-throated opposition in the early 1960s.

Chapter Two

Rethinking the Liberal Embrace of Government Agencies

"THIS BOOK IS AN ATTACK ON CURRENT CITY PLANning and rebuilding," Jane Jacobs bluntly declared in the opening sentence of her 1961 bestseller, *The Death and Life of Great American Cities*. Jacobs was a journalist and editor living in New York City who had written frequently about cities and urban planning for publications like *Architectural Forum*, *Fortune*, and *Vogue*. Her treatise on community-oriented urban design took aim at the government planners who, the book's advertising declared, were "ravaging our cities!" Instead of the highways, bridges, and housing projects celebrated by postwar urban redevelopers like New York's Robert Moses, Jacobs touted the complex hustle and bustle of busy and diverse streetscapes. In Jacobs's view, Moses and other city planners, in partnership with business leaders and construction unions, and backed by millions of dollars in federal funding, were tearing apart neighborhoods to create urban landscapes characterized by "monotony, sterility and vulgarity." Moses had "made an art of using control of public money to get his way," Jacobs said. The public interest and essential democratic processes, she warned, could be negated "just as effectively by honest public administrators as by dishonest representatives of purely private interests." As *Time* magazine explained the thrust of Jacobs's book, "U.S. planners and redevelopers, in trying to save U.S. cities, are in reality destroying them."[1]

Writer and activist Jane Jacobs, pictured here at a 1961 press conference, protested government development plans that she argued would destroy vibrant urban communities. Library of Congress.

Prominent public intellectuals in the early 1960s, including talented writers like Jane Jacobs, often had backgrounds in journalism and made their mark with a breakthrough book on a critical political concern of the postwar period. Mass-market publishing, including cheap and popular paperbacks, enabled these writers to shine a spotlight on pressing social issues and to become the spokesperson for a cause or a movement. Writers such as Jacobs, and influential critics such as Rachel Carson and Ralph Nader, did not create new arguments so much as they became powerful vehicles for amplifying existing ones. They frequently were gatherers and synthesizers. They drew on insights from experts in and out of government. The research and initial organizing that preceded their 1960s publications started in the 1950s. They were responding, particularly, to the expanded use of science and technology during the post–World War II economic boom, including the reorientation of the American landscape and economy around the automobile and the escalating use of chemical pesticides. With support from liberal charitable foundations, these independent writer-activists denounced the political establishment's plans to aggressively manipulate natural and social systems.

Rachel Carson's attack on pesticides in her 1962 bestseller *Silent Spring* powerfully illustrated these growing calls for greater attention to community, the environment, and the ordinary citizen. *Silent Spring* is remembered today primarily for the way that Carson urged Americans to make peace with the natural world. Nature, she wrote, did not exist solely "for the convenience of man." Carson celebrated natural biodiversity and condemned the biological simplification inherent to widespread pesticide use. Her description of natural ecosystems and her critique of high-tech industrial systems echoed the contrast that Jane Jacobs drew in the urban environment, between bustling street life and sterile urban redevelopment projects. The "control of nature," Carson famously said, was "a phrase conceived in arrogance."[2]

Considered in the context of changing 1960s liberal politics, however, a different theme stands out in Carson's work: *Silent Spring*'s forceful attack on government agencies for their misguided pursuit of risky, large-scale, capital-intensive chemical spray programs. Viewed from this vantage point, Carson, like Jane Jacobs, voiced a growing public interest critique of government that Ralph Nader and others would carry forward later in the 1960s and in the 1970s.

When Rachel Carson published *Silent Spring* in 1962, she was a science-and-nature author who already had a significant popular following. She had started her professional career in the late 1930s working as a science writer and editor for the Fish and Wildlife Service. In 1951, Carson achieved breakout literary success with publication of *The Sea Around Us*, a general-interest nonfiction book about ocean history and marine ecology. *The Sea Around Us* won a National Book Award and was made into an Oscar-winning documentary. With new financial independence, Carson left her government position as publications editor to write full-time. In the late 1950s she agreed to write a general-interest book for Houghton Mifflin that would draw attention to the threat that chemical pesticides posed to wildlife and human health.[3]

Carson was not the first person to warn of the dangers of chemical pesticides, just as Jacobs did not initiate the liberal critique of urban highways and redevelopment projects. As Carson herself candidly explained in a 1962 speech to the National Parks Association, "The concern expressed in *Silent Spring* is not mine alone, nor is it new." Starting in the late 1950s, for example, the National Audubon Society had hired a research biologist named Harold Peters to travel the country and raise the alarm about the threat to wildlife posed by the "massive spraying of toxic chemicals." Peters gave interviews to local newspapers, spoke on radio shows, and pressed his case to whoever would listen. As Carson explained to her *New Yorker* editor William Shawn, she aimed to achieve "a synthesis of widely scattered facts, that have not heretofore been considered in relation to each other."[4]

Audubon's Peters was one of many scientists and others who corresponded with Carson about escalating local and national conflicts over chemical pesticides. In a June 1959 letter, Peters detailed for Carson the dangers posed by the US Department of Agriculture's (USDA's) fire ant program, which he had been studying in six southern states over the previous year. In 1957 the USDA had initiated what would become a massive, decades-long campaign to eradicate the red fire ant, whose population had exploded after it arrived in the United States in the 1930s or 1940s. To accomplish this objective, government agencies were spraying insecticides over tens of millions of acres in the American South. Peters also described for Carson local skirmishes over chemical pesticides like dieldrin, a potent organochloride that has since been banned because of its dangers to animals and to human health. In a letter full of outrage and dotted with exclamation points, Peters recounted how Memphis Garden Club members were driven to protest the mass application of dieldrin to fight the white-fringed beetle.[5]

As Carson investigated the growth in pesticide use, she heard from Peters and others that government agencies themselves were a chief source of the problem. The USDA was "the demon," according to a former president of Audubon. Local insect-control boards often sprayed chemical pesticides to combat infestations. The Department of Agriculture promoted these kinds of chemical controls, Carson was told, even to the extent of suppressing scientific information about the risks. The USDA and local control agencies paid no attention to critics, Peters complained to Carson in the summer of 1959. The government had treated Memphis-area properties without determining whether they were infested and against the wishes of property owners. "Control forces," as Peters called the government agents and corporate spokesmen pushing for increased spraying, spouted the "usual type of USDA propaganda." In Nashville, the pest-control agency blew dieldrin throughout one city park to combat the Japanese beetle. The sprayers, mounted on jeeps, left recreational "picnic tables covered with the snow-like granules" of toxic chemicals. Peters lamented the government's approach to chemical treatment and the deceptive information used to support spray programs. "You can't trust those folks, you can't believe what they say," Peters told Carson. "They falsified in testimony before Congressional committees on appropriation, they are underhanded in trying to have fired 4 or 5 biologists who found harmful side-effects from the fire ant program, and they refuse to admit their heptachlor is killing livestock, poultry, wildlife, and that it presents a hazard to people!"[6]

In *Silent Spring*, Carson embraced and amplified this growing criticism of public agencies for their implementation of spray programs. Excessively close ties between government and industry, she argued, exacerbated a misguided vision of a simplified, pest-free landscape. Government campaigns against the gypsy moth and fire ant, Carson wrote, were "ill-conceived, badly executed, and thoroughly detrimental." Government agencies relied on "undocumented claim[s]" and "propaganda" to justify spray programs "drenching millions of acres with poisons." Carson's critique of the quest for biological control attacked the concentrated power of government institutions. "The fundamental wrong," Carson explained in a 1963 speech, "is the authoritarian control that has been vested in the agricultural agencies." These agencies, which operated at local, state, and federal levels, acted as if the "agricultural interest were supreme, or indeed the *only* one."[7]

What about the public interest? Carson asked. Her question would echo through the growing environmental movement for the next decade. "People are beginning to ask questions instead of meekly acquiescing in whatever spraying programs are proposed." Americans had to wake up to their civic responsibilities, Carson argued, and stop trusting the government to act responsibly. "Until very recently," she explained, "the average citizen assumed that 'someone' was looking after these matters and that some little understood but confidently relied upon safeguards stood like shields between his person and any harm. Now he has experienced, from several different directions, a rather rude shattering of these beliefs."[8]

Carson envisioned a growing movement of citizens rising up in opposition to both industry and government. "A new spirit is abroad in this land," Carson declared in a 1962 speech on pesticides. "In the past, most communities could be counted upon to acquiesce in whatever spraying was done. They assumed that someone was 'looking after things'—that the spraying must be 'all right' or it wouldn't be done. Now they are beginning to challenge and ask questions." Communities were canceling spray programs and questioning their rationale. Carson characterized *Silent Spring* as "a rallying point for an awakened public." Advocacy organizations, such as the National Parks Association and the Audubon Society, she said, need to "show these people that they are not alone."[9]

Complicating Carson's harsh criticism of USDA propaganda and government spray programs, Carson's pesticide research relied heavily on government and industry informants who shared research and ideas with her. Carson's archive of personal correspondence is full of her letters to experts, seeking copies of the latest study, and asking whether her correspondent might have learned something about a thread of her investigation. Experts at the Fish and Wildlife Service, the Food and Drug Administration, and the Interior Department, in particular, aided Carson throughout. Many government employees sought to help in "relative anonymity," as an Interior Department staff member explained to Carson. The Kennedy and Johnson administrations, from the top level to the rank and file, thus served Carson both as a foil for opposition, and as a source of allies and encouragement.[10]

Carson, who lived most of the year in a Washington, DC, suburb, also had strong and active Democratic connections and ties to the government. She served on a natural-resources committee charged with developing proposals for the Democratic Party on resources and the environment during the 1960 campaign. She attended a "Women's Committee for New Frontiers" meeting at Senator John Kennedy's home in Washington, DC, shortly before the presidential election. After becoming president, Kennedy himself cited "Miss Carson's book" favorably at a press conference in the summer of 1962 and appointed a committee to study pesticide use. At the Department of the Interior, Secretary Stewart Udall paid tribute to Carson's work and highlighted the problem of pesticides in the environment. Carson, Udall declared in 1963, was a "great woman" who had "awakened the Nation" to the ways that humankind was "part of the balance of nature." Udall personally inscribed to Carson a copy of *The Quiet Crisis*, his book on conservation.[11]

Many liberal critics of the government in the 1960s shared Carson's complicated relationship to the federal government and its scientific and technical experts. As the historian Brian Balogh has argued, the growth of the administrative state after World War II and its deepening investment in science and technology produced diverse centers of expertise within national and state governments. As experts specialized and proliferated within the federal bureaucracy, they increasingly came into conflict. Their disputes spilled out from insular administrative forums into the public arena. Experts of all kinds, including university researchers, grew increasingly available to government critics, and opposition to government and industry proposals increasingly rested on technical challenges to government actions. The ecologist Barry Commoner, for example, raised questions about the prevalence

Rachel Carson, author of Silent Spring, *testifies before a Senate subcommittee studying pesticide spraying in 1963.* Library of Congress.

of strontium-90 from nuclear fallout in the fight over nuclear testing, while the Harvard geneticist Matthew Meselson questioned the safety for humans of the chemicals in Agent Orange during the Vietnam War. The Sierra Club's scientific experts similarly debated evaporation rates and sediment flows to challenge the economic viability of federal agency proposals to build dams around Grand Canyon National Park. Expertise was both the basis for the rapid expansion of government and corporate power, and a chief means for contesting that expansion.[12]

The importance of expertise in the fight over large-scale development projects explains why chemical companies and trade associations and critics in the press targeted Rachel Carson in a concerted campaign after the publication of *Silent Spring*. Calling Carson "emotional and inaccurate," they questioned her "worthless" evidence and her "mystical attachment to the balance of nature." Carson and her book were "poisonous" and "reckless," they said, and a tool of "food faddists" and "health quacks." Why had Carson never married? they asked. Was she secretly a Communist? Carson, they argued, stood against the progress of humanity and the contributions of scientists and technologists to a more prosperous future. "If man were to follow the teachings of Miss Carson," one of her chief scientific opponents declared in 1963, "we would return to the Dark Ages, and the insects and diseases and vermin would once again inherit the earth." The attacks on Carson paradoxically drew attention to her book, boosting its sales and encouraging more coverage, including a lengthy *CBS Reports* television segment in April 1963 that was viewed by an estimated ten to fifteen million people. Shortly after the CBS feature aired, Carson was invited to testify on the hazards of pesticides before a Senate committee. At the peak of her public influence, however, Carson died, just one year later, of heart failure associated with the breast cancer that she had battled for many years.[13]

✦

WHEN RALPH NADER AGREED to write *Unsafe at Any Speed* for publication in 1965, he followed many aspects of Rachel Carson's playbook. *Unsafe at Any Speed*, in fact, was the "*Silent Spring* of traffic safety," according to the journal *Science*. Comparing Nader's book with Carson's attack on chemical pesticides made sense. Although Nader is not always remembered as an environmentalist, his auto safety advocacy emerged from some of the same wellsprings as the environmental movement, part of an increasingly shared postwar concern about the "harmful and insidious impacts of new technologies and processes." To Nader, automobile safety meant creating a safe environment for the driver, and environmentalism meant protecting people. Nader saw automobile safety, and environmentalism more broadly, as part of a "bodily rights revolution" whose origin lay in the idea that the physical bodies of American citizens should be protected against external hazards. The tragedy of automobile accidents, Nader wrote, was one of the most serious "manmade assaults on the human body." Nader's campaign for highway safety was inseparable from his subsequent advocacy for clean air and clean water and his fervent opposition to toxic chemicals and nuclear power. "The battle of the environmentalists is to preserve the physiological integrity of people by preserving the natural integrity of land, air, and water," Nader would declare in 1970. Carson similarly spoke of "the right of the citizen to be secure . . . against the intrusion of poisons." Radioactive and chemical contamination threatened the "internal environment within the bodies of animals and men," Carson explained. She called protection against environmental hazards one of the "basic human rights."[14]

Nader's political analysis also shared much with *Silent Spring*. Nader, like Carson, particularly blamed government "obsolescence and bureaucratic inertia" for the highway safety problem. Like the local pest-control boards and the USDA that Carson criticized, traffic safety agencies too often served the interests of private enterprise and treated citizens with "contempt or indifference." The traffic safety establishment, Nader wrote, was a "great power with no challengers." Like Carson, Nader thought an "awakened public" provided the key to countering concentrated government and corporate power. Nader particularly called on independent, civically active lawyers, engineers, and scientists to oppose the powerful alliance between government and business. These "professionally qualified citizens" looked an awful lot like Nader himself. They could force the government to protect American consumers from dangerous cars and badly designed roads.[15]

◆

NADER STARTED INVESTIGATING the highway safety problem as a Harvard law student in the late 1950s. He had grown up the youngest of four siblings in a small industrial town in northwestern Connecticut. His parents had immigrated to the United States from a village in Lebanon, and they ran a small bakery-restaurant on Main Street in the town of Winsted. The area, Nader later recalled, had "a lot of nature around it; rivers, lakes, hiking paths, meadows." But Winsted itself struggled. Its factories were in decline, and the Mad

River, which ran through town, was badly polluted. While the town had a strong community sensibility, many outsiders, including state planners, viewed Winsted largely as a place to pass through on the way to the more touristy areas of northwestern Connecticut.[16]

The Nader family restaurant served as a town meeting place for discussing public affairs, and the four Nader children developed a common passion for civic action and legal reform. "My father would take me down to the county courthouse, which was, like, three blocks down the same street, the Main Street," Nader would later recall. "And I would sit and watch the lawyers go at it, and the jury and judge. And he always wished he could have become a lawyer, because we equated being a lawyer with spearheading justice." The political culture of Winsted's town-meeting government, with active participation by citizens of all kinds, became Nader's ideal. Winsted and the family restaurant also cultivated a small-business mentality in Nader, as well as his suspicion of centralized big government and big business.[17]

After completing his undergraduate degree at Princeton University's Woodrow Wilson School of International and Public Affairs in 1955, Nader enrolled at Harvard Law School. There he grew increasingly disdainful of the typical law student's track and interested in the possibilities of law as a strategy for reform. In his third-year research paper, Nader tackled the problem of automobile design. Nader argued that vehicle accidents consist of two collisions: first, the car hitting another object, and second, the occupant striking the interior of the vehicle or being ejected from a door that opened on impact. It was the second collision that caused human injury, he claimed. In a companion piece published in the *Harvard Law Record* in 1958, Nader called on the auto companies to redesign car interiors to protect people against the car itself.[18]

After graduating from law school, Nader continued to explore the auto safety issue over the next several years. He wrote occasional columns on the topic in the *Hartford Courant* and the *Christian Science Monitor*. Nader also closely followed congressional hearings on automobile health and safety, and the role that "unsafe *automobile design* plays in the millions of accidents and casualties." In 1959, Nader criticized Connecticut governor Abe Ribicoff in the *Courant* for not pressing for improved car engineering, and for instead placing too much emphasis on changing driver behavior. In 1960, five years before publishing *Unsafe at Any Speed*, Nader sought to mount a public relations campaign through the national Junior Chamber of Commerce to increase demand for safer cars. Nader also worked closely with his local state representative in Connecticut to get legislation introduced that would mandate stronger door latches, recessed knobs, padded interiors, and other interior safety changes.[19]

Nader approached the highway safety issue from the perspective of legal reform and citizen action, with clearly defined views on government accountability and transparency. After a trip to Scandinavia, he became enthusiastic about a new innovation: the "ombudsman." The Scandinavian ombudsman was an independent public official empowered to investigate government wrongdoing and publicize it widely. In early 1963, Nader helped to get an ombudsman proposal introduced to the Connecticut House of Representatives. Representative Nicholas Eddy proposed that Connecticut create a nonpartisan office to which citizens could complain about state agencies. The ombudsman would provide "practical remedies against state abuses," Nader explained in a letter to the *Hartford Courant*. In an April 1963 editorial in the *Christian Science Monitor*, Nader described the ombudsman as a tool that might be adopted across the nation. He touted the way an ombudsman would interact with the press, gaining an impact through "stimulation . . . of the public's morality." Government administrative power had grown "vast" in recent decades, Nader argued, echoing Charles Reich's arguments about the expanding federal government. The ombudsman would "help strengthen the system of checks and balances which has been rendered somewhat lopsided by the fast growth of the Executive branch." In a 1965 essay advocating the creation of ombudsmen for state governments, Nader warned that citizens needed to be protected against "administrative abuses." The "bureaucratic apparatus of all state governments share similar traits which do violence to equal protection for citizens," Nader wrote. While Nader's proposal to create an ombudsman position in Connecticut did not succeed, the concept of the ombudsman remained central to Nader's self-conception and political program. In the late 1970s he would campaign to establish consumer advocates in federal agencies to serve this same kind of ombudsman role.[20]

The problem of highway safety provided Nader with a defining issue of great concern to Americans and a focal point for reform. With highway construction booming and car use rapidly expanding, the automobile was transforming American daily life. Between 1946, when transportation patterns had largely returned to prewar levels, and 1965, when Nader published *Unsafe at Any Speed*, US automobile ownership tripled from twenty-eight million to seventy-five million vehicles. Automobile use increased even more quickly. Vehicle miles traveled rose from 340 million miles to an astonishing 887 *billion* miles over the same time period—an increase of more than 250,000 percent. Automobile executives saw their interests as almost inseparable from those of the nation. "For years I thought that what was good for our country was good for General Motors, and vice versa," declared the president of General Motors at his 1952 confirmation hearing for the position of US secretary of defense.[21]

The automobile business thus provided an attractive target for Nader when he moved to Washington, DC, in 1963 to work with Daniel Patrick Moynihan at the Department of Labor. Moynihan was responsible for addressing occupational hazards affecting government employees, including traffic accidents. Moynihan shared Nader's interest in making both highways and automobiles safer, and he considered traffic accidents the nation's top public health problem. In the late 1950s, as an aide to New York governor Averell Harriman, Moynihan had advocated for traffic safety. In 1959, Moynihan wrote "Epidemic on the Highways," a widely circulated essay that laid out many points similar to those that Nader would develop in *Unsafe at Any Speed*.

Like Nader, Moynihan was heavily influenced by the work of the physician William Haddon, who conducted pioneering studies on traffic safety for the New York State government. Moynihan argued in his essay that traffic hazards should be approached from an epidemiological or public health perspective. Moynihan attacked the industry-dominated National Safety Council for blaming drivers for traffic accidents instead of pressing for better design. Moynihan called for "packaging" drivers to protect them against injury within the environment of the automobile. Seat belts, secure doors that did not pop open upon impact, recessed knobs, cushioned interiors, and other innovations all could protect the driver, Moynihan argued. Above all, Moynihan favored federal regulation of traffic safety, contending that the "only organization big enough to take on the automobile industry is the Federal government itself." After the publication of "Epidemic on the Highways," the Knopf publishing house contracted with Moynihan to write a popular book on auto safety, along the same muckraking lines as Upton Sinclair's classic 1906 novel, *The Jungle*. Moynihan planned to emphasize his epidemiological approach to "thinking about controlling the environment and the agent of a disease."[22]

Moynihan never completed his own book, leaving the field open for an auto safety exposé. Richard Grossman, a new independent publisher, eventually reached out to Nader to see whether he would do it. Nader already had completed much of the research in his capacity as a consultant to the Department of Labor, and he had tried unsuccessfully to sell it as a book. In turning down Nader's initial book proposal, one publisher reportedly called it likely "of interest only to insurance agents." Grossman saw the potential for something more. Grossman worked closely with Nader to complete a manuscript in just a few months, hoping to publish it before planned congressional hearings on auto safety. In the final editing stages, Grossman and Nader reportedly set up typewriters side by side in a Washington motel. As Nader finished a page, he would hand it to Grossman to edit. Nader's years as a journalist writing for the *Christian Science Monitor* had honed writing skills that he now used to write a popular book. Like Carson, Nader famously worked a national network of contacts in industry and government. He was a kind of "one-man C.I.A.," gathering intelligence from all quarters, according to a 1967 profile. Nader also carefully cultivated sympathetic journalists and distributed information for them to publish in order to influence government agencies or congressional proceedings. Of Drew Pearson, a muckraking columnist at the *Washington Post*, Nader said he would "go over at night and slip something through his door at Georgetown. And a day and a half or so later, I'd see it in the *Washington Post*."[23]

Unsafe at Any Speed attracted modest attention in its initial print run, selling some twenty-two thousand copies in the first three and a half months. In March 1966, however, Nader's popularity exploded in the public consciousness. James Roche, the chairman of General Motors, was forced to publicly apologize for the company's hiring of a private detective to follow and investigate Nader, and even try to entrap him. In the same way that the chemical industry's clumsy public relations campaign against Rachel Carson had helped to elevate her book and make Carson a household name, the auto industry's effort to discredit Nader raised his profile and strengthened his hand. General Motors' public exposure fed into a narrative of corporate malfeasance and generated tremendous momentum behind automobile safety legislation.

During the spring and summer of 1966, the outcry over General Motors' harassment and Nader's effective congressional testimony helped elevate Nader as an auto safety spokesperson and key broker on the final legislation. Nader's "passion and inexhaustible energy was the greatest moving force behind that law," recalled Michael Pertschuk. Pertschuk, a key legislative aide then working on the legislation for the Senate Committee on Commerce, remembered this about his relationship with Nader during that time: "Apart from my wife and children, I spent more time talking with him than with anyone else. From early morning to late at night he would call me at home, alerting me to auto lobbyists' schemes and pressing me, always civilly, to work harder." In the closing moments of legislative drafting, Nader sat in one Senate anteroom while Lloyd Cutler, a Democratic lobbyist representing the auto industry, stayed in another. The old Democratic

Ralph Nader testifies on automobile safety before a Senate subcommittee in March 1966. Congress passed bills governing traffic and highway safety the following September. AP Photo.

Party establishment, with its interwoven ties between government and business, was being forced to negotiate with its new liberal critics. Pertschuk went back and forth between Nader and Cutler as they hammered out the final details of the bill.[24]

On September 9, 1966, Lyndon Johnson signed the Traffic Safety Act and the Highway Safety Act. The two measures aimed to force manufacturers to design safer cars and to press states to carry out a highway safety program. Minimum safety standards for automobiles and clearer tire standards were key parts of the legislation. Over Labor Day weekend alone, Johnson noted in his remarks, 29 American servicemen had been killed in Vietnam, while 614 Americans had died on US highways. Johnson lamented this "raging epidemic of highway death." More than fifty thousand Americans would die in traffic accidents in 1966, fourteen thousand more than had died on the roads in 1960. House Speaker John McCormack credited the final legislative outcome to the "crusading spirit of one individual who believed he could do something. . . . Ralph Nader." The *Washington Post* similarly called Nader the "gadfly" responsible for "arousing public demand for safer automobile design" and showed a picture of LBJ shaking hands with Nader on the paper's front page. "LBJ Signs Two Road Safety Bills as Nader Looks On," read a *Post* headline.[25]

The final congressional bill was ultimately tougher than the Johnson administration initially proposed. As the legal scholars Jerry Mashaw and David Harfst have argued, the National Traffic and Motor Vehicle Safety Act included two important innovations that rejected previous approaches to automobile regulation. First, a new federal highway safety agency would act proactively to set industry-wide standards, rather than adjudicate cases involving specific individual firms. Initially called the National Highway Safety Bureau, the agency later would become known as the National Highway Traffic Safety Administration (NHTSA). Second, the law embraced the epidemiological perspective championed by Nader, Moynihan, and others. Vehicle design, rather than driver behavior, would be a primary focus of government regulation. To establish the new highway safety agency along these lines, President Johnson appointed as director William Haddon, the public health scientist who had long promoted the epidemiological perspective on traffic accidents and had shaped Nader's and Moynihan's views. Congress's role pushing federal agencies to act more forcefully, and to deploy science-based regulatory approaches, anticipated the direction that environmental regulation would take in the early 1970s.[26]

After his breakthrough success attaining auto safety legislation, Nader sought to carve out a role as an influential voice within the Washington policy community. He did not want a staff appointment in the Johnson administration, in Congress, or with a Washington think tank or law firm. Nader, still just thirty-three years old, instead became a "self-appointed lobbyist for the public interest," according to a 1967 article in the *New York Times*. Nader quickly branched out beyond automobile safety to tackle meat inspection, natural-gas pipeline safety, and radiation safety. He notched additional victories with the 1967 Wholesome Meat Act and 1968 passage of pipeline and radiation safety bills. *Newsweek* magazine boosted Nader's savior image by picturing him on the cover in knight's armor. *Time* magazine ran a similarly flattering profile, calling Nader a "one-man scourge of dangerous cars, diseased meat, dirty fish and innumerable other public nuisances." The presidential ceremony for the meat bill explicitly linked Nader to a longer progressive tradition. The eighty-nine-year-old Upton Sinclair, author of the classic 1906 muckraking book *The Jungle*, attended in a wheelchair to witness the signing of the new law to enforce federal standards for meat. President Johnson credited Sinclair's efforts decades earlier and nodded to more recent advocates, such as Nader, also in attendance, saying that "other writers have carried on a crusade, too."[27]

Nader wanted to do more, however, than just carry on an individual crusade. And so, in late 1967, he decided to distinguish himself from book-writing peers like Rachel Carson and Jane Jacobs. Over the course of the next decade, Nader would found dozens of public interest organizations and draw thousands of idealistic young people into careers as advocates of social change. Carson died too soon after *Silent Spring* to become an organizational entrepreneur. She succumbed to cancer at age fifty-six in 1964, less than two years after the publication of *Silent Spring*. Jacobs, who had helped organize grassroots protests in New York City, left the United States for Canada in 1968 in opposition to the Vietnam War. Nader stood apart for the way that he helped to institutionalize the role of the active citizen in the American political economy. The roots of Nader's success lay in his vision for public citizenship and the strategies that he embraced for mobilizing idealistic young people as professional citizens outside any previously existing institutional framework. In the process, Nader would help create a new institutional landscape—the nonprofit public interest movement of the late 1960s and early 1970s.

Part II

"WHO REGULATES THE REGULATOR?"

Chapter Three

Creating Public
Interest Firms

"PROJECT THE SCENE," RALPH NADER TOLD A *WASH-ington Post* reporter in 1971. "Start with *Unsafe at Any Speed* and then you put out a book a year on each industry. See? You get a law through and you just repeat the same cycle. . . . Very nice, very comfortable. You know, the Lone Ranger. The establishment loves Lone Rangers. Because they can always point to them and say, SEE, this country can do it. They love the prop."[1]

But Nader didn't want to be a prop, and he rejected this comfortable path. Instead, Nader self-consciously sought to become, as the *Post* awkwardly put it, an "Institutional Lone Ranger." More important than one person's heroic efforts to write books and influence policy, Nader contended, was "to train people and get a lot of people to do this thing and to develop the concept of public interest firms." Smart, hardworking citizens with access to information could become experts capable of pressuring wayward governments and profit-seeking corporations to serve the public interest. Even more than peers like Rachel Carson, Barry Commoner, and Jane Jacobs, Nader wanted to create institutions that would mobilize and nurture other citizen activists. "We are creating a new professional citizen role," Nader told *Time* magazine.[2]

And so, in the fall of 1967, after his success with auto safety and amid new campaigns on gas pipelines, meat inspection, and radiation from X-ray machines and televisions, Nader searched for ways to extend his reach and build something larger than an individual crusade. The "lone campaigner," reported the *Wall Street Journal*, planned to "go institutional." Nader was going to create a "public-interest law firm" to fight air and water pollution and to challenge special treatment for businesses. His concerns fit broadly under the rubric of ensuring safety in every setting where Americans might find themselves: workplace, home, doctor's office, highway, or just outside, breathing the air. Nader's strategy was to enlist energetic young researchers and professionals to press government agencies to fulfill their public missions and their regulatory roles. The media, the courts, and administrative and legislative processes would be their field of operation.[3]

By the spring of 1968, Nader had incorporated a new nonprofit charitable and educational trust, the Center for Study of Responsive Law. The center proposed to research how "law and legal institutions meet the needs of the public." Unusually, rather than positioning himself as an employee of the organization, Nader became the center's legal, governing "trustee." Nader's position overseeing the organization that he founded, rather than working for it, characterized his quirky leadership style. The independent-minded Nader anticipated that he would help fund the center, rather than draw his own salary from it. By creating an organization, yet not placing himself within its structure, Nader sought to bridge two operational modes: continuing to act as a freewheeling individual crusader of the 1960s, and also institutionalizing his causes through the kinds of formal structures and organizations that would characterize the 1970s.[4]

As Nader worked to establish his new organization in 1968, political tumult gripped the nation and the world. The assassination of civil rights icon Martin Luther King Jr. in early April provoked popular outrage and protest, and the assassination of Democratic presidential candidate Robert Kennedy in June further shocked the nation and fed the sense that things were spinning out of control. University students and other young Americans figured prominently in the organized protests that year. At Columbia University, for example, civil rights activism and antiwar protest intersected in a violent clash with the academic and city establishment. In late April, students occupied Columbia University buildings to denounce the school's military research contracts and its collaboration with military recruiters, as well as its displacement of Harlem residents through construction of a new gymnasium. After a weeklong standoff, New York City police evicted the protestors in a confrontation that resulted in more than seven hundred arrests and more than a hundred injuries. The violent conflict at Columbia was one of many clashes drawing energy that year from young people disillusioned with their political leaders and questioning the fundamental institutions of the system itself. At the Democratic National Convention in August 1968, antiwar and leftist activists clashed with Chicago police during five days of televised riots and protests.

Yet Nader did not join this popular rebellion and protest. Nor did he embrace the students' more radical politics. Demonstrations in the streets instead created a window of opportunity for the thirty-four-year-old Nader to advance his health, safety, and public accountability agenda. "We owe these young people who got beat up on the streets on Civil Rights a debt for letting us go up on Capitol Hill and [get] a hearing," Nader recalled in a 2018 interview. Over the summer of 1968, Nader enlisted several law students and recent law school graduates to investigate the Federal Trade Commission. Nader and his team plunged ahead with the investigation, even though his new Center for Study of Responsive Law hardly existed yet. The center still lacked an executive director, and the IRS didn't formally approve its tax exemption until September.[5]

Although a somewhat obscure agency, the Federal Trade Commission provided Nader with a particularly attractive target that summer. Nader considered the commission essential to the federal government's regulation of markets and corporate behavior. The agency, he believed, had the potential to expand "consumer democracy" and represent the citizen's voice in government. Yet rather than protect Americans from dangerous and unhealthy products, ranging from automobiles to drugs and personal health products, the FTC allowed companies to exploit and endanger consumers. Nader believed that the commission had become a "self-parody of bureaucracy, fat with cronyism, torpid through an inbreeding unusual even for Washington, manipulated by the agents of commercial predators, impervious to governmental and citizen monitoring." According to Nader, the agency too often relied on voluntary compliance by companies and ineffectual cease and desist orders, instead of vigorously enforcing laws and making policy proactively. The agency also focused inordinately on small outlier companies and business fraudsters rather than addressing large-scale consumer exploitation and endangerment closer to the heart of the US economy.[6]

To investigate the FTC and expose its shortcomings, Nader enlisted a prestigious group of students to comb through agency records and interview agency staff. The student group did their research over the summer and then went back to school, reconvening for several weeks over the winter holidays to write their final report. Nader's young researchers drew from Harvard, Yale, and Princeton, and from the highest echelons of the American political elite. William Howard Taft IV was the great-grandson of President Taft and had just completed his second year at Harvard Law School. While working for Nader in the summer of 1968, Taft attended a classmate's wedding in "stroller coat" and a "white shirt with French cuffs." But even Taft wasn't insulated from the war; in October 1968, he learned that one of his St. Paul's prep school classmates had been killed in Vietnam. Another researcher, Edward Cox—a descendant of the Winthrop, Livingston, and Schuyler families—had just graduated from Princeton, where he had taken an undergraduate seminar with Nader on corporations and American democracy. While working for Nader, Cox dated and then, in 1971, married Richard Nixon's eldest daughter, Tricia Nixon. These weren't "nobodies," another of Nader's early employees later recalled a journalist telling him. "If you look at the names, it's like you're looking at the names on the Pullman cars at the train station." In a sign of Nader's politically ambidextrous positioning, both Taft and Cox would later go on to successful careers in and around Republican politics.[7]

The Nader Report on the Federal Trade Commission, released in January 1969, sent a shot across the bow of traditional big-government liberalism. The nascent public interest movement, the Nader report demonstrated, would not coexist easily with the mainstream Democratic establishment. The students had initially enlisted the support of Paul Rand Dixon, the Democratic chairman of the trade commission. Dixon was a prominent Democrat and veteran New Dealer. He had worked as a staff member at the FTC starting in 1938, and also served as counsel to the Senate antitrust committee before President Kennedy appointed him chairman. Now the students' blistering report shredded Dixon's reputation and called on the chairman to resign "from the agency that he has so degraded and ossified."[8]

The Nader group deliberately wrote sections of its report "to attract the attention of the new Republican administration," explained Edward Cox. The report particularly highlighted extensive Democratic Party patronage at the agency, "with the thought that the incoming Republican administration would be motivated to clean it up." The first major news coverage from the Federal Trade Commission study ran in the *Wall Street Journal* in November 1968, right after Nixon's election. The story exposed a peculiar and isolated office in Oak Ridge, Tennessee, entirely created for and "manned by a friend of Chairman Dixon's." The final report presented a more sweeping set of claims. The agency's senior staff, the report alleged, was plagued by "alcoholism, spectacular lassitude, and office absenteeism, incompetence by the most modest standards, and a lack of commitment to the regulatory mission."[9]

Dixon denounced the study as a "hysterical, anti-business diatribe and a scurrilous, untruthful attack." Beyond his bitterness at being attacked personally, Dixon's defensive reply revealed the different attitudes toward government held by the students and by agency leadership. "There is a gap as wide as the Atlantic Ocean between Mr. Dixon's philosophy of what a regulatory agency should do and the philosophy expressed by the Nader-organized investigatory team," explained the syndicated columnist John Chamberlain. Dixon thought that the American political system should not pass laws and make rulings that could not be enforced. "This attitude," Chamberlain noted, "results in such things as 'advisory opinions,' 'consent decrees,' promises to 'cease and desist,' 'voluntary compliance' and other things which the Nader-recruited law school students regard as horrifying softness." The Nader group, by contrast, thought that an expanded agency staff should engage in "positive detective work," employing its own experts to investigate the workings of appliances, construction materials, and the performance of automobiles. They wanted the trade commission to force American corporations to change how they were doing business.[10]

With the FTC report Nader charted a path for citizen activists separate from, and even in opposition to, government agencies touted by New Deal Democrats to serve the public welfare. "So far as anybody can remember nothing quite like this has happened in Washington before," the *Christian Science Monitor* reported in January 1969. "A group of unofficial but informed outsiders . . . as a sort of civilian posse, has descended on a rather stuffy government commission, poked under sofas, and asked some rough questions." William Greider of the *Washington Post* called the task force team "Nader's Raiders." *Life* magazine amplified the name as the title for an article about Nader in the fall of 1969. "Nader's Raiders" proved a catchy and enduring label that captured the aggressive generational attack by young researchers on what they called the FTC's "tired blood" and "malaise of apathy, non-responsiveness and limited vision." The *Post* considered Nader's trade commission report "totally devastating" in its portrayal of a government agency that had "lost sight of its mission." Nader himself touted the student project as a model for how public interest advocacy could improve government and make the public sphere more inclusive. Fixing government agencies and democratic processes, Nader contended, depended on professional citizens like his student investigators. "A countervailing force in the private sector against the special interests and lobbyists is a vital condition if a regulatory agency is to perform its task well," Nader wrote in his preface to the FTC report.

Following the report and further investigation by the American Bar Association, Congress gave the Federal Trade Commission enhanced enforcement powers and mandated greater citizen participation in the agency's proceedings.[11]

As the waves created by Nader's FTC investigation started to ripple out during the fall of 1968, Nader sought financial support from several major liberal foundations to expand his efforts. In a grant proposal to the Carnegie Corporation, Nader explicitly proposed a fundamental change to the American political and economic model. Referencing John Kenneth Galbraith's influential 1952 book *American Capitalism: The Concept of Countervailing Power*, Nader explained that American society "has been described as one of 'countervailing powers,' with three major forces—big government, big labor, and big industry—each pursuing its own interest and balancing off the interests of the other." This prevailing model, however, was flawed. The three-legged stool of government, business, and labor, Nader argued, "accepts as given the absence of the ad hoc force of the public or the citizen-consumer. It omits it for the very obvious reason that this group has had virtually no focused force; it is for the most part unorganized and powerless." Galbraith himself would concede this point in a 1981 memoir, writing, "Countervailing power often does not emerge. Numerous groups—the ghetto young, the rural poor, textile workers, women clerical workers, many consumers—remain weak or helpless."[12]

Nader's proposal to create a new Center for Study of Responsive Law sought to "remedy this impotence" and to create an "organized structure for making heard the voice of the public in all levels of government and government sanctioned private institutions." The federal regulatory process especially showed the need for this effort, Nader explained. Federal regulatory agencies, including an alphabet soup of New Deal and Progressive Era agencies like the "FTC, SEC, ICC, CAB, FPC, [and] FCC," as well as branches of executive departments, "exist ostensibly to pursue the 'public interest.'" The agencies made policy through action and inaction in their power over standards, rates, licenses, approvals, and so on. But there was a "gap between the citizen and his government," Nader said, and a growing "feeling of powerlessness and the inability to acquire facts and tools of participation."[13]

Program officers at liberal foundations such as Carnegie shared Nader's critical view of bureaucracy and impersonal federal power, and supported his call for citizen empowerment and action. Carnegie Corporation program officer Eli Evans had provided Nader with important advice and contacts in 1967, even paying a law firm to advise Nader on how to legally tackle "controversial public issues" through a federally tax-exempt educational organization. Now Evans raved about Nader's proposal to his Carnegie colleagues, urging them to support a $55,000 grant to help start Nader's new center. Nader specifically sought Carnegie money to finance the creation of a handbook that would teach citizens how to participate in the federal regulatory process. "For the past five years Ralph Nader has lived the life of a lonely reformer in Washington concerned with the great issues of the relationships between the consumer, private industry, and government," Evans explained in November 1968. Nader had successfully navigated the press, Congress, and the White House to force congressional hearings and legislation. Concurring with Nader's analysis, Evans told his colleagues that the "problem of citizen access to government" would be a crucial issue during the next decade. American citizens, Evans said, were increasingly frustrated "dealing with the massive impersonality of so many of the institutions of American life." Nader's study, Evans hoped, could help fend off "a growing feeling of citizen helplessness in the face of a distant bureaucracy." Funding Nader's proposed handbook would mean "starting his Center for Responsive Law" by bolstering Nader's efforts with formal institutional support. Evans was eager to put Carnegie's ample resources behind Nader's cause.[14]

✦

NADER AND EVANS weren't the only liberal advocates hoping to launch a new public interest legal movement to shake up federal agencies and create a counterforce to industry lobbyists and bullheaded bureaucrats. Conservation leaders at the National Audubon Society and the Sierra Club, as well as other young, up-and-coming lawyers and scientists, also were exploring new legal strategies to protect the environment. Inspired by the effectiveness of civil rights and antipoverty lawyers, Audubon Society executives in late 1967 discussed the idea of creating a "Conservation Legal Aid Society," a nonprofit, tax-exempt entity able to litigate on behalf of other groups. "At the present time," an Audubon consultant reported that fall, "there appears to be no national organization which finances court actions brought to achieve specific conservation objectives." The Boston-based Conservation Law Foundation, established in 1966, was perhaps the closest to fulfilling that early vision of an independent environmental law firm, though it focused almost exclusively on New England. The San Francisco–based Conservation Law Society of America, a small group started by Sierra Club–affiliated activists in 1963, articulated a similar legal mission but had yet to file its first lawsuit in 1967. The group referred cases to volunteer lawyers and did legal research on issues related to the preservation of parks, wilderness, and open space. But the San Francisco group was "not in a position to finance, even in part, litigation conducted by other groups," and the group itself declared that it could not be considered a "conservation legal aid society at the present time."[15]

In October 1967, after discussions about possible litigation strategies at its September national convention in Atlantic City, the Audubon Society voted to finance a new "Environmental Defense Fund" led by a group of Long Island scientists and lawyers. The group was established as separate from Audubon because it planned to venture into uncharted legal territory that Audubon's leaders feared might threaten the organization's tax-exempt status. The Environmental Defense Fund's brash lawyer, Victor Yannacone, declared that the new litigation group "would be to conservation what the Legal Defense Fund of the National Association for the Advancement of Colored People has been to civil rights or the American Civil Liberties Union to civil liberties." Fittingly, since the Environmental Defense Fund initially focused on combatting DDT spray programs, Audubon's initial support came from the organization's Rachel Carson Fund, established after her death in 1964. The Environmental Defense Fund's legal campaign against DDT and the government agencies promoting the chemical's use would be another fitting legacy for Carson.[16]

Like Nader's nascent Center for Study of Responsive Law, the new Environmental Defense Fund was a poorly financed, ramshackle affair. During its first few years, the organization operated out of "an attic room in the post office in Stony Brook," according to a 1970 EDF newsletter, near where some of the organization's cofounders worked as scientists at SUNY Stony Brook and at the Brookhaven National Laboratory. The organization's governing executive committee met in the evenings at one of their houses. When the organization finally moved out of its attic offices in 1970, EDF took up residence in a hundred-year-old farmhouse that initially had "no heating system in it" and had "antiquated" plumbing and electrical systems. To clean up the old house, an "army of EDF volunteers, trustees and staff" spent a Saturday scrubbing and painting it, sanding and varnishing the floors, and mowing and weeding the overgrown vegetation. Charles Halpern, the cofounder of another fledgling public interest law group, similarly recalled that for the first six months, the Center for Law and Social Policy was "housed, rent-free, in the row house of one of its four attorneys; the Xerox machine sat on his kitchen table." Public interest law, at its inception, had elite origins and connections, but it also was still a bootstrap affair.[17]

Around the same moment when the Audubon Society and its Long Island partners created the Environmental Defense Fund, the Natural Resources Defense Council also took shape. Over time, NRDC also would develop into a powerful law and science advocacy organization with a multimillion-dollar annual budget. But in the fall of 1968, it was just a new concept. James Gustave Speth, then a third-year student at Yale Law School, circulated a proposal to fellow Yale law students for "a legal action organization analogous to the NAACP Legal Defense and Education Fund, Inc, in the area of environmental defense." Speth imagined creating an organization with about twenty lawyers, with offices around the country. "Decisive action is necessary," Speth's draft proposal explained, if the United States was going to save its "natural heritage." He warned about a possible future of a "frightening world with few if any natural areas, unpolluted streams, or fresh breezes." Private legal actions, Speth argued, could be "an effective instrument for curbing an industrial civilization's abuse of nature."[18]

After a complex courtship brokered by the Ford Foundation, the Yale Law School students joined forces with older and better-established New York lawyers who had ties to the Sierra Club. These lawyers included people like Whitney North Seymour Jr., a Princeton and Yale Law graduate and the son of a former president of the American Bar Association. Seymour was elected to the New York State Senate in the late 1960s and became a United States attorney in 1970. Seymour and some of the other older NRDC founding board members were liberal Northeast Republicans, including members of legendary families in national conservation politics, such as Pinchot, Rockefeller, and Roosevelt. Their new younger colleagues, like Speth, were almost entirely Democrats. With Ford's financial support, these two groups of lawyers together created the Natural Resources Defense Council.

✦

THE FORD FOUNDATION, more than any other major foundation, provided vital early funding to the public interest law movement. In contrast to the $55,000 grant from Carnegie to Nader's center, Ford's generous grants, totaling more than $2 million between 1967 and 1972, propelled the environmental law firms, and the public interest movement, much further and faster than otherwise might have happened. Ford helped launch the Environmental Defense Fund, the Natural Resources Defense Council, the Sierra Club Legal Defense Fund (now called Earthjustice), and other new law groups with a significant environmental portfolio, including the Center for Law and Social Policy, as well as Public Advocates. With additional funds,

during this same period Ford also helped create new civil rights litigation groups, including the Mexican American Legal Defense and
Education Fund and the Puerto Rican Legal Defense and Education
Fund, with a particular emphasis on employment discrimination and
school funding cases.[19]

The Ford Foundation funded these new public interest law firms
because of the remarkable ideological agreement between the foundation and its grantees. The foundation's leaders shared the view of their
grantees that aggressive litigation might make the government work
better. Ford Foundation president McGeorge Bundy, a quintessential
establishment insider who had stepped down as national security advisor in 1966 to lead the foundation, felt strongly that the public interest was "not adequately represented" by the government in a range of
fields, including the environment, communications, and energy policy. Ford program officer Gordon Harrison, who oversaw the foundation's environmental law grants, explicitly declared that government
agencies were the primary target of the new public interest firms. The
law firms, Harrison explained, needed "to bring suits against government agencies, to oversee the performance of government agencies
and take other legal actions to provide the agencies with a broader
view of social interests than they normally get." Public interest law
was one of the foundation's "more important undertakings," Harrison
reflected in 1972. "Government should not be all-powerful." Society
needed a "counterforce" to government that was "not beholden to the
government in any way." Ford's public interest grants aimed to create an "antagonist of government" that would stay clearly within the
bounds of the American legal system, in fact becoming an integral
part of that system.[20]

With backing from Ford and from insiders like Bundy, the field
of public interest environmental law that appeared at the close of the
Johnson presidency thus constituted an attack on federal agencies
from within the liberal establishment itself. The new environmental
lawyers shared Nader's aspiration to perfect the American system of
governance, and they were idealistic and hopeful about peaceful social

change overseen by the courts. In their efforts to uplift the professional citizen, they explicitly distinguished themselves from protesters and rioters, and they believed that the system would respond to their legal claims. "We're hawks," EDF cofounder Charles Wurster told *Sports Illustrated* in 1969, "but we operate entirely within the sociolegal structure. We don't block traffic. We don't sit in. We don't riot." NRDC "believes in the legal process," Stephen Duggan emphasized at the organization's founding conference. "We want to work within it." NRDC could help "renew this country through the time-honored method of using the judicial system for change." Senator Clifford Case, a liberal Republican from New Jersey who supported NRDC's work, felt the same way. Case called NRDC's legal reform efforts a worthy substitute for "demonstrating in the streets and picketing." The *Washington Post* similarly praised the environmental lawyers for "doing exactly what the establishment advised—working peacefully within the system to change the system."[21]

The environmental lawyers' faith in the responsiveness of the legal system reflected the fact that the firms were founded by idealistic, ambitious, and highly educated professionals, almost entirely white men. They believed in the system's capacity for reform because they were privileged products of it. For the most part, like Nader himself, who graduated from Princeton and Harvard Law School, the new environmental lawyers had excelled educationally and professionally. James Gustave Speth, a leader of the Yale student group that cofounded NRDC, graduated from Yale College and Yale Law School and was a Rhodes scholar and a clerk for Justice Hugo Black on the US Supreme Court. The other NRDC cofounders were equally credentialed, with Yale law degrees, editorial positions on the *Yale Law Journal*, and district, appellate, and Supreme Court clerkships. The students' glittering resumes were crucial to persuading the Ford Foundation to invest in the new venture. Ford's Frank Barry was "not particularly moved by the specifics of our proposal," Speth reported to his fellow students about a 1968 telephone call, "but they were very impressed by our vitae. I quote: 'Our eyes popped out.'" Barry told

Speth that "we were 'too good for the big law firms.'" The founders of the Center for Law and Social Policy (CLASP), which started operations in late 1969, also came from elite educational backgrounds, with college degrees from Harvard and Duke, and law degrees from Harvard, Yale, and Duke law schools.[22]

These graduates of elite colleges and law schools were products of the system and believed in its responsiveness, yet they also had been radicalized by the historical events of the 1960s, particularly the civil rights movement and the Vietnam War. Indeed, it is impossible to imagine the public interest law movement emerging in the form that it did separately from civil rights and the war. The experience of Geoffrey Cowan, who cofounded CLASP soon after graduating from Yale Law School, captures some of these direct ties to both civil rights and antiwar activism, and to structural reform efforts within the Democratic Party itself. Cowan grew up in New York City in a wealthy, assimilated Jewish family with a strong commitment to social justice and a deep involvement in Democratic politics. Louis Cowan, Geoffrey's father, was an executive at CBS, responsible for the breakaway success of the network's famous quiz show *The $64,000 Question*. Louis worked during World War II in the Office of War Information and as head of Voice of America, and he served as Adlai Stevenson's media advisor during the 1952 presidential campaign. Pauline Cowan, Geoffrey's mother, who also worked in radio and television, became active on civil rights. Pauline helped initiate "Wednesdays in Mississippi," an effort that brought interracial and interfaith groups of northern women to Mississippi to support racial justice and connect with their southern counterparts. Through their mother's connections, both Geoffrey and his brother, Paul, participated in the Freedom Summer campaign to register Black voters in 1964. In a series of "Letters from Mississippi," published in *Esquire* in September 1964, the two brothers shared their experience in the South and their perceptions of Black disenfranchisement and oppression. Geoffrey Cowan returned in 1965 to help start the *Southern Courier*, a new weekly publication that covered civil rights issues in the South from 1965 to

Geoffrey Cowan interviewing Bobby Bell about school integration in Montgomery, Alabama, for the Southern Courier *in 1965. The civil rights movement and Vietnam War powerfully influenced public interest advocates, inspiring them to social action and deepening their distrust of government authority.* Photo by Jim Peppler, Alabama Department of Archives and History.

1968. Through activism, Cowan later recalled, he came to see that it was possible to make change and accomplish things.[23]

While a student at Yale Law School, Cowan became involved in the antiwar movement and in the "Dump Johnson" campaign to push President Lyndon Johnson off the Democratic presidential ticket. Following the contentious 1968 Democratic National Convention, Cowan played a significant role opening up the party's nominating process for future presidential campaigns. Cowan, who had worked on the unsuccessful campaign of Eugene McCarthy in Connecticut in 1968, helped organize and lead a committee that successfully proposed changes to how convention delegates would be selected. The new system weakened the power of state party leaders and increased the participatory role of voters in selecting delegates through the Democratic primary elections. The official restructuring of the presidential primaries delivered another blow from within against traditional Democratic power structures.[24]

Cowan also continued to follow developments in the Vietnam War closely. In late 1969 and early 1970, even as Cowan and Charles Halpern and other young lawyers started the Center for Law and Social Policy out of Cowan's Washington, DC, townhouse, Cowan also wrote a column on political affairs for the *Village Voice*. Cowan and his coauthor, Judith Coburn, harshly criticized the "war criminals" responsible for the Vietnam conflict. In one December 1969 essay, they denounced the lack of accountability for leaders who had welcomed the opportunity to wield power, but then had not spoken out against the war. "Few declined to enter that 'Vietnam situation' room," Cowan and Coburn wrote, "and not one man chose to leave it and tell the country what went on there." Key figures seemed to suffer no consequences, they fumed. "A criminal war should not be like a poker game where the players can cut their losses, shake hands, and come back to play again." In another December 1969 essay, Cowan and Coburn revealed details about Operation Phoenix, a secret CIA program against the Viet Cong that involved "kill quotas" for American advisors working with teams of foreign mercenaries.[25]

Fury and disillusionment about the war fueled a broader critique of the liberal establishment, including leaders of the mainstream press who acted almost as a "fourth branch" of government. "Perhaps no institution so deserves to be indicted for society's active or passive support of the war," Coburn and Cowan wrote of the *Washington Post* in January 1970. The newspaper had "played cheerleader to official Washington, praising and justifying each new group increase." The mainstream press lived in a cozy world, Coburn and Cowan argued, where editors "tend to believe government officials and to distrust controversial stories which can't be officially confirmed." To Cowan, the infamous story of the My Lai Massacre illustrated this complicity. After an initial report that dozens of civilians had been killed by American soldiers in a village in South Vietnam in the spring of 1968, mainstream newspapers did not follow up on the story. In October 1969, however, Cowan learned that a secret army court-martial proceeding was underway. Cowan tipped off the investigative reporter Seymour Hersh, who tracked down the story. Major newspapers refused to run Hersh's account, but the shocking report of the massacre, in which, it turned out, hundreds of villagers had been killed, became one of the most significant and damning events of the entire Vietnam War.[26]

"There was something about that period," Ralph Nader later recalled of the late 1960s and early 1970s. "Vietnam. Civil rights. Coming off the struggles of the '60s—it did something to people that age." Geoffrey Cowan's personal journey encapsulated many of these crucial elements. A child of significant privilege, Cowan had a series of life-altering experiences with civil rights and antiwar activism, and with the push for political reform within the Democratic Party. Cowan was unusual in that he touched each of these developments at such a high level. He would even marry within the public interest movement, joining forces with Aileen Adams, a graduate of Smith College and former Peace Corps volunteer in Brazil. Adams worked part-time on truth-in-advertising campaigns at Ralph Nader's Center for Study of Responsive Law while attending law school at Howard University.[27]

The Vietnam War and the civil rights movement served as defining issues for the young public interest lawyers, shaping their views of the government and their ambitions for their own lives. During the summer of 1965, Charles Halpern, who would cofound CLASP along with Geoffrey Cowan and others, was preparing to join the law firm Arnold, Fortas & Porter, an influential and politically connected corporate law firm whose named partners had deep ties to the Democratic establishment going back to the Roosevelt administration and the New Deal. (Fortas was about to be appointed to the Supreme Court by Lyndon Johnson.) Halpern had recently graduated from Yale Law School and had clerked for a federal judge on the District of Columbia Court of Appeals. The summer before taking the new law job, however, he spent a month in Louisiana volunteering to do civil rights work with the Lawyers Constitutional Defense Committee. Halpern later particularly recalled visiting a rural Black church to

hear the charismatic civil rights leader James Farmer speak, and sing-
ing "We Shall Overcome" with the mostly Black attendees. The experience of volunteering and traveling in the South, and the inspiration
of being connected to the civil rights movement, prompted Halpern to
think about what kind of lawyer he would be, and about whether his
work would have meaning and purpose.[28]

Pro bono work particularly engaged Halpern while he was at the
law firm. In 1967, two years before he launched CLASP, Halpern
and two friends started the *Selective Service Law Reporter* to gather
and share information on Vietnam War draft resistance cases, which
were unreported and largely unknown. The group collected military
draft cases from around the country and developed a network of
lawyers doing that kind of work. Halpern recalled feeling that they
knew they were doing something significant when the director of
the Selective Service System, General Lewis B. Hershey, ordered
ten copies of their publication for his own office, perhaps because the
agency did not have its own compilation of the draft resistance case
records. About the early years at CLASP, Halpern later recalled,
"We had anti-war people passing through our place. We were part
of the anti-war left."[29]

The war and conflicts over civil rights also had a defining impact on
Harrison Wellford, a Harvard political scientist whom Nader hired to
run the new Center for Study of Responsive Law. A professor at Yale
Law School had reached out to Wellford to tell him about Nader's new
project. At the time, Wellford had completed his doctorate in political
science at Harvard and was working with Richard Neustadt, a leading
presidential scholar, and also with Henry Kissinger. Wellford shared
the elite background of many of Nader's early followers, coming from
a politically connected and prominent white Virginia family with roots
going back to the early seventeenth century. After graduating as vale-
dictorian of Davidson College, Wellford had been a Marshall Scholar
at Cambridge University before enrolling in the graduate program at
Harvard. One summer while in graduate school, Wellford taught at
LeMoyne College, a historically Black college in Memphis. Several of

his Black students were arrested for picketing a department store that refused to hire Black store clerks. Writing about the incident several years later, Wellford recalled seeing the "façade of racial tolerance" pulled back to reveal a "carnival of humiliation" for African Americans encountering the court system. His students had been tried "en masse" rather than as individuals, and all were pronounced guilty, including one teenage girl who had simply been "walking home from a movie when she was caught up in the police drag net."[30]

Following Nixon's election in 1968, Henry Kissinger tried to hire Wellford to join him at the National Security Council. One of Wellford's best friends had been killed in Vietnam, however, and he fiercely opposed the war. Wellford instead took the job with Nader. He moved to Washington in May 1969, just before another onslaught of young student researchers, about a hundred of whom arrived that summer. Wellford later recalled working at Nader's center during the day, and protesting at Lafayette Park or outside the Pentagon at night. His wife "would put a baby on her back, I'd put a baby on my back, and we had to be really, really careful about not getting teargassed," Wellford later recalled. "You can't imagine how thrilling it was."[31]

✦

IN LIGHT OF THESE transformative experiences, perhaps it is no surprise that, despite the elite connections and privileged educational backgrounds of people like Cowan, Nader, and all the others, foundation program officers considered this new generation of legal advocates as in need of some supervision. Both the Ford Foundation and the Carnegie Corporation looked on public interest law, their new creation, with trepidation and anxiety, in addition to pride. In creating the Natural Resources Defense Council, Ford forced the Yale law students to join with the older, more established New York law group in a kind of shotgun marriage. The rebellious law students, who initially aspired to an egalitarian organizational structure with no single chief executive, quickly found themselves working under a former assistant United States attorney with an inaugural board that included prominent New

York lawyers and civic leaders. To persuade Ford to finance the Center for Law and Social Policy, Cowan and CLASP's other cofounders similarly were forced to consult with prominent judges, private lawyers, and government attorneys and academics. Former Supreme Court justice Arthur Goldberg supported CLASP as an active chairman of the board. CLASP partnered with leading law schools, including Yale, Penn, Michigan, and Stanford, for financial backing and to gain the schools' stamp of legitimacy and educational purpose.[32]

The Ford Foundation pushed its public interest grantees to partner with members of the establishment elite because it feared the political and legal risks inherent to funding this new approach to the law and to challenging the government. The foundation itself had come under congressional attack in 1968 for grants that were seen as too political in nature, including travel grants to members of Congress and to former staff members of Senator Robert F. Kennedy. In the midst of a congressional review of rules governing private foundations, Wilbur Mills, the powerful chairman of the House Ways and Means Committee, twice wrote to Bundy to ask about "allegations" that the Ford Foundation planned to fund the Natural Resources Defense Council's "novel approach" to environmental law. Foundation president McGeorge Bundy consequently worried about the "precarious state of the consensus" underlying the public interest law firms' legal strategies. According to Gus Speth, one of the NRDC student founders, Bundy "told us to get lost until the foundation tax legislation passes both houses." Other foundations also were putting pressure on the Ford Foundation, concerned that "Ford was endangering the whole foundation world by funding us." Fearing that the whole venture was collapsing, Speth wrote despairingly to his mentor Charles Reich in October 1969, "What do you think, were we merely naïve players in the game of grantsmanship or were we a potential danger that the power structure had to reach out and crush?"[33]

Bundy and Speth rightly worried about the prospects for launching public interest law firms. President Nixon and his advisors pressed the Internal Revenue Service to "take a close look at the activities of left-wing organizations which are operating with tax-exempt funds," according to a staff memo to the president in June 1969. "I want action," Nixon scrawled on the memo, demanding that his staff "follow up hard on this." In 1970, the IRS initially denied NRDC its nonprofit tax exemption, by extension threatening the entire foundation-supported public interest law sector. IRS staff questioned whether broad, cause-oriented litigation around the environment qualified as a charitable activity in the same way that poverty or civil rights law did. Following a brief but aggressive campaign that engaged prominent congressmen, including House minority leader Gerald Ford, the IRS reversed course and granted NRDC its tax exemption in November 1970. According to Bundy, it was "critically important in the early stages of this new kind of law that we should avoid the appearance that politics and philanthropy are entwined."[34]

The Ford Foundation therefore carefully monitored the fledgling public interest law firms to ensure that the foundation and the firms complied with IRS guidelines and insulated themselves from criticism for being overly political or irresponsible. A committee of four former presidents of the American Bar Association vetted the Ford Foundation's public interest law grant docket. These "wise counselors," whose meetings Ford president Bundy regularly attended, helped "tranquilize the doubters," according to one Ford program officer, protecting the grant-making program against trustees, regulators, and other potential critics. Each organization also had an internal litigation committee to review proposed lawsuits. During their first few years of operation, Ford Foundation consultants visited each public interest law firm for a couple of days every few months and filed lengthy reports to Ford program officers on the legal cases and management of the office.[35]

The Carnegie Corporation, like the Ford Foundation, conditioned its grant to the Center for Study of Responsive Law on Nader's creating a structured organization with a legitimate and formal board of trustees. Nader only partially bowed to Carnegie's demands. He created a board for the center, but stacked it with his sister Laura Nader, his cousin Edmund Shaker, himself, and two longtime collaborators.

Carnegie's program officer Eli Evans interviewed prominent lawyers and legal academics to vet both Nader and his proposed trustees. The foundation's decision to award the grant helped give Nader "legitimacy," recalled Harrison Wellford, the Harvard political scientist whom Nader hired to run the center. Nader's growing personal celebrity, however, also made it possible for him to stand apart as something larger than other emerging 1970s nonprofit legal advocates. His unusual leadership style and public profile continued to fuse two distinctive personas: the iconoclastic 1960s public intellectual, along the lines of Rachel Carson and Jane Jacobs, and the ambitious new 1970s organizational entrepreneur, like the lawyers and scientists launching the Environmental Defense Fund, Natural Resources Defense Council, and Center for Law and Social Policy.[36]

The pressure to play by establishmentarian rules rippled out from the Internal Revenue Service to the foundations, and then was imposed by the foundations on their grantees. The liberal public interest organizations sought to change the system from within. They used the system's tools—law, science, and the media—to appeal to the system's ideals. The organizational founders, graduates of elite law schools, saw themselves as restoring democracy by engaging American citizens in the nation's civic institutions. The civil rights and antiwar movements exposed how the traditional establishment could entrench power in unaccountable government institutions that would use lies, violence, and other tactics to retain control and pursue their objectives. Nader and his public interest allies showed how these institutional flaws and weaknesses also were manifest in the environmental crisis and in the exploitation and suffering of other marginalized groups, including workers, the poor, and the disabled. The system, they argued, required a new understanding of power and new institutional checks on the dominant institutions of the postwar period.

Chapter Four

"Insecure" Power and the Nonprofit Rationale

WHY CREATE A PROLIFERATING ARRAY OF SMALL, independent, issue-based nonprofit organizations, often staffed by just a handful of underpaid young people, rather than try to seize control of the government itself or pursue reform through well-established labor organizations? In the late 1960s and early 1970s, the answer to this question lay in a new understanding of power that emphasized the corrupting influence of institutional structures and societal position. The veteran community organizer Saul Alinsky explained this perspective in his 1969 book *Reveille for Radicals*. Recounting his experience confronting "fat-bellied, fat-headed, and cynical" labor leaders, Alinsky described how he came to understand their leadership failings as situational. "Through experience you learn to see people not as sellouts and betrayers of moral principles," Alinsky wrote of the individuals who had disappointed him. "I now see these people as having moved from the Have-Not's to the Have's." Alinsky, in other words, no longer perceived corrupt labor leaders as individually flawed, but rather saw them as having been led astray by virtue of their place in a larger system of power. Morality, Alinsky argued, was "largely a rationalization of the point you happen to occupy in the power pattern at a given time."[1]

Alinsky's understanding of institutional power systems and their warping effect on individuals had important strategic implications:

improving the ethical character of leaders would not necessarily change the behavior of those individuals when they held institutional power. Rather, any concentration of power tended, inevitably, toward misuse and the abuse of the powerless. To activists on the left at the end of the 1960s and in the early 1970s, the list of corrupting and potentially oppressive institutions increasingly included the very government bureaucracies intended to serve the public, as well as labor unions created to empower workers. The structures of the system, they argued, mitigated against the moral individual in positions of institutional leadership and necessitated a counterforce in the form of participatory democracy, community organizing, and citizen advocacy.

Ralph Nader and the founders of other public interest nonprofit organizations agreed with many aspects of this critique. In a 1971 interview with the *New York Times*, Nader explained his own "theory of power." If power is "going to be responsible," Nader said, "it has to be insecure, it has to have something to lose." Nader's theory of insecure power explained why he had so little interest in state socialism as an alternative to corporate capitalism. Nader had traveled to Moscow in the summer of 1962 on a special tour sponsored by the Soviet tourist agency. He came away dismayed by "how orchestrated" the tour was, constantly reinforcing the "whole Kremlin party line." Nader concluded that "social justice delivered tyrannically is verbiage."[2]

Nader rejected the idea that socialism presented an alternate path to human liberation. "Putting all economic power in the state would be disastrous," Nader argued, "because it would not be insecure." The problem with socialism, he said, came down to "one word—it's called bureaucracy." Advocates of socialism failed to recognize that "if the government becomes a bureaucracy with its own momentum and ability to be secretive, heady, corrupt, introverted, then the society is basically trading one master for another." Despite its rhetorical commitment to equality, socialism tended toward bureaucratic injustices, Nader believed.[3]

Yet Nader also saw democratic institutions as suffering from some of the same corrupting forces. In a democracy, Nader noted, power comes from the people. But the "administration of government begins to erode this principle in practice immediately." As democratic power concentrated in bureaucratic public institutions, it increasingly became unresponsive and even oppressive. Nader thus sidestepped the Cold War conflict over whether capitalism or socialism was a superior economic model and the traditional left-right debate about whether power should be in private or public hands.[4]

Nader argued instead that power in the American system could be kept "insecure" through the creation of independent, nonbureaucratic, citizen-led organizations that existed somewhat outside the traditional American power structure. He also believed that traditional institutions, including government agencies, needed internal mechanisms that facilitated accountability and participation. Nader's democratic vision had its roots in his childhood experience in northwestern Connecticut, in a restaurant-owning immigrant family that participated actively in the local New England town meeting–style governance. In Nader's view, both public and private institutions, as they grew in scale, tended to monopolize power and oppress individual citizens. Nader's philosophy emphasized open and competitive markets, small private businesses, and, most important, an active citizenry.

Nader's theory of power explains the complicated attitude that he and many liberal and leftist activists like Alinsky had toward labor unions in the late 1960s and early 1970s. Nader believed in the power of unions to represent workers, but he was also deeply skeptical that union leaders would be reliable agents for progressive reform. In Nader's view, union bosses since World War II had too often positioned themselves as partners with industry and government, striking bargains that yielded economic growth, higher wages, and union jobs at the expense of the health and well-being of workers, communities, and the environment. Labor was thus a third major target of Nader's reform effort. "When he tilts," one journalist wrote of Nader in 1971, "it is not at windmills, but at Big Business, Big Labor, and even more important, Big Government." It was this constellation of power, the postwar alliance between business, labor, and government at the heart of the "New Deal Order," that Nader sought to disrupt and break apart.[5]

After the highway safety victory in 1966, Nader turned immediately to other health and safety issues, including workplace hazards. Nader's investigations and his public pressure on Congress drew attention to worker safety and helped advance a series of laws to protect workers, including the 1968 Natural Gas Pipeline Safety Act, the 1969 Federal Coal Mine Health and Safety Act, and the 1970 Occupational Safety and Health Act. Even as Nader allied with labor reformers to protect workers and advocate for legislation, however, he denounced union leaders who he thought did too little to protect workers on the job. "Too often there has been silence," Nader said about union leaders in a speech to the 1967 convention of the Oil, Chemical, and Atomic Workers Union. "Too often there has been lip service." Nader called on the union to "recover its nerve" and advocate for protections against explosive pipelines, radiation, and other threats.[6]

Nader particularly criticized the leadership of the United Mine Workers of America (UMWA) union. In February 1968, Nader wrote an article in the *New Republic* on coal pneumoconiosis, or "black lung" disease. Nader urged Congress to force extractive industries like coal to take "preventive measures to diminish the bodily depletion of their employees." Protecting coal miners fit into Nader's conception of "bodily rights." Nader noted that little action had occurred in the five years since a 1963 Public Health Service study of the black lung problem. He blamed government officials, corporate executives, and cooperative labor leaders. "Inert administrators who are surrounded by indifference," Nader said, had failed to address coal mining's "human wreckage." Coal operators and UMWA labor leaders together were permitting "slow death in the mines." Nader demanded a congressional inquiry to generate momentum to combat the "insidious ravages of coal dust." The following month, Nader wrote to Secretary of the Interior Stewart Udall, calling Udall's agency "the captive" of coal operators. Nader's public letter derailed a sanguine report to Congress from the US Bureau of Mines, scheduled for the following day but never

An explosion in a coal mine near Farmington, West Virginia, in November 1968 killed seventy-eight miners and sparked intense criticism of federal worker protections. Congress passed the Coal Mine Health and Safety Act the following year, one of a series of laws to strengthen health and safety regulation by federal agencies. Mine Safety and Health Administration.

released. By contrast, Nader argued that the coal operators, the miners union, and the government cared more about keeping down production costs than they did about protecting miners themselves. The UMWA, Nader wrote, had chosen the "alleged health of the industry over the health of its workers. . . . The *UMWA Journal* devotes endless space to the threat of other energy sources to coal but virtually nothing to the crucial matter of coal dust hazards."[7]

In September 1968, President Johnson introduced a new mine safety bill that extended federal enforcement to the face of the mine and to surface coal mines, and addressed the problem of coal dust. Nader and several outspoken doctors working with miners in West Virginia played crucial roles in getting respiratory health standards into the new legislation. A series of devastating mine explosions, including one near Farmington, West Virginia, that killed seventy-eight men in November 1968, also generated momentum for the bill. "There is nothing accidental about these disasters—they are caused by unsafe practices," Nader said about the November explosion. Coal miners, he said, faced a situation "reminiscent of medieval times." Udall eventually conceded that the Department of the Interior could do more to safeguard miner health and safety. "In all honesty, Ralph Nader was right when he wrote me earlier this year," Udall acknowledged in December 1968, though he continued to deny undue industry influence.[8]

In January 1969, Nader escalated his attack on UMWA leaders, writing a harsh two-and-a-half-page statement that Democratic congressman Ken Hechler read on Nader's behalf at a rally in Charleston, West Virginia. In the statement, Nader accused UMWA president Tony Boyle of getting too close to the coal operators. Nader called for Boyle's ouster. Nader said, "I doubt whether there is any union in this country whose highly paid leadership has been as insensitive and inactive toward health and safety conditions." Boyle had failed in his responsibility to protect the coal miners. The miners, Nader said, "may conclude that Mr. Boyle is no longer worthy of being your leader, that you need new leadership that will fight for your rights and not snuggle close to the coal operators and forget about the men who are paying the dues and paying the price."[9]

Nader worked with dissidents within the UMWA to press for federal and corporate action on black lung disease. "An epidemic of black lung disease is raging," Nader declared. The "dank, dark, and damp interiors of these coal mines represent inhuman environments," he said. Greater mechanization of mining had produced a "finer dust" that increased the threat to miners. Yet union leaders, including Boyle, were not pursuing federal health benefits and worker protections aggressively enough. In April 1969, Nader attacked Boyle again, accusing the union leader of corruption and nepotism, and of conspiring with coal industry leaders. Nader alleged that there were four hundred "bogus" union locals with voting rights that helped entrench the leadership. Union leaders, Nader charged, were conspiring with the industry in "secret meetings" to avoid action on health and safety protections. The union leadership,

Joseph Yablonski, candidate for United Mine Workers president, speaking to the press in Washington, DC, in May 1969. Yablonski's murder on New Year's Eve, on the order of the incumbent president, Tony Boyle, revealed the depth of corruption within the miners' union and spurred calls for accountability and democratic reform. AP Photo/Henry Burroughs.

he said, was using its pension fund to aid the union-owned National Bank of Washington, rather than pay benefits owed to miners.[10]

Nader encouraged union reform candidate Jock Yablonski to campaign to oust Boyle from the union presidency in the December 1969 UMWA election. When Yablonski came to Washington to seek support, Nader helped with logistics and arranged press coverage. Yablonski's candidacy, however, first ended in defeat in the fall of 1969, and then in horrible tragedy. On New Year's Eve 1969, three weeks after Boyle resoundingly won reelection, Boyle's henchmen murdered Yablonski, his wife, and his daughter at their Pennsylvania farmhouse. The killings, which eventually sent Boyle to prison until his death in 1985, demonstrated to Nader the potential depths of union corruption. Power "can corrode or corrupt regardless of what crucible—corporate, governmental, or union—contains it," Nader declared in his 1971 book, *Action for a Change.*[11]

The focus on worker safety thus led unexpectedly to direct conflict with union leaders and, as in the UMWA case, into active involvement with the union democracy movement. "Safety got us in the door and then when we got in the door we looked around and said, 'Oh my gosh!'" recalled Alan Morrison, a lawyer who started working with Nader in the early 1970s. The public interest movement's pursuit of highway safety, for instance, sparked significant conflict with the teamsters union. Trucks posed a serious threat to automobile drivers, and tired truck drivers, using unsafe vehicles, were more likely to get into accidents on the highway. Yet the union leadership in the late 1960s and early 1970s focused more on wages than on safety. Morrison recalled, "The ethos of the union was that you drove what you drove and you drove hard and you drove long hours." Drivers benefited financially when they pushed the limits of their time on the road, and companies preferred to pay a smaller number of drivers to work harder and longer. The public interest lawyers opposed this arrangement and petitioned the government to regulate hours of service. They also sought to protect against retaliation those workers who complained about the unsafe vehicles they were forced to drive. As with miner safety in UMWA negotiations with coal operators, the teamsters union leadership often was willing to trade concessions on driver protections for other union priorities, particularly wages.[12]

Union activists who sought to shake up their leadership confronted undemocratic processes within the union. Morrison and other lawyers sued to counter censorship in union newspapers, to force union votes on contracts, and to facilitate democratic participation in union governance. The public interest criticism of the unions was complicated, and resembled its relationship to government regulatory agencies. Nader and his allies supported unions in principle and on specific issues of common agreement, and they also forcefully attacked the unions for not doing enough to protect worker safety and health or to allow worker participation in governance. Morrison explained, "We were for organized labor but we were also for the worker. This caused a lot of tension, but we brought a number of cases against the Teamsters and against other people as well." The critique of labor organizations, of course, drove a wedge between unions and liberals, and between unions and the Democratic Party, that would help undermine unions in the years ahead.[13]

✦

DISILLUSIONMENT WITH the performance of public institutions and skepticism about union leadership pushed Nader and other citizen activists toward an alternative: nonprofit organizations independent of government, industry, and unions. To be sure, citizen groups had organized to protect rivers and forests and to fight pollution long before the 1970s. In the United States, a robust tradition of citizen protest against government and industry runs back to the early republic. Fishermen and farmers fought early milldams to protect access to common property resources and private landholdings. Society women in the Progressive Era created state Audubon clubs to promote conservation and protect wild birds. The Idaho Wildlife Federation, Izaak Walton League, and Sierra Club led key post–World War II campaigns against western dams. The League of Women Voters pushed for water pollution controls and watershed planning.[14]

But these earlier activists often differed from those of 1970s antiestablishment critics in their prescription for change. The League of Women Voters, for example, strongly deferred to government experts in the 1950s and 1960s, and emphasized the value of "wise planning and intelligent, persistent, cooperative action." Rather than stridently oppose the government, the league sought to cooperate with officials and experts. Some League of Women Voters leaders criticized the "emotionalism and rhetoric" of newer antiestablishment activists and identified instead, as historian Terrianne Schulte has argued, "with the political actors they were trying to influence." Their emphasis on collaboration contrasted strikingly with the harsh, outraged tone of the Nader FTC task force, which called explicitly for the resignation of the Federal Trade Commission's chairman.[15]

The American nonprofit sector surged during the 1970s, fueled by dissatisfaction with both government and industry. New applications for nonprofit status would average about thirty-six thousand per year between 1977 and 1980, nearly triple the rate a decade earlier. Americans were creating thousands of organizations to address ecological issues, consumer rights, public interest law, and other causes, with perhaps forty thousand local environmental organizations created in just a few years. An influential 1975 report by the Commission on Private Philanthropy and Public Needs concluded that Americans turned to voluntary organizations in response to a "sense of alienation" that they felt "in the face of giant, impersonal institutions of government and business." Voluntary organizations, which drew their support from interested citizens, operated on a more human scale. The growing voluntary sector also reflected a political philosophy that "there is no one body, one governing structure, that holds the answers to society's problems." According to the 1975 report, Americans had become "less persuaded than ever to stake our destiny totally on the wisdom or beneficence of centralized authority." The weakness of centralized power structures had shown "the virtues of a vigorous public-minded and independent sector."[16]

A new understanding of political economy emerged in the early 1970s that characterized *both* business and government as flawed institutions that needed to be counterbalanced by a "third sector," consisting of nonprofit and public interest organizations. This perspective, which drew on a Progressive Era legacy of civic reform, reflected disillusionment with both capitalism and socialism as monolithic governing models. "No single institutional mechanism, private or public . . . is capable of correcting all the shortcomings of an economic and social system," wrote the economist Burton Weisbrod and his colleagues in a seminal multiyear study of public interest law sponsored by the Ford Foundation and published in 1978. "A variety of institutional devices are needed."[17]

Liberals had long emphasized how the concept of market failure or inefficiency justifies government's regulatory role. And the new regulation of the early 1970s appropriately aimed to remedy classic examples of market failure, such as air and water pollution. But the public interest movement that Nader and his allies sought to create aimed at a different problem: what some observers awkwardly called "*government market failure.*" As Weisbrod and his colleagues explained, the public interest movement assumed "both types of failures—the market and the government." "Political and economic pressures on the decision-making process" caused failures that could be solved only by "extra-*governmental* efforts."[18]

Nonprofit organizations provided a remedy for the "serious limitations" of both business and government, Weisbrod would later elaborate in his 1988 *Nonprofit Economy*. Profit-seeking businesses "cannot be relied on to undertake activities, such as pollution control and consumer health and safety protection, that would be unprofitable even if consumers valued them highly." And government agencies "face political pressures that make them excessively responsive to well-organized demands from industry and other pressure groups but far less responsive to the interests of poorly organized groups such as consumers." Americans turned to nonprofits as a "potential safety valve," Weisbrod wrote.[19]

The expansion of the nonprofit sector in the 1970s coincided with what sociologist Robert Putnam has characterized as a decline in the "social capital" of the United States. Fewer Americans, Putnam argued, participated in clubs, leagues, and voluntary associations. How does the proliferation of nonprofit organizations in the 1970s make sense in the context of Putnam's account of declining social engagement? One explanation lies with Nader's "professional citizens." By the 1970s, nonprofit organizations had shifted increasingly from voluntary labor to a more corporate paradigm based on "trained employees." Nonprofit advocates, whether based within the emerging Nader network or at new environmental organizations such as the Natural Resources Defense Council and Environmental Defense Fund, frequently worked on behalf of members and donors who did not themselves actively engage in civic action. Citizen involvement in these groups usually entailed paying dues or reading a newsletter. The growth of these membership organizations coincided, Putnam noted, with a sharp decline in more active voluntary church groups, unions, fraternal and veterans' groups, and parent-teacher associations.[20]

◆

FOR ADVOCATES LIKE Ralph Nader and the lawyers at EDF and NRDC, reimagining the role of "the State" and creating new nonprofit public interest groups especially meant rethinking the role of lawyers in American society. Professor Charles Reich mentored many of the new public interest lawyers as a faculty member at Yale Law School. "The lawyer must carry the responsibility of his specialized knowledge," Reich argued in an influential 1965 essay on the "humanistic study of law." Rather than be a secondary or supporting character who was shielded by attorney-client privilege and who simply fulfilled the wishes of corporate and government clients, Reich urged lawyers to play a more central part in the pursuit of justice. In a frequently repeated phrase in his essay, Reich declared, "In a society where law is a primary force, the lawyer must be a primary, not a secondary, being." Reich himself had graduated from Yale Law in the early 1950s and then clerked for Supreme Court justice Hugo Black. While in Washington during his clerkship and afterward, Reich grew friendly with another justice, William O. Douglas, a passionate conservationist and outspoken New Deal liberal who had grown disillusioned with federal administrative agencies. Reich shared with Douglas a deep love of the outdoors from summers spent at his own family's house in the Adirondacks, and he would join the justice on long weekend walks along the Chesapeake and Ohio Canal towpath. After returning to teach at Yale Law School in the early 1960s, Reich expressed an increasing skepticism about the growing federal bureaucracy and argued for the need to secure individual rights against the government's overweening power. In his constitutional law classes at Yale, Reich led students to question traditional liberal approaches to government. Reich went so far as to camp out with students in a shantytown in the Yale Law School courtyard in 1969 to protest the "establishment." Roderick Cameron, executive director of the Environmental Defense Fund, channeled Reich's vision when he declared in 1970, "In the Ralph Naders we see lawyers as catalytic agents in our society."[21]

Many of the public interest law advocates like Nader and Cameron particularly distinguished themselves from the Washington lawyers who defended corporations before the government, and who worked to align government regulation with their clients' business interests. Lloyd Cutler was a Democratic Party stalwart, cofounder of the powerful firm Wilmer, Cutler & Pickering, and perhaps "Washington's most successful lobbyist," according to the *Los Angeles Times*. Active on civil rights issues and influential with the Kennedy and Johnson administrations, Cutler also represented the automobile trade association and the pharmaceutical lobby. Cutler embodied many of the contradictions of liberalism in the late 1960s. When the highway safety bill became unstoppable in 1966, Cutler lobbied successfully to weaken disclosure requirements and block criminal penalties for corporate safety violations. The scene in the closing moments of legislative drafting, when Nader camped out in one Senate anteroom and Cutler, representing the auto industry, stayed in another, was a metaphor for Nader's new model of governance: industry lobbyists countered on equal terms by public interest lawyers representing citizens.[22]

In his analysis of power in the United States, Nader considered Washington lawyers like Cutler, pillars of the liberal establishment, a central obstacle. Nader called corporate lawyers the "chief power broker between the special interests and the government." Corporate lawyers, Nader said, hid behind the lawyer-client relationship to "pursue all kinds of antisocial behavior." The lawyers helped thwart efforts to address air pollution, mine safety, and other societal problems. Corporate lawyers, of course, countered that they simply sought to persuade the government that their clients' cases had merit.[23]

Nader's campaign for ethical lawyering resonated strongly with law students, young lawyers, and faculty allies, such as Reich, within the top law schools. In 1969, Nader-affiliated students picketed and protested outside Cutler's office, arguing that lawyers had an obligation to serve the "public interest." The students criticized the law firm's "use of its skill and wide influence" on behalf of polluting industries. Picket signs blasted Cutler's ethical failings. "Lloyd Cutler & General Motors. More air pollution for your lungs," one sign read. The students specifically protested a decision by the Justice Department to settle an antitrust suit over antipollution devices for motor vehicles. Cutler had brokered the deal. While the students denounced Cutler to the press, Nader hovered in the background on the sidewalk, looking favorably over the protest. Cutler, in turn, criticized the student protest as a form of "McCarthyism." The "extremism on the right," Cutler complained, was close to the "extremism on the left." Nader, like Senator Joseph McCarthy in the 1950s, Cutler said, "believed he had a divine monopoly on knowing where the public interest lies."[24]

The same week that the students and Nader picketed Cutler's office, Nader published a blistering attack in the *New Republic* on law schools and law firms. Nader used Harvard Law School, his alma mater, to illustrate how legal training took "bright young minds and conditioned them to the demands of the corporate law firm." Nader lamented lawyers' "escape from responsibility" for justice. The nation's legal crises, he argued, had their origins in legal education. Problems associated with access to government, environmental regulation, and international justice all resulted, in part, from a litany of failures of the legal profession. "Lawyers labored for polluters, not anti-polluters, for sellers, not consumers, for corporations, not citizens, for labor leaders, not rank and file." Lawyers, Nader continued, too often advocated for weakening regulatory standards, displacing residents to build highways, granting subsidies to the rich rather than the poor, and using government to create special tax breaks and other privileges. "None of this and much more seemed to trouble the law schools," he lamented.[25]

Nader had a different vision for lawyers. "I really literally want to see 5,000 public interest lawyers in this town in six years," Nader told a reporter in 1971. "It's just got to be that big. At least a one-to-two ratio compared with the private-interest lawyers." Nader called for "building a new way of life around citizenship action." Nader complained that the society had "thousands of full-time manicurists and pastry-makers but less than a dozen citizen-specialists fighting full time" against water pollution or hunger. As someone who dedicated his career to a range of public problems, he modeled this idea of a "professional citizen." In Nader's conceptualization, active citizens were "not part of any governmental, corporate, or union institutions. Rather they are independently based, working *on* institutions to improve and reshape them or replace them with improved ways of achieving just missions." Nader's model involved "taking a serious abuse, laying it bare before the public, proposing solutions, and generating the necessary coalitions to see these solutions through." His system depended on people acting as individuals rather than "as cogs in large organizational wheels."[26]

In addition to lawyers and other professionals acting in the public sphere, Nader called for "on-the-job citizenship." He urged employees to break the "complicity of silence" to reveal institutional abuses and counter "organizational tyranny." Nader's investigative research depended heavily on informants and whistleblowers within companies and within government agencies who provided him with crucial information. Employees, in their capacity as citizens, he suggested, needed to maintain their own individual ethical standards, and not allow themselves to be corrupted by their employer. Everyone with a job, Nader wrote, knew about some abuses in their industry or agency. He urged them to act on this information. "Until unstructured citizen power is given the tools for impact, structured power, no matter how democratic in form, will tend toward abuse, indifference, or sloth." The corruption of power, he argued, occurred within "supposedly democratic governments," as well as "unions, cooperatives, motor clubs, and other membership groups."[27]

Where Saul Alinsky's model for social change called for an extended process of community empowerment by organizing groups around salient issues, Nader emphasized individuals. Nader's proposed mass movement by professional citizens necessarily attracted individualistic middle-class and educated followers. What Nader and his followers seemed to be calling for, one commentator wrote in the *Baltimore Sun* in 1970, "is a hero, someone with all the answers, a great deal of muscle and a large amount of courage to battle industries, congressmen, cabinet officers and bureaucrats. The unanswered question is where are such heroes supposed to come from?"[28]

Chapter Five

Making Regulation "Government-Proof"

ON A FRIDAY NIGHT IN EARLY NOVEMBER 1968, Ralph Nader delivered a lecture at Harvard Law School, where he had graduated ten years earlier. It was just days before Richard Nixon's election, ending eight years of Democratic control of the White House. Only a week later the *Wall Street Journal* would publish the first report from Nader's Federal Trade Commission investigation, exposing favoritism and malfeasance in that agency, including the "peculiar tale" of a remote office in Tennessee set up as a sinecure for one of Chairman Paul Rand Dixon's friends. The Carnegie Corporation was in the process of making a grant to Nader to start his new Center for Study of Responsive Law.

The success of that summer's investigation of the trade commission made Nader want to marshal more smart, idealistic young people in his campaign to expose problems with the administrative agencies and in industry. In a speech entitled "Law Schools and Law Firms: The Mordant Malaise or the Crumbling of the Old Order," Nader exhorted a crowded auditorium of nearly four hundred students to join him in creating new public interest law firms. Together, he said, they could counter the "power brokers" who typically dominated Washington policy-making. If just a few hundred lawyers would dare to bring professional representation to the public, they could rip "aside the curtains of secrecy," Nader declared. "Official Washington would never be the same again."[1]

Nader's visit generated an enthusiastic student response. An editorial in Harvard's student-run law paper touted Nader as the law school's "most outstanding" graduate. Nader wasn't rich and hadn't written any judicial opinions, the *Harvard Law Record* explained, and as a student Nader hadn't even joined the *Harvard Law Review*. But he'd "done something that no other graduate has accomplished. He has challenged with notable success irresponsibility at the highest echelons of corporate power." Students could help Nader by "contributing their talents during the summer to Nader's investigation of federal regulatory agencies."[2]

Inspired by the opportunity to make change, and willing to overlook the tedium of wrestling with the bureaucracy, more than a thousand young people applied to work with Nader in Washington during the summer of 1969. He chose ninety-five young researchers. He sought out self-starters who could "combine moral indignation with laborious research." Many were graduate students in law, medicine, and engineering. Others were college students or recent college graduates. Only two of those selected were African American, and only ten were women.[3]

Young lawyers serving as project directors oversaw task forces of seven to fourteen young researchers. One team studied the Department of Agriculture, focusing on food inspection, pesticides, and programs for poor and minority populations. Another group scrutinized the Food and Drug Administration's standards and regulatory enforcement. A third tackled the Interstate Commerce Commission's regulation of trucking, railroads, shipping, and pipelines. Other research teams examined air and water pollution control and occupational safety. Each task force aimed to research and then write its report within a year or, at most, two. Grossman, the independent publishing house that had released Nader's *Unsafe at Any Speed*, would publish the reports as books. Nader's Center for Study of Responsive

Ralph Nader poses with "Nader's Raiders" on the steps of the US Capitol, Washington, DC, 1969. Copyright © John G. Zimmerman Archive.

Law retained the copyright to these books, plowing royalties back into further research efforts.[4]

Many of the Nader task force reports focused on pollution and related environmental concerns and fed directly into new regulatory initiatives. These environmental investigations expanded upon Nader's auto safety work. His concern for bodily rights meant addressing the ways that government and business shaped the environment within which Americans lived and worked. Nader placed so much emphasis on environmental threats because he believed that their physical toll far exceeded other, better-known, forms of violence, such as street crime and urban unrest. In a 1969 essay in the *Nation*, Nader called car crashes and workplace accidents and diseases the primary forms of violence that threatened Americans. Fewer than three hundred people had died in urban riots during the previous three years, Nader observed. By contrast, each year more than fourteen thousand people died on the job. Exposure to toxic and hazardous materials, including asbestos, coal dust, pesticides, and radiation, greatly endangered the long-term health of workers. Nader urged that the word "pollution" simply be abandoned in favor of "violence." Writing in the context of controversial US military spraying of the toxic defoliant Agent Orange in Vietnam, Nader compared air pollution to "domestic chemical and biological warfare." "Our children," Nader said, "are children of smog, who have never known fresh water, or clean air. They are the sufferers of our biological warfare."[5]

◆

NADER SITUATED ENVIRONMENTAL and consumer threats at the center of domestic politics, showing how they revealed the pervasive failures and corruption of American industry and government. Environmental hazards like air and water pollution also made particular sense as a target for citizen-centered investigations and campaigns. Pollution of common resources like air and water often creates diffuse sets of victims with neither the financial resources nor the individual incentive to pursue legal claims. Citizen activists like Nader and his followers in the early 1970s sought to force governments and industry to account for these external costs of pollution, and for the common interests that often were lost when only narrow economic concerns were heard.

Nader's air and water investigations starting in the summer of 1969 illustrate his strategy for using student research teams to expose and challenge the regulatory establishment to do more to prevent pollution. John Esposito was the twenty-nine-year-old lawyer who led the air pollution task force that produced *Vanishing Air*, a scathing 1970 critique of federal air pollution control efforts. Esposito had graduated from Harvard Law School in 1967 and worked for Nader on the FTC report during the summer of 1968. He was a "dark-haired, brooding man with penetrating eyes and penchant for sports shirts and bell-bottom trousers," according to

Urban air pollution, including smog from motor vehicles in Los Angeles, prompted fierce criticism of the federal government's collaborative approach to regulation and yielded a new Clean Air Act with strict Congressional mandates in 1970. Keystone Press / Alamy Stock Photo.

the *New York Times*. The *Times* also described Esposito as drawn to conflict and public confrontation.[6]

The air pollution investigation led by Esposito naturally extended Nader's ongoing attack on the automobile industry. Much of the nation's most serious air pollution came from motor vehicles. Congress had passed clean air legislation in 1967 to expand the federal role in air pollution control. The 1967 legislation, however, took a collaborative approach by pushing state and local governments, rather than federal agencies, to determine regulatory policy. The legislation embraced regional diversity by allowing air standards to vary by location. The law also expressed concern for the cost of containing pollution, and instructed regulators to take expense into account in setting regional air quality standards. These cost considerations provided an easy way to avoid taking action. If the federal government wanted to override state pollution controls, it had to convene a conference of interested parties, including industry representatives, to guide its regulatory decisions. The industry itself was determining how its pollution would be regulated.[7]

Vanishing Air blasted the 1967 Federal Air Quality Act as a "hopeless failure." The National Air Pollution Control Administration and other federal regulators, *Vanishing Air* argued, were a "disorganized band of government officials acting out a pollution control charade." The essential characteristic of federal air pollution control was its "basic irrelevance to the problem." Regulators failed to provide adequate oversight of emissions control devices, and they neglected enforcement. Given free rein, automobile companies delayed technological improvements and obstructed progress on pollution control. Electric utility companies and other industries deceived the public by pretending to abate pollution while investing the minimum possible. To combat "militant corporate radicalism," the Nader group called for antitrust enforcement, tougher controls, stiffer penalties, and more money and staffing for antipollution efforts. In his foreword to *Vanishing Air*, Nader argued that the "deep loss of popular belief" in government's ability to fight air pollution was part of "a broader absence of confidence, particularly among the young, that government can be honest and courageous enough to administer law for the people." Polluted air, in other words, revealed corrupt and cowardly political leadership on a broader and more pervasive scale.[8]

To illustrate this failure of leadership, the Nader report chose an unlikely target for special criticism: the liberal icon Senator Edmund Muskie, Democrat from Maine, 1968 vice-presidential candidate, and chair of the Senate Subcommittee on Air and Water Pollution. Muskie had a national reputation as "Mr. Pollution Control," and he sought to burnish his environmental credentials in advance of his planned 1972 presidential campaign. Muskie allied himself with the rapidly emerging environmental movement. On April 22, 1970, just a few weeks before *Vanishing Air* was released, Muskie spoke at three large Earth Day rallies. "You can't stand in front of a group like this without feeling the power which can flow from it," Muskie told the crowd. Americans needed to "make every day Earth Day."[9]

Yet the Nader task force ripped into Muskie and declared his environmental halo unwarranted. Going after Muskie exemplified Nader's instinct for attacking liberals who he thought did not go far enough to protect the public interest. Muskie, according to *Vanishing Air*, had "failed the nation" on air pollution. The report described the "collapse of the Federal air pollution effort starting with Senator Edmund Muskie." Instead of providing leadership, the Senator merely offered up "politically expedient platitudes" even as he gave out a "business as usual license to polluters." Muskie, the report contended, had weakened the 1967 air pollution bill in part to help powerful pulp and paper mills in his home state of Maine. According to the report, Muskie continued to offer weak solutions. *Vanishing Air*, in its closing pages, linked Muskie with Nixon, arguing that the "environmental bandwagon is the cheapest ride in town." At their press conference releasing the report, Esposito and Nader flatly declared that Muskie did "not deserve the credit he has been given." Muskie's actions, Nader contended, had deflected more forceful leadership by other senators, such as Walter Mondale, Gaylord Nelson, and Warren Magnuson.[10]

Nader's criticism produced a political crisis of sorts for the Maine senator. The day after Nader and Esposito's press conference, Muskie held an hour-long meeting with the press to rebut Nader's charges. Muskie rejected the report's "personal attack" on him, and insisted that he had fought hard to counter "public apathy, industry resistance and presidential and Congressional reluctance." Muskie defended himself as someone who tried to accomplish things. He called Nader "a newcomer to this cause" and urged him to participate in a "constructive effort" to address pollution problems. Americans needed to find ways to "move across the lines of confrontation and reach agreements and get results." Muskie conceded, however, that new air legislation would have to include tougher national standards, which his 1967 legislation had eschewed in favor of regional rules. In a sign of how Nader's group embraced confrontational tactics, John Esposito showed up at Muskie's press conference and issued a dueling statement that criticized Muskie's "disappointing record" and urged Muskie to address the "outrageous environmental crisis."[11]

In addition to its attack on Muskie, a leading Democratic presidential aspirant, *Vanishing Air* sharply criticized Jennings Randolph, a veteran Democratic senator from West Virginia. Randolph chaired the Senate Committee on Public Works; Muskie chaired its Subcommittee on Air and Water Pollution. Like Paul Rand Dixon, the subject of Nader's FTC report, Jennings Randolph was a longtime New Deal Democrat, first elected to Congress in 1932. Randolph strongly supported many liberal causes, including the 1964 Civil Rights Act, Medicare, and antipoverty programs. Yet Randolph and Nader had clashed over coal-mining health and safety legislation. Now the Nader task force accused Randolph of weakening air pollution legislation to protect West Virginia's coal industry. Randolph blasted *Vanishing Air*'s "excesses of exaggeration and vituperation" and warned that Nader and his staff wanted to "destroy the coal industry." Nader proposed "impossible-to-achieve requirements" that would wreck the West Virginia economy, Randolph warned, creating "unemployment and hunger and privation."[12]

Nader's attack on Randolph's and Muskie's pollution control records illustrated his ambivalent relationship with the Democratic Party. In response, many leading Democrats rushed to share their disdain for Nader's methods. The day after Muskie's defensive press conference, Jim Wright, a Texas congressman who would later become Speaker of the House of Representatives, took to the floor of the House to express the contempt many Democratic elected officials felt toward Nader. Wright denounced the Nader group's "juvenile, gratuitous, and fulsome flutter of personal criticism" of Muskie. To Wright, Nader and his team were a group of "self-appointed overseers" who needed "to recognize who is on what side." The attack on Muskie, Wright said, was like a rookie football player "who thinks the way to win games is to tackle his own quarterback." Instead of blaming Muskie for the 1967 act's deficiencies, Wright said that Nader and his team should recognize that "except for Senator Muskie, there might not even be an Air Quality Act." Blaming legislators like Muskie was "utterly stupid, counter-productive, and self-defeating." Representative Edward Boland from Massachusetts, another staunch liberal, joined Wright to "deplore the unjustified charges" against Muskie in the Nader report.[13]

Muskie and his allies might have bemoaned Nader's charges, but the tactics seemed to work. By going after the Democratic Party's leading presidential candidate on his signature issue, Nader helped produce legislation tougher than it otherwise might have been. Leon Billings, Muskie's chief aide on the clean air legislation, later described Nader and the task force report as "the gel" responsible for "a lot of the debate" on the 1970 Clean Air Act. *Vanishing Air* was "a frontal assault on my boss," Billings recalled in 2014. Muskie was "stung" both personally and politically by the Nader report, and it prodded him to further action. Along with Muskie's competition with Nixon and the broader popular movement represented by Earth Day, Billings said that Nader's direct attack "provided the political stimulus" necessary to drive the clean air legislation forward. A central part of Nader's strategy, and essential to his ultimate political effectiveness, was that "Nader believed that you didn't attack your enemy if you wanted to accomplish something, you attacked your friend." Nader would withhold his support as a bargaining strategy and urge congressional liberals to do the same in order to get tougher legislation. "If Muskie shows he's too satisfied he restricts himself from getting more," Nader told Muskie's staff privately.[14]

The Clean Air Act of 1970 differed from earlier regulatory models in important ways that directly reflected the critique of federal agencies articulated by Nader and others. "The idea of Congress actually, specifically, directing the executive branch what to do, when to do it, how to do it, and what the consequences were if they didn't do it or didn't do it adequately was precedential," Leon Billings said of the 1970 air pollution law. "It had never happened before." The leg-

A coal barge moves past a United States Steel Corporation coke plant on the Monongahela River near Pittsburgh, Pennsylvania, in 1973. The U.S. Environmental Protection Agency previously had cited the plant for air pollution violations under the new Clean Air Act. Photo by John L. Alexandrowicz, U.S. National Archives and Records Administration.

islation rejected the Great Society's deference to state regulators and its reliance on intergovernmental conferences and voluntary industry compliance. The new air quality law also made clear that executive agencies could not be trusted to strictly enforce air pollution controls. Pollution standards, Nader argued, worked only if they were "adequately drafted, kept up to date, vigorously enforced, and supported by sanctions." The tough legislation thus signaled a profound and pervasive distrust of government even as it expanded federal regulatory powers.[15]

Reflecting this distrust of executive agencies, the Clean Air Act sought to rebalance power between the three branches of national government. Under this new legislation, Congress gave the executive branch detailed mandates and stipulated dates by which specific pollution reductions should be attained. Courts stood ready to enforce those mandates. Congress also empowered citizens to file lawsuits to force state and federal agencies to comply with the law. The Clean Air Act thus epitomized "command-and-control" regulation in the lack of discretion that it afforded to both regulatory agencies and regulated industries. "Deadlines, mandatory statutory requirements, citizen suits and judicial review"—these marked a clear separation from earlier regulatory strategies and were hallmarks of the clean air legislation and other early-1970s environmental laws, Leon Billings later explained.[16]

✦

NADER'S FIGHT AGAINST water pollution followed a script very similar to the clean air struggle, and also yielded tough new legislation: the Clean Water Act of 1972. David Zwick was a Harvard Law School student in his second year when Ralph Nader came to campus in the fall of 1968. Zwick had an unusual background for a law student. He had attended the US Coast Guard Academy and served for two years in Vietnam, some of that time as captain of a patrol boat in the Mekong Delta. Zwick returned home from Vietnam in 1967, thinking that the war was a "big mistake" and feeling very "skeptical of what government tells us." Ten days after coming back to the United States, he enrolled at Harvard. Zwick volunteered for Eugene McCarthy's 1968 presidential campaign and attended the 1968 Democratic convention as an alternative delegate. Zwick protested—and was teargassed—in the famous clash at Grant Park in Chicago during the convention.[17]

In his speech at Harvard Law School just before the November 1968 election, Nader argued that government was so captured and overwhelmed by special interests that it couldn't protect the public on its own. In an interview more than thirty-five years later, Zwick recalled being blown away by Nader's visit. Zwick "ran up after his speech and joined a small group of students gathered around." Nader "scribbled my name" on a piece of scrap paper, he recalled. A few days later, someone working with Nader called Zwick to invite him to come work in Washington that summer for $50 per week.[18]

Zwick joined a team of graduate students studying water pollution. Although he knew little about the subject, Zwick was older and more experienced as a result of his Vietnam service. He soon found himself in charge of the group, assigning research tasks and assembling interview reports. As with the air pollution study, the researchers concluded that a collaborative approach that emphasized regulatory actions by state governments also did little for water pollution control. More than a hundred water conferences had been held to address specific pollution problems, but no regulatory enforcement had followed. For other highly polluted waters, no enforcement conference had ever taken place.[19]

Zwick returned to law school in the fall of 1969, working on the water book while continuing his classes. At first Zwick traveled back and forth between Cambridge and Washington, DC, still hoping to pass law school classes that he had mostly stopped attending. He eventually dropped out of law school to work full-time for Nader, returning to complete his degree a few years later. Zwick rented a single room in a basement a few blocks from the Nader offices and threw himself into the water work. Things were moving fast. Following passage of the Clean Air Act, which President Nixon signed on December 31, 1970, Edmund Muskie, chairman of the air and water pollution subcommittee, held extensive hearings on water pollution starting in early 1971.[20]

Coinciding with the congressional investigations, Zwick's task force released its seven-hundred-page study, *Water Wasteland*, in April 1971. *Water Wasteland* came to the same conclusions as *Vanishing Air*, calling the federal water pollution program a "miserable failure." The water report had taken a full year longer than the air study, in part because Zwick and his chief coauthor, Marcy Benstock, went back to redo some of the work by the student researchers. In his introduction to *Water Wasteland*, Nader called water pollution a "crime against humanity." Federal water pollution control efforts were a "complex charade" carried out by "long-faltering, if not pathetic, bureaucracies." Even William Ruckelshaus, administrator of the Environmental Protection Agency, declared of their critique of federal water pollution control, "I agree with Ralph Nader."[21]

On the water issue, Nader's group followed a similar political strategy as with the Clean Air Act. They positioned themselves as independent, unaffiliated outside experts, vigorously attacking both Nixon and Muskie for inadequate proposals. The enforcement mechanisms were too weak to guarantee compliance and to improve water quality, the Nader team argued. In September 1971, Zwick testified before Congress in his role as project director for the water pollution project. The nation's water remained "dirty," Zwick declared. Federal officials could not point to a "single major body of water" that federal efforts had "restored to any of its original uses as recreation spot, fish and wildlife habitat, or public drinking water supply." Zwick urged Congress to write laws that would be "government-proof." By this he meant that Congress should design regulations that "defy administrative bungling, timidity, or dereliction." While Americans could "hope for aggressive and competent administration of pollution laws," they could not "unfortunately, count on it."[22]

Distrust of federal agencies lay at the heart of Zwick's policy recommendations, as with the clean air policy proposals. To Zwick and many other antipollution activists, the failure of water regulation resulted from discretion granted to federal regulators. Zwick called for a "national water quality standard" and for using suitability for fishing and swimming as a "clear yardstick" to measure progress in reducing bacteria and other contamination. Setting a firm federal standard with a target date, Zwick argued, would force the development of new technology and prompt action by polluters and agencies that might otherwise drag their feet. Mandatory penalties and aggressive enforcement would back up the strict standards. Congress needed to "insulate" administrators from external pressures by "depriving them of the discretion to choose not to enforce the law." Zwick's distrust of agency enforcement efforts also explained his call on Congress to authorize citizen lawsuits, as it had with the Clean Air Act. Litigation initiated by citizens—when the government couldn't or wouldn't enforce standards—was the "only real guarantee, in the end, that the law will work." Zwick explicitly rejected the idea that the government should have a "monopoly on enforcement."[23]

Zwick helped mobilize political support for passage of the Clean Water Act, and he left his mark on the specific legislative provisions. Behind the scenes, Senate staff members contacted Zwick for information and sought his approval of draft provisions. Zwick sometimes waited outside the Senate staff room to consult with committee staff members, including Leon Billings, on the Democratic side, and Tom Jorling, legislative counsel on the Republican side. To advance the legislation, Zwick and Nader, with support from sportfishing equipment manufacturers, also created the Fishermen's Clean Water Action Project during the summer of 1971. The group, which sought to amplify the political voice of sport and commercial fishermen on behalf of pollution control, later became Clean Water Action, an advocacy organization that Zwick led for more than thirty years.[24]

◆

VANISHING AIR AND *WATER WASTELAND* were just two of more than a dozen major investigative reports produced by Nader's teams. Other studies, such as *The Chemical Feast* (1970) and *Sowing the Wind* (1972), contributed to changes in pesticide regulation, food safety, and drug safety. Nader had "thrown open the entire catacomb," Leonard Ross, a Columbia law professor, wrote of several Nader reports for the *New York Times* in August 1971. Ross saw the books as a powerful indictment of the regulatory structures established in the early twentieth century. "Every page of these books answers the question, who regulates the regulator?" Ross wrote. Nader's studies showed that the answer, at the close of the 1960s, usually was the regulated industries themselves. "Why has business been able to boss around the umpire?" Ross asked. "What went wrong with the brave new alphabet agencies of the New Deal?" The revolving door between business and government explained a great deal. Nine of the most recently retired members of the Interstate Commerce Commission later worked as lawyers or executives in the companies that they had recently regulated. But the Nader reports showed that individual self-interest alone was not a sufficient reason. "Many of the regulatory agencies didn't have to be corrupted—they were designed from the outset to strangle competition and succor monopoly." Ross concluded that regulatory reformers from an earlier generation had been "taken for a ride." Industry had "simply used regulation to escape the risks of the marketplace." To be sure, not all the reviewers were as enthusiastic about the lessons of the Nader task force reports. One critic complained that *Water Wasteland* read "like an unedited collection of seminar papers in Poly Sci 300: Politics of Pollution." Another called the report on the Food and Drug Administration "a disorganized rant."[25]

While the Nader reports occasionally slipped into extravagant youthful criticism and overheated outrage, for the most part the reports were earnest, high-minded, academic in style, and, frankly, boring to read. Agency budgets, congressional committee structures, and legislative proceedings were their typical focus. Robert Fellmeth, who worked on the trade commission report in 1968 and supervised the 1969 study of the Interstate Commerce Commission, explained, "It's not the dashing young Cossack charging in and laying waste to the establishment. It's working long hard hours, reading day after day what is boring trivia, hearings, memos, letters, scholarly treaties. It's just hard tedious work." Colman McCarthy, writing in the *Washington Post* in 1970, similarly described Nader's acolytes as smart, motivated young men and women possessing "the rarest of all assets among reformers—an acceptance of plodding." "Tedious study" was Nader's chief weapon, another *Washington Post* writer explained in a 1971 article: "By his own assessment, consumer advocate Ralph Nader's only power is the power of the information his corps of 'raiders' ferrets out and discloses, coupled with the power of lawsuits and petitions to government agencies."[26]

Despite the tedium, young people flocked to work with Nader. At a time of tremendous social turbulence and political uncertainty and conflict, Nader's reform strategy was optimistic in its assertion that careful research and reasoned argument would change policy. More than four thousand students reportedly applied to work with Nader in the summer of 1970, including a third of the Harvard Law School student body. Nader chose about two hundred participants to work on projects that summer.

Nader further tapped into college student enthusiasm by encouraging the creation of student-led Public Interest Research Groups. Starting in Oregon and Minnesota after Nader's campus speaking tours, student activists persuaded university administrators and fellow students to create, often through student referendums, a new student activity checkoff fee to fund public interest research and advocacy. The activity fees were small, initially just a dollar or so per student, but aggregated across a large student body, the fees could create a fund adequate to hire employees to coordinate and mobilize volunteer student labor. The Public Interest Research Groups (commonly known as PIRGs) often focused on state-level policy issues, including enforcement of clean water standards, consumer protections, and energy policy. PIRGs also advocated for state bottle bills that imposed a deposit fee on cans and bottles to encourage recycling. Students often were able to receive course credit for internship projects that they undertook with the PIRGs.[27]

Public interest groups were "sprouting like daisies" across the country, according to the *Los Angeles Times*. Working with Nader, though, wasn't all sweetness and flowers. Student workers during the summer of 1970 complained of "dictatorial treatment, poor supervision, lack of meaningful assignment," according to one report. Nader himself blamed the students for their lack of discipline and focus, and their lack of commitment to the cause. "Some of them wanted, you know, soft-ball teams," Nader said dismissively. "They wanted to develop a sub-society, they wanted people to sit with them in the morning and say, 'How are you doing?' Hand-holding." Nader expected his followers to share his maniacal work habits and single-minded devotion. Asked how many hours per week his acolytes should work, Nader told a reporter half-jokingly, "The ideal is 100." Nader would call his project leaders when they were on vacation and complain that they weren't working on their project. Nader regularly telephoned colleagues late into the night to discuss strategy and research. The long hours also came with low pay. "They could earn much more working for a corporation," Nader said righteously about his employees, "but it's a labor of love, and they won't starve."[28]

Nader's style characterized many of the new nonprofit organizations—an experiment in "*not* developing a bureaucracy." Mark Green, one of Nader's top lieutenants, called it simply "orchestrated chaos." "Have you been down to that office?" Green asked a reporter in early 1971. "It's impossible. I work at home because I can't get anything done when I go down there." Instead of sound management principles, Nader relied on youthful idealism and passion. He gave student researchers ample freedom and opportunity to take on big research projects, but he also was "an authoritarian with a mania for detail and perfection." His style inspired many young people, though it particularly attracted highly educated, white liberals. Few Black activists found Nader's approach appealing, or were actively recruited by him.[29]

For those individuals who thrived working with Nader, however, the opportunity launched them into prominent careers in public affairs. "I'll still be a Raider when I'm 60," the twenty-five-year-old Green declared proudly in 1971. Green continued to work for Nader through the 1970s, eventually becoming the director of Congress Watch. Later in his life, Green was elected the first public advocate for New York City, and he ran unsuccessfully for mayor, senator, and state attorney general. John Esposito, lead author of *Vanishing Air*, became one of the directors of the Nader-initiated Campaign GM, an effort to pressure the auto company to adopt "corporate responsibility" and address issues related to safety, pollution, and minority hiring. Esposito later became chief counsel for the New York State Consumer Protection Board. David Zwick, who coauthored *Water Wasteland*, led Clean Water Action, a grassroots lobbying group, for decades. Marcy Benstock, who coauthored the water book with Zwick, returned to New York City, where she waged a lengthy, and ultimately successful, fight to block a highway down the west side of Manhattan. Jim Turner, who wrote *Chemical Feast*, continued to work on food safety and food additives, such as saccharine. Turner participated in efforts to pass an organic food safety bill and to regulate dietary supplements.[30]

Other young Nader followers leveraged their research and writing skills into careers as journalists. James Fallows, lead author of a Nader book on industrial pollution in Savannah, Georgia, and another key Nader report on Congress, became a speechwriter for Jimmy Carter and then an award-winning political journalist and the editor of *U.S. News & World Report*. Michael Kinsley, author of a 1976 book on the regulation of commercial satellites, subsequently became the editor of the *New Republic* and the founding editor of *Slate* magazine.[31]

Nader himself became the leader of a growing nonprofit empire with wide-ranging policy influence. By 1971, Nader had surrounded himself with what the *Washington Post* called a "bewildering network of organizations, all devoted to a staggering array of public issues." In keeping with Nader's antibureaucratic mentality, the array of organizations consisted of many small ventures specializing in particular issues. Public Citizen, the largest entity and the closest to a conglomerate, housed Nader projects focused on congressional reform, public health, energy, and public interest litigation. Other independent Nader ventures dealt separately with auto safety, airlines, disability rights, and corporate accountability. A proliferating number of other unaffiliated nonprofit organizations joined Nader's sprawling collection of investigation efforts and policy ventures. These citizen activists included a new group of public interest law firms that used litigation and the courts to fight the destructive tendencies of misguided and captured government agencies.[32]

Chapter Six

"Sue the Bastards"

On Friday, March 20, 1970, a group of promi-
nent environmental leaders, New York lawyers, and philanthropists
gathered at the Princeton Inn in Princeton, New Jersey, to officially
launch a new public interest environmental law group, the Natural Resources Defense Council. The stately mansion in which the founding
conference took place matched the new organization's high-powered
boosters. US senator Clifford Case, a liberal Republican in his third
term representing New Jersey, attended, as did John B. Oakes, the
influential editorial-page editor for the *New York Times*. W. R. Hearst
Jr., the powerful editor of the Hearst papers, sent a representative. David Brower, the former head of the Sierra Club who now led Friends
of the Earth, also participated. Representatives from other fledgling
law groups, including the Center for Law and Social Policy and the
Environmental Defense Fund, showed up to help set in motion the
new litigation group.[1]

NRDC represented a different approach from the one initially
modeled by Nader and his research teams. Nader and his citizen
researchers aimed to pressure Congress to pass tough new federal legislation. The Princeton conference attendees, by contrast, proposed to
influence government agencies by suing them in court and intervening
formally in their administrative proceedings. In a panel discussion
entitled "The Role of the Natural Resources Defense Council" confer-

ence speakers explained that NRDC and the other environmental law firms had to hold government true to a public purpose that was going unfulfilled, either because private interests dominated and "captured" the agencies, or because the agencies themselves were isolated and misguided bureaucratic fortresses.

David Sive, a pioneering environmental lawyer active in the Sierra Club who was an early NRDC trustee, described the problem of pervasive bias toward industry on the part of regulatory agencies: "The Federal Power Commission is power-oriented, the Atomic Energy Commission is atom-oriented, the Interstate Commerce Commission is railroad-oriented. The general interest must often fight not only the developer, which may be a private company, but the very governmental agency which is supposed to regulate that company." Sive's comments echoed a critique of regulatory agencies going back to James Landis's 1960 report to President Kennedy and then more recently articulated by Ralph Nader's student researchers. By embracing the private objectives of the companies that they were meant to regulate, Sive and others argued, federal agencies themselves had become an environmental threat.[2]

The idea that litigation by citizen groups might usefully counter agency power was becoming an increasingly widely held view by liberals. Just a week before the NRDC conference, George McGovern, Democratic senator from South Dakota and the eventual Democratic presidential nominee in 1972, introduced federal legislation to expand the legal grounds available for environmental litigation. McGovern's measure was entitled "The Environmental Protection Act of 1970." It sought to establish a "federally guaranteed right to a pollution-free environment." The legislation, which was modeled on a similar bill introduced to the Michigan state legislature, proposed to open the federal and state court systems to environmental lawsuits by citizens. McGovern's measure never passed. But provisions from the bill, including the ability of citizens to sue to protect the environment, were incorporated successfully into other 1970s environmental legislation, including the Clean Air Act of 1970 and the Clean Water Act of 1972.[3]

The proposal to establish a formal "right to a pollution-free environment" reflected the concern that government agencies had lost their way. "Traditionally, environmental protection has been left to the Federal and State Governments and their regulatory agencies," McGovern explained when he introduced the legislation. "They were supposed to act to protect the environment on behalf of the public." But increased litigation in the late 1960s to challenge highways, pollution control, and industrial activities revealed a "widespread feeling the public agencies regulating private interests often end up not regulating but representing that private interest." A January 1969 oil spill off the coast of Santa Barbara, California, made the results of this situation "painfully clear," McGovern said. The Department of the Interior had avoided holding a public hearing on the federal oil leases on the grounds that a hearing might stir up public opposition. Santa Barbara residents who sought to block the oil leases lacked the standing to sue, however, because the Interior Department was the official "protector of their interests." The federal oil leases had been issued over their resistance. And then their worst nightmare occurred.[4]

McGovern's legislation sought to remedy this lack of standing to sue in order to give citizens a chance to appeal to a different branch of government: the judicial system. "The Bill," McGovern explained, "rests on the assumption that the courts, when prompted by concerned citizens, are fitting instruments for developing and enforcing society's rules of self-preservation." Faith in the courts as a potential safeguard ran through the nascent environmental law movement. "We must use the courts because administrative agencies are not working properly," said James Moorman, the lead environmental lawyer at the Center for Law and Social Policy. Speaking at a panel at the NRDC founding conference, Moorman praised courts over specialized agencies. "Courts still can be shocked," Moorman argued. Courts also provided a level playing field: "a one to one situation no matter how rich or powerful or influential one side may be." In a speech the following month to mark the first Earth Day, Roderick Cameron, executive director of the Environmental Defense Fund, likewise described courts as

"largely free of the economic and political pressures of vested interests." Courts "stand on a higher plane," Cameron said, and could serve
as the "one social institution" that might provide "powerful therapy for
the unresponsiveness of the political branches of government." Congress and the federal agencies were too vulnerable to corporate influence, Cameron thought. In contrast to independent courts, Cameron
argued, "industries who profit by rape of our environment see to it that
legislators friendly to their interests are elected, and that bureaucrats
of similar attitude are appointed."[5]

The newfound liberal faith in courts expressed by McGovern and
others flipped on its head 1930s New Deal thinking. During the New
Deal, independent executive agencies were touted as the solution to
major social problems. Back then, liberal lawyers like James Landis
had criticized litigation as "overheated" and praised the "calm of scientific inquiry" carried out by agency experts. Agencies such as the
Securities and Exchange Commission, where Landis served as a com-
missioner, or the Tennessee Valley Authority were seen as possessing
the necessary expertise to best represent the public interest. Economic
management programs, overseen by federal bureaucrats, were imagined as a promising way to balance supply and demand and bring
economic recovery. At that time, the new federal agencies and liberal
regulatory schemes had famously clashed with a more conservative
judiciary. When the Supreme Court struck down both the National
Industrial Recovery Act and the Agricultural Adjustment Act in the
1930s, President Franklin D. Roosevelt went so far as to threaten to
pack the court with liberal justices to force it to back his expansion of
executive power.

By the late 1960s and early 1970s, however, the script had reversed
for many liberals. Now they had more faith in courts than in agencies.
The perceived limitations of federal agencies justified expanded oversight by judges. Agency deficiencies also led courts to welcome new
litigants into the courtroom and to entertain new kinds of legal claims.
A 1966 civil rights case, *United Church of Christ v. Federal Communications Commission*, involving a Mississippi television broadcaster,

proved crucial for expanding access to federal courts so that citizens could sue federal agencies. The broadcaster had aired discriminatory coverage of civil rights protests, in clear violation of the fairness doctrine that governed federal broadcast licenses. Despite complaints by citizens and civil rights organizations, however, the Federal Communications Commission had still renewed the broadcasting license.

Judge Warren Burger, then on the Court of Appeals for the District of Columbia, wrote the opinion in *United Church of Christ* that encouraged citizen lawsuits and participation in agency decision-making. Burger might seem an unlikely judicial spokesperson for a civil rights plaintiff, and an unusual jurist to help lay the foundation for public interest law. He was an Eisenhower appointee to the appellate court whom Richard Nixon soon would name as the next chief justice of the Supreme Court. Yet Burger's ruling showed how widespread the critique of agencies had become.

New parties had to be allowed to intervene in administrative proceedings, Burger explained in his opinion. The idea that the Federal Communications Commission could "always effectively represent the listener interests," Burger wrote, was "one of those assumptions we collectively try to work with," until it no longer "stands up under the realities of actual experience." Federal agencies like the FCC, Burger concluded, did not always effectively represent the public, and their failures left a void for outside third parties to fill. Consumers could help an overtaxed public agency identify issues and problems, Burger wrote. Consumers were "generally among the best vindicators of the public interest." Without consumer input, in fact, the agency might not act successfully alone. "In order to safeguard the public interest in broadcasting," Burger concluded, "some 'audience participation' must be allowed in license renewal proceedings."[6]

Burger's *United Church of Christ* opinion provided a "foundation-stone" for the larger field of public interest law, according to Charles Halpern, cofounder of the Center for Law and Social Policy. The case might have focused on the rights of African American consumers in Mississippi, but the ramifications of opening regulatory proceedings to the listening audience were far-reaching. Burger's ruling, according to Halpern, showed that the "traditional regulatory model didn't work" as long as regulatory agencies heard only from corporate interests. Burger also signaled—in Halpern's phrase—that "the courthouse door is open." Citizen groups could sue agencies over their regulatory decisions.

For activist lawyers, like Halpern, looking for new tactical opportunities in the late 1960s, Burger's decision in *United Church of Christ* justified establishing elite, specialized public interest law firms. Burger's "landmark decision," Halpern and the CLASP cofounders explained to the Ford Foundation in their grant application, "underscored the need for public interest advocacy." Halpern later recalled the reasoning: "The black tenant farmers in Mississippi don't know how to do this game. What we need is people who know how to play the Washington game, to really monitor administrative agencies on an on-going basis, and become players." Few Washington attorneys, however, served unrepresented groups. The "Washington bar . . . skilled in dealing with the Federal government" was "rarely available" to serve clients without a lot of money. Organizations like the Center for Law and Social Policy, Halpern believed, could fill the void. The same aspirations animated the founders of the Natural Resources Defense Council, who aimed to bring elite representation to legal interventions by citizens to protect the environment.[7]

With rulings like *United Church of Christ*, the federal courts increasingly expanded standing to sue beyond narrow economic interest. Previously, under the guidelines of the 1946 Administrative Procedure Act, federal regulatory proceedings had emphasized purely economic considerations; only parties threatened with a financial loss generally had the legal right, or "standing," to participate formally in the proceedings. The opening of the courts now reflected a profound change in thinking about what mattered in society and who had the right to contest it.

Changes in standing doctrine correlated with the new theories about "public goods" articulated by economists like John Kenneth

Galbraith. In his 1958 book, *The Affluent Society*, Galbraith rejected "the myth that the production of goods . . . is the central problem of our lives." A wealthy society such as the United States, he argued, needed to move beyond its narrow focus on economic production to emphasize better quality of life, including environmental amenities. Changes in legal standing recognized these new social claims, and encouraged lawsuits to safeguard less direct economic interests. The litigation also expanded the policymaking role of the courts. Admitting new legal claims enhanced the federal judiciary's power to review agency decisions and elevated the courts as a means to respond to critical social problems.[8]

In a pivotal lawsuit over a proposed hydropower facility in New York, the federal courts granted legal standing to plaintiffs concerned about the "aesthetic, conservational, and recreational aspects of power development." In the case, *Scenic Hudson Preservation Conference v. Federal Power Commission*, conservation activists sought to block industrial development on Storm King Mountain, a popular recreational destination along the Hudson River. Consolidated Edison, the regional utility, proposed to pump river water up Storm King into a storage reservoir during inexpensive off-peak hours, and then release it to power hydroelectric generators during peak times. The Storm King project, in some ways, was ahead of its time—the kind of energy storage system now contemplated as a means to integrate variable renewable energy into the electrical grid. Yet the pipes, pumps, turbines, and wires would have industrialized a celebrated mountain landscape and threatened recreational fishing.

The Federal Power Commission, the agency in charge, argued that the conservationists who sued to block approval of the project had suffered no "personal economic injury" meriting court review. The agency's argument about who had standing matched historical precedent, but times had changed. The court of appeals allowed the litigation to proceed, and the proposed project was eventually canceled. In addition to encouraging more environmental lawsuits, the *Scenic Hudson* case led directly to the founding of the Natural Resources Defense Council. Buoyed by their successful litigation, several veterans of the case decided to create a specialized national organization to sue for environmental protection. More broadly, the *Scenic Hudson* case also inspired others in the late 1960s to see the potential for environmental lawsuits. Storm King was the "talk of Yale Law School students concerned with the environment," recalled one student, who saved press clippings on the case and went on to a career in environmental law after graduation. Some of those Yale Law students also helped create NRDC.[9]

The *Scenic Hudson* decision contributed to the larger judicial shift in the 1960s to embrace a more expansive definition of the "public interest." In *Udall v. Federal Power Commission*, a 1967 Supreme Court case concerning hydroelectric power plants proposed for the Pacific Northwest, Justice William O. Douglas argued that determining whether projects served the "public interest" involved a much broader calculation than just economic estimates of future power supply and demand. Agencies also had to assess "the public interest in preserving reaches of wild rivers and wilderness areas, the preservation of anadromous fish . . . and the protection of wildlife." Douglas, who was an avid outdoorsman and fervent environmentalist, insisted that "all relevant issues" had to be explored. Wildlife and fish conservation, in fact, might prove "all-important." Douglas's intervention signaled the judiciary's heightened concern for environmental considerations, its skepticism toward agency planning, and its openness to the lawyers who sought to represent environmental claims in court. Justice Douglas's attack on the agencies for their destructive environmental role particularly illustrated how things had changed since the New Deal. An FDR ally who had chaired the Securities and Exchange Commission in the 1930s, Douglas now echoed James Landis's 1960 report to President Kennedy on the problem of agency capture. In another environmental case from 1972, Douglas wrote that federal agencies were "notoriously under the control of powerful interests," and described a "web spun about administrative agencies by industry representatives." Douglas thought that the courts had an obligation to defend the public interest against these captured agencies.[10]

The harsh criticism of federal agencies by veteran New Dealers like William Douglas often still venerated the memory of the New Deal itself. Critics told a story of New Deal agencies that had been led astray from their founding ideals during the postwar period. "Although the power of the administrative agencies has grown since the New Deal, there has been increasing recognition that the agencies have not fully lived up to their mandate to serve the 'public interest,'" the Center for Law and Social Policy explained in a grant proposal to the Ford Foundation. At NRDC's founding conference in March 1970, Harvard Law School professor Louis Jaffe, a leading theorist of administrative law, declared that environmental litigation promised to revive the administrative magic of a previous generation. Jaffe said, "Administrative agencies could be effective once again, as they were with the beginning of the New Deal, if they get into the act—if they are given something pertinent to do." Environmental litigation, Jaffe said, sought "to stimulate these agencies."[11]

The public interest law organizations leaned into the idea that a more publicly interested government had once existed, and needed to be restored. An early NRDC fundraising letter explained that the Tennessee Valley Authority, that triumphant symbol of the New Deal, had once been a "benevolent government agency" but had since become the largest "offender," its strip mines polluting streams and reducing people to poverty. Another NRDC appeal letter complained that the "Good Forester," who cared "for the forest as a natural whole," now had been replaced by the "Sales Agent," who listened only to the timber industry. Public interest lawyers described their litigation as an effort to make federal agencies fulfill broader public missions that included the health of forests and streams and the well-being of the people who used these resources in different ways.[12]

✦

THE ENVIRONMENTAL MOVEMENT of the 1960s and 1970s is often viewed in terms of the expansion of government. The Environmental Protection Agency, created in late 1970 by Richard Nixon's consolidation of various smaller federal units and their thousands of employees, grew rapidly into a large federal agency. Tough new environmental laws provided fresh legal muscle for government regulators. During the first two years, the agency undertook over a thousand enforcement actions, with another five thousand following during the next two years. Empowered by the Clean Air Act, Clean Water Act, and other legislation, the EPA directed much of its regulatory fire at local governments and private businesses. The agency forced municipalities like Detroit and Atlanta to install modern sewage treatment facilities costing hundreds of millions of dollars, and required cities to develop controversial transportation control plans to combat smog. The EPA also made companies like U.S. Steel and American Electric Power install expensive equipment to clean up their industrial air emissions. The agency mandated that lead additives be phased out of gasoline and that American farmers and pest-control agencies stop using DDT.[13]

All of these actions represented an expansion in federal regulatory power. Yet in order to understand the historical roots of Americans' lack of trust in government today, the environmental and broader public interest movement also has to be seen in another light—as a legal attack, led by liberals, on the post–World War II administrative state. Resource policy in the United States, including rules governing rivers, pesticides, and highways, needed to move away from "government agency monopoly planning," argued Michigan law professor Joseph Sax. Like other public interest advocates at the time, Sax questioned "whether public agencies adequately protect the public interest." The decision-making process needed "external scrutiny" and a "prod," he wrote. Private groups needed to "intervene in the enforcement process as a 'third force.'"[14]

Lawsuits directed at government agencies reflected a fresh twist in long-standing debates over the public interest. Nineteenth- and early-twentieth-century debates defining the public interest had turned on what kinds of private business activities should rightly be subject to government regulation. When a business was "affected with the public interest," government, embodying the "public," could properly regulate

it. Now in the early 1970s, the new public interest law firms asserted
the reverse: government agency activities affected a broad public interest that justified private involvement in government decision-making.
The public interest, they asserted, lay outside government in an unrepresented citizenry whose cause the new law firms would champion.
The very name of the "public interest movement" implied that government was no longer the locus for the public interest, and that civic-
minded citizens instead had to force public agencies to represent the
public interest.[15]

The litigation pursued by the public interest environmental law
firms shows how the lawyers saw themselves fulfilling Joseph Sax's
call for an independent counterforce to government. When public
interest lawyers boasted of their eagerness to "sue the bastards," they
referred, in practice, to lawsuits against government officials and agencies. The lawsuits were a repudiation of the government's modernist
developmental plans, as represented, for example, by the Tennessee
Valley Authority. "We were, by nature, skeptical of all of the big
Roosevelt-era public works projects," one NRDC lawyer later recalled.
"We didn't like big dams, we didn't like big power plants, we didn't
like big transmission lines." The lawyers questioned technological and
scientific strategies to manipulate nature to boost economic production. They challenged the administrative proceedings that generated
and approved these plans.[16]

Litigation by leading public interest environmental law firms in
the early 1970s almost exclusively targeted the government for legal
action. The Sierra Club Legal Defense Fund boasted of seventy-seven
legal accomplishments between 1971 and 1973. Approximately sev-
enty sought to block government actions, or to intervene in public
proceedings to influence government regulatory and permitting practices. The Environmental Defense Fund similarly began its 1972 case
summary with a list of acronyms for the ten federal agencies named in
its legal interventions. In more than sixty of its sixty-five listed legal
actions, the Environmental Defense Fund either intervened in public proceedings, such as government permitting processes for private

projects, or directly assailed a government-led initiative. Fewer than five of EDF's legal actions directly targeted companies or private parties. Similarly, only three out of twenty-nine of NRDC's legal action initiatives from its first seven months directly named a corporate defendant. To be sure, these legal targets reflected the comparative feasibility of suing government entities rather than corporations, but they also showed the extent to which public agencies were implicated in environmental pollution, expansive development projects, and the reshaping of the American landscape.[17]

Lawsuits against government agencies and legal interventions into public proceedings ranged widely and opportunistically, illustrating a growing scope of ambition on the part of the emerging environmental movement. Government projects under attack included new highways, bridges, airports, and dams, and the dredging of harbors. Other government initiatives prompting lawsuits included pest-control efforts such as DDT spray campaigns and water management plans.

Lawsuits against new highway construction, such as the proposed Interstate 40 through Overton Park in Memphis, placed environmental advocates in direct opposition to state and federal highway engineers. Transportation officials developed highway plans in close partnership with private boosters, including auto clubs, construction firms, and oil and motor vehicle companies. In her 1970 book *Superhighway—Superhoax*, writer Helen Leavitt described the meetings of the "Road Gang," a secretive group consisting of company representatives and state highway officials. Leavitt particularly attacked the federal Highway Trust Fund, which established a separate financing scheme for highways that insulated them from competing budgetary demands and democratic controls. Highway supporters vigorously defended the freedom of state highway commissions to use dedicated highway funds for the exclusive benefit of highway users. Highway opponents struggled to have their criticism heard in a policy process dominated by what they decried as "The Freeway Establishment." Critics denounced freeways through city neighborhoods as "an instrument of war against the urban population." Federal highway construction, the New York–

based Conservation Foundation explained, was, on the one hand, "the greatest public works program in the history of man" and a "boon to the freedom, mobility and pleasure of the individual American," and, on the other hand, "a grossly expensive, narrowly planned mistake in priorities—an insult to humanity and the human environment." The highway system was creating a "vast web of concrete" that was "disrupting neighborhoods and degrading the environment."[18]

Public interest litigation was deeply seductive. Small organizations could punch far above their weight class. The firms could define their vision of the "public interest" and then pursue it in court. The Environmental Defense Fund argued that the group's litigation produced results "faster than by lobby, ballot box, or protest." An April 1970 fundraising letter from EDF explained that teams of scientists and lawyers "on a shoestring budget but armed with enthusiasm, commitment, and a lion's share of truth, can be hard to beat in a court of law where the ground rules are fair and applied equally to both sides. The strategy compels action and results." The very success of public interest law led its founders away from a more movement-centered approach to social change. They embraced professional expertise, elite knowledge production, and inside-the-Beltway strategies, rather than mass protests and political action.[19]

After passage of the National Environmental Policy Act (NEPA) in January 1970, lawyers often could halt proposed development projects, at least temporarily, by demanding that agencies produce the environmental impact statements newly mandated by the act. Once an impact statement had been written, the lawyers then could contest that statement's adequacy, its conclusions, and its underlying assumptions. In one of the very first uses of NEPA, the Center for Law and Social Policy sued the secretary of the interior in March 1970 on behalf of The Wilderness Society, Friends of the Earth, and the Environmental Defense Fund. Their lawsuit, which also hinged on right-of-way specifications from the 1920 Mineral Leasing Act, prompted a court injunction halting construction of the Trans-Alaska pipeline for several years. James Moorman, CLASP's lawyer on the project,

*Public interest environmental law firms sued to block the Trans-Alaska
pipeline, pictured here under construction in the Brooks Mountain
Range, south of Prudhoe Bay.* Alaska State Archives, Trans-Alaska Pipeline
Construction Collection, 1976-1977, ASL-P2-6-14.

later described his feeling when the judge declared the injunction over
the objections of the government. "At that moment I was so overcome
that all the voices and the scene just faded into the distance. For a few
moments, the talk seemed a long way away, and then it all came back.
I remained in a euphoric mood for at least two weeks. I've never had
an experience quite like it. Never have I accomplished anything in the
practice of law which has had such an emotional impact on me as that
injunction did." CLASP, a tiny law firm run out of a dingy office in
Washington's Dupont Circle, barely even existed as a going concern,
and now it had helped stop one of the most costly and ambitious engineering projects in US history.[20]

◆

IN THE DECADES to follow, as environmental law organizations
honed their expertise and grew increasingly powerful, critics com-

plained that technocratic professionals and Washington insiders were undermining the environmental movement's potential as a radical and grassroots force. The environmental law organizations were nominally membership organizations, and within the first few years of operation, their thousands of members were "numerous enough to give standing on every legal issue," as the Environmental Defense Fund explained to the Ford Foundation. Yet most members were check writers, contributing to an organization but doing relatively little else to advance its cause. The membership programs served primarily as vehicles for lawsuits and fundraising, and were a programmatic afterthought. The Supreme Court's *Mineral King* decision, for example, which barred the Sierra Club from suing over a proposed Disney resort in the Sierra Nevada because of a lack of legal standing, prompted the Natural Resources Defense Council to create membership programs so that it could litigate on behalf of its members. An NRDC membership appeal letter in 1972 explained frankly that the *Mineral King* decision "forced us to launch a membership campaign."[21]

More recent critics of the environmental movement have lamented lost opportunities to partner with labor organizations, communities of color, and grassroots advocacy organizations—partnerships that might have generated a more political and disruptive movement centered on social justice. To be sure, some of this coalition-building did occur in the late 1960s and early 1970s. The threat of pesticides to farmworker health, for example, prompted collaborative efforts between the Environmental Defense Fund and labor groups, such as Cesar Chavez's United Farm Workers union. Ralph Nader fought aggressively to help coal miners get protection and compensation for black lung disease, and to pass sweeping occupational health and safety legislation. Conflicts over highway construction in urban areas also could unite environmental groups and civil rights organizations. The potential for this kind of coalition-building, however, went mostly unfulfilled and did not produce robust, lasting alliances. The emerging environmental movement too often conceived of its public health mission in broad terms. Environmental organizations emphasized the health of Amer-

A miner at the Black Lung Laboratory in the Appalachian Regional Hospital in Beckley, West Virginia, has his lung capacity tested to determine whether he has the disease. The fight for worker safety offered one potential area for alliances between environmental and labor advocates. Photo by Jack Corn, U.S. National Archives and Records Administration.

icans in general, rather than focusing on specific injustices suffered by disadvantaged communities. Despite being founded at the height of the civil rights movement, the environmental organizations paid relatively little attention to distinctive connections between racial injustice and environmental degradation.[22]

The public interest lawyers' efforts to embed themselves within the system as reformers did not sit well with less establishment-oriented activists in the early 1970s, particularly those focused on organizing for racial and economic justice. "Foundations demand nice, respectable boards—it's a front," complained Marion Wright Edelman of the Washington Research Project, a law group focused on federal programs for low-income families that later became the Children's Defense Fund. "You have to have Arthur Goldberg as chairman of your board to get two cents." Edelman urged avoiding big foundations. "I wouldn't go to Ford for money, because I don't want their conditions. The little foundations are the most gutsy. That is why we have deliberately sought broad support, so no foundation can cripple us." A 1971 meeting of public interest lawyers organized by the Center for Law and Social Policy—whose board Goldberg chaired—erupted in racial and class conflict over close ties between the major foundations and leading public interest law firms. George Wiley, a formidable and outspoken African American leader who headed the National Welfare Rights Organization, criticized the exclusion of groups, like his, working on the front lines of the civil rights movement. Public interest law firms seemed to provide mainstream philanthropies like the Ford Foundation with a safe way to do something about environmental and civil rights issues. The comfortable relationship between McGeorge Bundy, president of the Ford Foundation, and the establishment board members who advised CLASP and other nonprofit law firms "drove Wiley nuts," Charles Halpern later recalled of the failed conference. "The tensions were so high, there was so much anger . . . it was terrible."[23]

At the time, the public interest lawyers and their financial supporters touted their constructive role. NRDC's John Adams called the "opportunity for change 'within the system' . . . a unique safety valve in the often volatile political process." The Ford Foundation's program officers who were funding the new organizations similarly celebrated the fact that public interest lawyers showed "such constraint and respect for the legal system" that courts viewed Ford's grantees as "private attorneys general, not as rebels and troublemakers." As it made its early grants, Ford deliberately sought to situate public interest law within the system as a permanent, constructive addition to public administrative processes. Carefully selecting and managing the legal grantees helped ensure Ford's success. The American legal system was a "damn good system and . . . capable of a large amount of reform," Ford's Gordon Harrison said in a 1972 interview. Environmentalism, Harrison thought, might be a "truly radical movement" in its challenge to the "growth dogma." Ford's public interest law grantees certainly sparked ample controversy with their lawsuits. Yet Ford's grantees, Harrison argued, were "careful to act so clearly within the system that in order to attack them you really have to attack the system."[24]

In retrospect, some of the founders of the environmental law firms themselves later worried that they had taken a wrong turn by embracing legal strategies to the exclusion of political movement building. Looking back, in 2014, on a more than "forty-year experiment on whether mainstream environmentalism can succeed," NRDC cofounder James Gustave Speth regretted that "we opted to work within the system of political economy that we found, and we neglected to seek transformation of the system itself."[25]

Part III

"GOVERNMENT IS THE PROBLEM"

Chapter Seven

Institutionalizing the Public Interest Movement

IN A COMMENCEMENT ADDRESS AT CORNELL UNI-
versity in June 1968, the liberal reformer John W. Gardner described
twentieth-century democratic institutions as "caught in a savage
crossfire between uncritical lovers and unloving critics." Gardner explained that the defenders of the system's features "tended to smother
them in an embrace of death, loving their rigidities more than their
promise, shielding them from life-giving criticism." The major institutions, including the government, corporations, unions, and profes-
sions, each were trapped in their "own impenetrable web of vested
interests." At the same time, Gardner also warned against "a breed of
critics without love, skilled in demolition but untutored in the arts by
which human institutions are nurtured and strengthened and made
to flourish." Many critics, Gardner thought, seemed more eager to
pull down social institutions rather than do the drawn-out and often tedious work to improve them. Gardner was a liberal Republican
who had served as head of the Department of Health, Education,
and Welfare under President Lyndon Johnson. Gardner helped the
Johnson administration implement many of its most ambitious domestic policy programs, including the creation of Medicare and the
expansion in federal funding for primary and secondary education. In
January 1968, however, Gardner resigned from the Johnson administration. He criticized the escalating conflict in Vietnam and the way

Common Cause chairman John W. Gardner being interviewed on Face the Nation, *May 20, 1973.* Everett Collection Inc / Alamy Stock Photo.

it undermined urgent domestic policy ambitions, such as the need to address poverty, health care, and the urban crisis.[1]

Gardner considered himself a loving critic, and he sought to invigorate and strengthen American democratic institutions. In August 1970, Gardner launched Common Cause, a new nonpartisan citizen lobbying group to advocate for political reform. According to Gardner, Common Cause would provide "some sort of countervailing power" to offset the influence of corporations on government and politicians. Gardner thus echoed Ralph Nader and other public interest advocates in their critique of the political economic system described by John Kenneth Galbraith in the 1950s. Common Cause would organize a new "constituency for good government." Among the group's priorities were removing barriers to voter registration, implementing campaign finance reform, lowering the voting age to eighteen, and revising the congressional seniority system. The group also called for legislation to set a date for withdrawing from the war in Vietnam.[2]

In Common Cause's reform strategy, Gardner imagined himself

and his organization standing outside and above traditional politics. With full-page advertisements in major newspapers and a direct
mail appeal to potential supporters, Common Cause enlisted more
than two hundred thousand members, each paying $15, in little
more than a year. Gardner wanted to work on reforming the political
system as an external "third force," rather than pursue change and
power through electoral politics and one of the political parties. The
parties themselves, Gardner said, were "virtually useless as instruments of the popular will." Common Cause instead needed to use
its multimillion-dollar budget to "revitalize and needle both of the
parties." Gardner colorfully described Democratic and Republican
politicians like "people sitting in an ancient automobile by the side
of the road. The tires are flat and the drive shaft is bent, but they're
engaged in a great argument as to whether they should go to Phoenix or San Francisco. In my imagination, I am standing by the road
saying, 'You're not going anywhere till you fix the goddamn car.'"
Until the system was reformed, in other words, both parties would
fail to lead the country forward.[3]

For Gardner and someone like Ralph Nader, electoral politics in the
first years of the 1970s held little appeal. "I have absolutely no political
ambitions," Gardner told reporters in 1970 about whether he might
pursue the presidency himself. "I don't believe that this effort can
work if the man running it harbors political ambitions." Ralph Nader
declared a similar view. "I'm not interested in politics," Nader said in
an interview that same year. "Not because I don't think people who
feel the way I do shouldn't go into politics but because I believe that
even good elected representatives, heading outmoded or bureaucratic
organizations, simply can't do anything about them." Democratic
leaders considered tapping into Nader's authenticity and popularity in
the summer of 1972. After Thomas Eagleton unexpectedly withdrew
from the Democratic ticket, Democratic presidential nominee George
McGovern reportedly asked Nader, among others, whether he might
consider seeking the vice presidency. Nader declined to be considered,
however, preferring to remain outside of electoral politics. Nader also

refused to run as a minor-party candidate challenging the major parties in the 1972 election.

Both Gardner and Nader thought that political institutions corrupted politicians and government policy makers, inevitably leading them astray or thwarting their efforts. "The department swallows up the man," Nader said about the idea of his taking a possible future cabinet appointment. Gardner said similarly, "As soon as a good man gets in, he's rendered incapable of being effective." Gardner's and Nader's attitudes captured a broader disillusionment with politics within liberal America. The new nonprofit advocacy sector that Nader, Gardner, and others were creating promised a purer, less compromised professional path to people who wanted to achieve reform.[4]

With the Nixon administration and the old guard of the Democratic Party as his foil, Nader was at the peak of his powers. He reveled in his ability, through his growing legions of followers and imitators, to shape US public policy. Congress was passing tough legislation, with specific mandates, to protect Americans' health, safety, and the environment. The federal government had begun to implement more than a dozen expansive new laws regulating air and water pollution, energy production, endangered species, toxic substances, workplace safety, and land use. The laws affected virtually every sector of the US economy. Clean air standards forced changes in automobile design and efficiency, and mandated pollution controls for factories and power plants. Water quality rules pushed states and municipalities to invest in treatment plants to clean up pollution in rivers and harbors. A broad interpretation of judicial "standing" enabled citizens and new environmental law organizations to monitor government activities and file suit over major development projects.

Yet even as the public interest movement established itself and made its mark, its position felt precarious and its future cloudy. How far would the regulatory expansion go? Would the public interest movement become a permanent part of American politics? Nader and other public interest activists had played a crucial role building support for the new regulations, pressing vigorously for expanded federal intervention. But their success was contingent on working closely with key allies in Congress and receiving strong backing from the Ford Foundation and other major liberal donors. By the mid-1970s, relations with both their congressional partners and their foundation backers were growing increasingly uncertain. The low-hanging legislative fruit had been picked, and start-up foundation grants were running out. The public interest movement also started pushing beyond specific issues, such as clean air and clean water, into the structure of US political institutions. Their broadening critique of American politics would deepen potential areas of conflict with the Democratic Party. At the same time, public interest advocates sought to professionalize and entrench their organizations in the nation's political economy. They campaigned for ongoing financial support from the very government that their movement had been created to watch over and sue. In the process of navigating these complicated waters, they established organizational structures whose forms, funding, and modes of operation would shape progressive politics for decades to follow.

✦

DURING THE SUMMER of 1972, Ralph Nader attempted his most ambitious, and perhaps most politically perilous, research project: a kind of consumer guide to Congress for the November 1972 election. Nader saw Congress as the best "hope of reclaiming America," but he also considered the institution a "continuous underachiever." To complete the Congress Project, about a thousand researchers—a veritable "citizen's army"—researched and wrote detailed profiles of all the members of Congress who would be on the ballot. "Nader's Biggest Raid," *Time* magazine called the report on Congress.[5]

It was an aggressive endeavor viewed unfavorably and suspiciously by many members of Congress. The "eager, mostly unpaid Nader's Raiders" were "stalking their prey," according to *Time*. Researchers gave congressional representatives a daunting ninety-six-page questionnaire with 633 questions. Project director Richard Fellmeth described the project as an effort to fact-check the congressional campaigns and bluntly warned that many profiles would "not closely resemble what members of Congress may be saying to their districts about themselves." A Brookings Institution congressional scholar more derisively called the endeavor a "fishing expedition." Perhaps most astonishingly, and a testament to Nader's influence in 1972, most members of Congress participated in the project. Yet many did so grudgingly. The congressional profiles, recalled one of Nader's project leaders, "caused a ruckus." In addition to the politician's voting record, each profile included a detailed report on the congressional district, including census data, data on grants and expenditures, and key staff people. Members of Congress had "never had an independent organization evaluate them the way we did," one project leader recalled.[6]

The Congress Project's approach inevitably meant clashing with the Democratic Party, which had dominated both legislative chambers in the decades since the 1954 midterm elections. "The Democrats were in total control of the Congress," the project organizer later recalled. "It wasn't a time, as it is today, where there's two vibrant parties. It really wasn't." Given the assumption of continued Democratic dominance, the Congress Project felt able to swing freely in all directions, and didn't see itself as supporting a particular political party in the 1972 elections. "Some members of Congress were really bad and others were fantastic." The complexity of the parties complicated the politics of the project. Liberal Republicans sometimes might favor the policy aims of the public interest community, while some of the more conservative Democrats might oppose them. "It was totally apolitical," in the sense that the report did not favor one party over another.[7]

The Congress Project's individual studies of members of Congress laid the foundation for a broader critique of the institution as a whole. In *Who Runs Congress? The President, Big Business, or You?*, a best-selling book published as a companion volume, Nader and three of his top lieutenants delivered a searing critique of American democracy. Congress, they said, had surrendered its democratic role to domineering and corrupt congressional committee chairmen, an overreaching executive branch, and corporate special interests. People like the Democratic lawyer-lobbyist Clark Clifford, an advisor to four presidents, earned a fortune helping business clients "wriggle around the laws and regulations he helped pass while he was in government." The book's authors—Mark Green, James Fallows, and David Zwick—urged citizens to take back Congress from the "domination of the White House and relentless special interests." American citizens, they said, had "abdicated their power" to oversee Congress. In turn, Nader lamented, Congress had "shackled itself with inadequate political campaign laws, archaic rules, the seniority system, secrecy, understaffing, and grossly deficient ways to obtain crucial information." Congressional committees had fallen under the sway of lobbies for special interests, including the mining, timber, oil, and dairy industries.[8]

Like Nader's 1969 report on the Federal Trade Commission, *Who Runs Congress?* particularly took aim at longtime Democratic politicians, who had run Congress for decades, and their financial patrons. Campaign contributions to congressional leaders, the report said, bought "an entire election or favored treatment or simply special access to politicians." Wayne Aspinall, a powerful Democratic congressman from Colorado and chair of the House Committee on Interior and Insular Affairs, was described as the key person to "determine the profit rates" in western mining, timber, and oil. Aspinall, the authors complained, raised most of his campaign funds from lobbyists and executives for whom he could "ease many of life's problems." Aspinall's backers included Kennecott Copper, Shell Oil, Humble Oil, and a mining company called American Metal Climax (later a subsidiary of Freeport McMoRan). A subsequent Nader study of the interior committee approvingly quoted an environmentalist who said that Aspinall had done "more damage to the American earth than any other human being in this century." Instead of "caveat emptor," or "buyer beware," the Nader report said, Bureau of Land Management leasing forms "should read, 'Let the Buyer Take What He Will.'"[9]

Wayne Aspinall became a key target for environmentalists in the 1972 electoral cycle, identified by the advocacy group Environmental Action in its "Dirty Dozen" campaign against the dozen biggest environmental enemies in Congress. In the contested Democratic primary, the League of Conservation Voters provided significant support to Aspinall's opponent, a thirty-eight-year-old liberal professor, lawyer, and land use advocate named Alan Merson. Merson previously had founded a legal services program for native Alaskans. Merson defeated Aspinall in the primary but then lost in the general election to a Republican candidate. Despite the loss of Democratic control of the seat, the League of Conservation Voters considered Aspinall's defeat a major victory and a template for future campaigns. After his defeat, Aspinall parted ways with the increasingly liberal Democratic Party. He joined the board of the conservative Mountain States Legal Foundation and supported Gerald Ford and Ronald Reagan, the Republican presidential nominees in, respectively, 1976 and 1980.[10]

Attacks on powerful Democratic congressional incumbents like Aspinall made partnering with Democratic allies and motivating them to lead on legislation increasingly fraught. Calling Congress "comatose" and "verging on the moribund" didn't make Nader and his team any political friends. Nor did accusing congressmen of using their power on committees to "pork-barrel funds" into their home states and districts. Many Democratic members of Congress were growing increasingly tired of Nader's badgering. They felt that Nader did not have their backs, or understand the strategic and practical considerations that elected officials had to consider. Nader, in turn, grew more distrustful and openly critical of Congress. Congress, he thought, needed citizen oversight and shaking up. *Who Runs Congress?* called for a "citizen's lobby" that could serve as a "political counterweight."[11]

After the 1972 election, when Richard Nixon returned to power in a landslide and Democrats retained control of both the House and Senate, the public interest movement placed increased emphasis on reforming Congress and other political systems. Nader established a new lobbying group, called Congress Watch, to press for reforms to congressional rules on seniority, secrecy, campaign finance, disclosure, and committee jurisdiction. Nader's Public Citizen Litigation Group, led by attorney Alan Morrison, pursued class action lawsuits on behalf of stockholders against companies, like American Airlines, whose executives or board members were diverting corporate money into secret political slush funds. The litigation group also sued the Nixon administration on behalf of taxpayers for using public funds to benefit Nixon's 1972 reelection campaign. Other public interest organizations, including John Gardner's Common Cause, also pressed for post-Watergate reforms to campaign finance and government information disclosure. The Watergate scandal, Gardner explained, was made possible only by "secret cash in . . . various black satchels."[12]

In Congress, the post-Watergate reforms weakened powerful committee chairmen, like Wayne Aspinall on the interior committee, in an effort to break the tight hold that industries had over the congressional committees that regulated them. Congressional reformers, however, had mixed results in producing a better Congress. They accomplished the goal of weakening the previous system. But the new structures of power did not necessarily produce the anticipated results. Less power concentrated in the hands of committee chairmen helped create a politics that was less transactional and more ideological. Party leaders would increasingly set policy across the Republican and Democratic conferences, and the parties would become more ideologically consistent. Yet the leaders themselves also lacked key tools for control and influence. Limits on campaign donations ironically pushed political funding into corporate political action committees and other extraparty vehicles that empowered lobbyists and corporate interests. The decline in congressional earmarks, which allocated funding to specific projects in individual congressional districts, weakened the ability of party leaders to bargain with members of their party and push through legislation. Looking back decades later at the congressional reform effort, some of the reformers would come to question the results, in terms of party polarization and institutional paralysis. "We came here to take the Bastille," recalled George Miller, a California Democrat elected to Congress in 1974 who steadily rose through the ranks into party leadership. "We destroyed the institution by turning the lights on."[13]

✦

THE POLITICAL REFORMS advocated by Nader and Gardner aimed not just at the operations of presidential campaigns and Congress, but more broadly at the openness and accountability of the government as a whole. Writing in a 1975 book profiling "public citizens in action," one of Nader's colleagues, Kenneth Lasson, explained that citizens needed to "regain control over decisions that affect their lives." Americans could not simply "stand idly by thinking their government is its own best watchdog, hoping for integrity without actively demanding it." Citizens had to serve as a bulwark against a corrupt and oppressive government and its leaders. "Deceit runs rampant through the highest levels of government," Lasson wrote, "public servants arrogantly renounce faith in the public's common sense, and the electorate's distrust of elected officials has become pervasive."[14]

Extensive documentary evidence and testimony confirmed public distrust of government officials. In 1971, the *New York Times* published the Pentagon Papers, a secret account of the lead-up to the Vietnam War. The documents showed that the nation's leaders had lied to the public about the nature of the Vietnam conflict. The Watergate scandal that became public in 1972 revealed pervasive political corruption up to, and including, President Richard Nixon, who ultimately resigned in August 1974.

In the face of this high-level deceit, strengthening access to government information through the federal Freedom of Information Act was one way to force greater transparency and accountability. The act, which President Johnson had signed in 1966, was a remarkable law mandating that government agencies release a broad range of internal operational information to American citizens. Nader's Public Citizen Litigation Group, among other organizations, waged a steady campaign in the early 1970s to set legal precedents in the area of information disclosure. One lawsuit brought by the group on behalf of an NBC news reporter was against the Justice Department and the Federal Bureau of Investigation. The reporter sought to force the FBI to disclose the existence of a federal counterintelligence program to infiltrate and disrupt domestic radical organizations, including by the spread of false stories and harassment of movement leaders, and through active instigation by informers. The judge declared that the reporter could have the documents, and the FBI's secret campaign against antiwar and civil rights organizations was suddenly revealed on national television.[15]

Despite successful efforts by public interest advocates to force agencies to release some documents, such as the counterintelligence program files, federal agencies generally continued to evade requests for information under the 1966 act. Federal employees delayed providing information, claimed that the records were exempt, charged excessive fees, and otherwise thwarted the law's implementation. Asked at a 1973 Senate hearing to name the federal agencies that were "particularly reluctant to disclose information," Ralph Nader answered, "Just knock on any door." The agencies had a "pretty uniform reluctance to disclose information." (The recently created Environmental Protection Agency, interestingly, was an outlier in displaying "an openness that is heartening.") Nader urged Congress to assert its inherent constitutional powers by challenging the executive branch. "The Congress has totally failed in asserting its right to executive information," Nader said. "It has growled, but it has never grappled." Nader and other citizen activists pushed Congress to pass legal amendments in 1974 and 1976 to further pry open the bureaucratic fortresses and empower civil society groups to challenge federal actions. The 1974 measure gave citizens the ability to see information about themselves and the right to sue to gain access; the 1976 law required that formal meetings of agency boards and commissions be open to the public and that the agency announce the event in the *Federal Register* at least a week in advance. The 1976 amendments, titled the "Government in the Sunshine Act," explicitly declared that "government is and should be the servant of the people, and it should be fully accountable to them for the actions which it supposedly takes on their behalf."[16]

✦

EVEN AS THE PUBLIC interest groups attacked the failings of key American political institutions and pushed for changes to Congress and to government information disclosure, the groups scrambled to secure their own position. By the mid-1970s, the public interest groups increasingly hoped to professionalize and institutionalize their operations. They were no longer fledgling start-ups, but rather going concerns with employees who wanted to build individual careers, have steady jobs, and raise families. At the same time, the major foundations backing the public interest movement wanted to move on from their primary financing role. The foundations sought to find ways to make the public interest law movement a sustainable and permanent part of the American legal system. The foundations sought to help the public interest law groups develop an agenda for advocacy and to establish structural methods for financial support, such as the award of attorney's fees.

The public interest groups had been founded in a flurry of creativity, volunteerism, and passion. Young staff members, often boasting elite educations and comfortable backgrounds, had been willing to work for relatively little money, in poorly outfitted offices, and in chaotic situations. "Many public interest institutions were candidly begun as experiments, without any expectation of permanence," explained Charles Halpern, cofounder of the Center for Law and Social Policy. Rapid growth prompted internal conflicts and management challenges as the public interest organizations sought to professionalize their operations and make them permanent. The Environmental Defense Fund executive committee spent much of 1973, for example, dealing with the structure of offices in five locations around the country, the "clarifying of administrative procedures," and the establishment of committees to oversee programs. EDF's executive director Rod Cameron candidly explained in the fall of 1973 that the organization was emerging from "a period of moderately severe growing pains." The governance structure that had worked when EDF was "small and fresh and innocent" no longer seemed adequate for an organization with five offices around the country and more than forty employees.[17]

In its early years, the founding board members had considered EDF more of a training organization than a permanent, professional staff. When the organization gave general counsel Lee Rogers a raise in 1972, for example, it stipulated that Rogers should plan to resign twelve months later, to "make room for others to become trained in environmental law." EDF's board leaders embraced a policy of "substantial turnover in EDF's professional staff." They did not imagine they were creating permanent jobs, but rather anticipated that young, early-career lawyers would cycle through EDF, gain training, and go on to other opportunities. It was only in the summer of 1973, almost six years after EDF was founded, that the group finally approved a formal job description for Cameron as executive director and granted him managerial authority to run the organization. The EDF board had conceded that the organization was no longer a start-up with a constantly rotating cast of young staffers, and needed a more stable and traditional organizational structure.[18]

As public interest law organizations like EDF sought to professionalize and institutionalize themselves, they consolidated their operations closer to the main centers of political and financial power. A new ecosystem of nonprofit public interest organizations, including offices for EDF and NRDC, formed in the Dupont Circle area where Ralph Nader also had his headquarters. EDF can be "most effective in Washington," Cameron argued. "The center of gravity of the environmental policy formulation process . . . is Washington, D.C." Making the case for moving EDF's headquarters, Cameron noted that other public interest lawyers and consumer groups had offices just "75 yards from EDF's Washington office."[19]

Moving to Washington provided access to the administrative state. Environmental policy, Cameron said, "emanates from the executive or administrative branch of government," and as the federal government expanded its role, "Washington becomes more significant as time passes." Public interest lawyers like Cameron increasingly conceived of themselves as "policy activists," responsible for persuading the public and pressuring the bureaucracy through regulatory proceedings and through Congress. For Cameron as early as 1973, this meant a reconsideration and shift in EDF's tactics, toward strategies more directly political. "In the past we have relied heavily—as a matter of faith—on litigation." EDF's successful campaign against DDT relied largely on legal actions. But the "shock value" of filing a lawsuit already had started to fade, Cameron told EDF's board of trustees in the fall of 1973. "Litigation, in my view, has also diminished as an educational tool. It has less ability to focus issues before the public. It receives less publicity than it did three years ago. The historic and inherent limitations on judicial proceedings seem to be reasserting themselves, as predicted by some." Cameron thought EDF needed to find other ways to bring pressure onto policy and to intervene directly in the legislative process. He told the board that EDF should "lobby for the right to lobby." If EDF had the ability to lobby, the organization could be more active in Congress and state legislatures.[20]

The fight over the Trans-Alaska pipeline particularly highlighted the importance of lobbying. Because public interest groups like the Environmental Defense Fund were founded as nonprofit organizations under section 501(c)(3) of the tax code, the organizations could not directly lobby Congress on legislation. Their role was limited to activities that counted as educational or legal assistance. In July 1973, after years of litigation and stalemate, the Senate voted on whether to set aside further legal challenges to the Alaska pipeline under the National Environmental Policy Act. The Senate vote resulted in a 49–49 tie. Vice president Spiro Agnew cast the deciding vote in favor of the override, thereby overturning years of successful litigation by public interest lawyers. Environmental activists, according to one of the lawyers involved with the case, couldn't help but feel "handcuffed by the Internal Revenue Service prohibition on lobbying by tax-exempt organizations." If the environmental groups could have lobbied Congress like the energy companies did, they felt they might have turned one more legislator their way. A coalition of charities formed to support a bill that would clarify how much charitable organizations could participate in the legislative process. Elvis Stahr, Audubon's president, explained, "We're not asking that the lid be entirely taken off, but that the law tell us where the lid is!" Stahr argued that uncertainty about what organizations could do "severely inhibits" responsible established organizations like Audubon, which wanted to stay on the right side of the law.[21]

The institutional growing pains of the nonprofit public interest law organizations were matched by their financial challenges. As early as 1971, public interest law firms worried about whether they could "keep the ship afloat." Even at the very height of the environmental movement, just three weeks after Earth Day, EDF's public relations advisor warned that the environment seemed to be slipping as a priority because of "a re-emergence of mass interest in the war." EDF and other environmental organizations needed to find ways to keep environmental issues before the public "with a similar intensity to that which preceded Earth Day."[22]

The Environmental Defense Fund continued to feel very dependent on the Ford Foundation. Cameron told his Ford program officer in October 1972 that EDF might be the "healthiest of the public interest law firms in terms of the diversity of its funding sources." Yet the organization was still far from financial independence. "We were deluding ourselves," he confessed, "as to the rate at which we were becoming self sufficient." In the fall of 1973, the Ford Foundation sought to start weaning its offspring by reducing its support for public interest environmental law firms. Ford's funding ranged from 12 to 50 percent of the organizations' budgets, so the potential cuts were a significant threat. EDF's Cameron predicted that there would be a "crash in the environmental law market" and warned that only some of the groups would survive. "Which ones—I don't know."[23]

The organizations and their foundation supporters started casting about for ways to make the public interest law movement more sustainable and a permanent part of the American legal system. "The firms now heavily dependent on foundation support cannot remain so," explained Sanford Jaffe, a key Ford Foundation program officer, in the *American Bar Journal* in 1976, "if for no other reason than that most foundations are reluctant to tie up their resources in long-term commitments." Public interest law had in common a "need for some kind of subsidy—whether from the government, private philanthropy, or the legal profession itself," wrote CLASP founder Charles Halpern in 1974. The proliferation of small public interest organizations might give an impression of a "massive build-up of powerful citizen advocacy entities," Halpern wrote, but that would be a "gross exaggeration." The public interest bar still numbered no more than a few dozen lawyers. The impressively named "Centers, Funds, Councils, and Institutes— were often facades behind which two or three relatively inexperienced lawyers stood."[24]

In 1974, Ford and other key foundation supporters organized the public interest law groups to form a Council for Public Interest Law to develop an agenda for advocacy and institutional sustainability. The council sought to expand opportunities for public interest lawyers to receive court-awarded attorney's fees following successful suits, and to explore the possibility of direct subsidies from government agencies or from a charitable fund for public interest law. At the same time, Nader's Congress Watch helped press the Federal Trade Commission to help finance participation by citizen groups in agency rule-making. As an *American Bar Association Journal* essay on the future of environmental law asked in 1975, "Should public interest environmental law become a permanent social institution itself, or should it play a catalytic role and stimulate the reform or creation of other, largely governmental institutions?" Nader and others advocated for the creation of a consumer protection agency that could serve as the citizen's representative within government. Nader had been enamored with the concept of the government ombudsman since visiting Scandinavia in the early 1960s. Now he sought to bring it to the US government. The consumer agency was described as functioning like a public interest law firm, working to "represent the public interest, in competition with special interests, before Federal departments and regulatory bodies."[25]

✦

FUNDING FROM INDIVIDUAL donors ultimately saved the most successful environmental law firms. Large and expensive direct mail campaigns generated a significant portion of organizational budgets. By the end of 1976, the Environmental Defense Fund was sending prospect mailings to more than 1.3 million nonmembers per year and had built up its membership to more than forty-four thousand people. Membership contributions provided roughly half of the organization's budget. Membership recruitment and renewal, however, grew more challenging over time, requiring an increasingly sophisticated direct mail operation. Where the early mailings in 1970 yielded $4 for every $1 spent, by late 1973 the return was only $1.23, and by 1976 it had dropped further, to $1.12. Fundraisers attributed the decline to a "saturation of the mails" by public interest causes and an overuse of the same lists by many environmental groups.[26]

The remainder of the funds came from foundation grants and gifts by major individual donors. For that reason, groups like EDF and NRDC needed access to money as much as access to the government. In the fall of 1977, the Environmental Defense Fund established its new national headquarters in New York City, close to crucial financial supporters. The group left its "lovely old white frame farmhouse in East Setauket, Long Island" and moved into a "modern office building." The shift in location reflected the modernization of the environmental movement. Environmentalists weren't "a bunch of naysayers chaining themselves to a tree," EDF announced. The movement was "a highly sophisticated, technologically competent, scientifically based collection of thousands of local groups and a dozen or so national organizations." While it maintained a large Washington, DC, office, the Natural Resources Defense Council also kept its national headquarters in Manhattan, near to major supporters in the finance and real estate industries.[27]

The financial strategy had significant consequences for the organizations themselves. A funding stream consisting primarily of dues-paying members and wealthy individual donors meant that the major environmental organizations became dependent on a largely white, middle- and upper-class constituency. Their fundraising appeals frequently catered to the interests of this group. The organization's boards also skewed heavily toward major donors from elite corporate, financial, and philanthropic backgrounds. It was an awkward financial basis upon which to build a transformative social justice movement.

Some envisioned a different outcome. Cross-class alliances around toxic hazards were one potential path toward a possible labor and environmental partnership, illustrated by efforts to protect farmworkers from pesticide poisoning and miners from black lung disease. And the ongoing fight over urban redevelopment and highways frequently centered the interests of low-income communities and communities of color. An assessment of the environmental law movement published in the *American Bar Association Journal* in 1975 posited that the commonality of interest between civil rights organizations and environmental groups around urban land use, highways, and other topics meant that "the essentially false juxtaposition of saving trees versus saving people has been put to rest." Yet the racial and class biases of environmental organizations persisted. Given the predominantly white staff, boards, and members of these organizations, internal institutional and cultural pressures mitigated against broader alliances.[28]

✦

AS THE NEW environmental organizations became more formally structured and professional in their operations and their fundraising efforts, federal regulators acknowledged the increasingly significant role that the nonprofits played in the regulatory process. Some environmental regulators welcomed scrutiny by environmental law firms because they saw their agencies as mediating between competing forces in society, rather than as independent, expert decision-makers. They seemed to agree with public interest advocates that the government agencies, by themselves, could not represent the public interest. Rather, as Nader put it, the "public interest can emerge only from an honest confrontation between differing interests presented with comparable intensity." Agency leaders counted on the public interest environmental lawyers to provide a counterpoint to industry and agency positions. Former EPA administrator Russell Train explained in a 1977 essay that the public interest law firms had "played an immensely important and valuable role, especially by holding EPA's bureaucratic feet to the fire." Increasingly, federal agencies seemed to feel that, as one public interest lawyer said about the Occupational Safety and Health Administration, "We must be right because everybody's mad at us." Public interest lawsuits contending that EPA was too slow or too lenient balanced industry lawsuits complaining that EPA was too strict. "I imagine that I was the most sued man in government," Russell Train recalled of his time at EPA, as if it were an accomplishment that he had managed equitably the competing pressures from both sides.[29]

Federal officials even spoke up to defend the funding of their outside critics. In 1973 the Ford Foundation, ready to move on to new projects, proposed phasing out its start-up grants for public interest organizations. John Quarles Jr., EPA's deputy administrator, wrote to Ford's program officer to express his dismay. "I have to say that when I read the story I was heartsick," Quarles wrote of Ford's plan to pull back its support. "Nationally recognized public interest groups fill a void in our political structure." Groups like NRDC and EDF had been "astoundingly effective" with limited budgets and staffing. The organizations had "emerged as vigorous and effective participants in the governmental process," monitoring the administration of complex programs and revealing weaknesses in government activities. The organizations reviewed permit applications, attended hearings, and, at times, sued EPA to force it to act. Quarles forcefully articulated the "irreplaceable role" of public interest organizations in 1970s environmental policymaking, saying that government operations needed to be "subject to constant public scrutiny" and "challenged through informed criticism, administrative proceedings, and judicial review." The business lobby, he said, needs to be "balanced by the active involvement of representatives of a broader public interest." Quarles told the National Council on Philanthropy in 1975 that without "public understanding and support," created in large part by nonprofit citizen groups, "EPA cannot do its job." The nonprofit organizations were "an integral part of the process which produces sound public policy. For all of these reasons, we cannot let them perish."[30]

William Ruckelshaus, a liberal Republican who served as the first EPA administrator, similarly saw the new nonprofit groups as a crucial antidote to what ailed American society and was eager to help them out. Ruckelshaus, who famously resigned as deputy attorney general in October 1973 rather than fire the Watergate special prosecutor, declared in a 1974 speech that the United States faced a "crisis of the spirit. A crisis of belief or trust in many of our basic institutions." To build faith that government acted in the interests of the people, he said, citizens needed to be involved in public affairs, and the public interest organizations provided a crucial vehicle. "The general public is often disorganized and sometimes powerless," Ruckelshaus explained in a fundraising letter on behalf of the Environmental Defense Fund. "With EDF's vigorous, effective representation, however, the public good has a better chance."[31]

◆

THE SIMPLE CELEBRATION of public interest law by Quarles and Ruckelshaus, however, was somewhat premature. The new federal regulations of the early 1970s, including laws like the Clean Air Act and Clean Water Act, prompted a vigorous counterattack by business lobbyists and the conservative movement. The regulations were prescriptive and combative, reflecting a lack of trust in both industry and the government. Opponents of the laws, with their mandates for pollution control and other expenditures, blamed people like Ralph Nader. To critics like future Supreme Court justice Lewis Powell, Nader was the "single most effective antagonist of American business." In an influential private memo written for the US Chamber of Commerce, Powell called Nader's campaign against corporate power a "frontal assault" on the American system of government and commerce. Powell urged the chamber and business leaders to muster a sustained ideological campaign to counter a left-wing attack on the "American free enterprise system." Such a campaign, he argued, would provide a "vast area of opportunity for the Chamber, if it is willing to undertake the role of spokesman for American business." Powell's memo helped mark the start of a corporate-funded counter-attack on the public interest movement.[32]

Already by the mid-1970s, the "public interest" had become an increasingly slippery concept, more capacious and contradictory than the idealistic founders of the liberal public interest groups initially intended. In a widely published 1972 editorial, the conservative publisher Eugene Pullman similarly warned about the "threat to freedom in America today . . . from a Federal bureaucracy which seems determined to gain control over every facet of American life." Pullman attacked Nader specifically, mocking the idea that he had a special claim on the "public interest" and denouncing Nader's ambitions to bring corporations to heel. "Here is a man without any official authority or credentials of any kind, forcing American industry into submission, threatening Federal prosecution if industry doesn't agree with his plans, bullying his way toward being the supreme dictator of all industrial production in this country." Pullman asked, "Who has appointed this man to play God over American business?" Conservative critics like the columnist James Kilpatrick mocked Nader for the way he equated himself with "the 'people' or with 'the public interest.'" Nader's approach suggested that "he alone . . . is qualified to proclaim what is good and wise and progressive. The possibility that he might be wrong—the possibility that decent men might take an opposite view out of pure motives and sound reasons—that possibility never crosses Mr. Nader's Olympian brow," Kilpatrick wrote in 1972.[33]

Nader provided a symbolic face for the public interest movement as its most prominent public figure. He gave critics a target for their ire. But conservatives did not just attack the public interest movement; they also emulated it. Seeing the success that liberal lawyers had with a receptive federal judiciary inspired a conservative countermovement to reshape the judiciary itself, and to create analogous public interest groups on the right. Nonprofit legal organizations like the Pacific Legal Foundation and the Mountain States Legal Foundation were founded in the mid-1970s to counter liberal groups, such as the Natural Resources Defense Council, Environmental Defense Fund, and Ralph Nader's legal network.[34]

The new conservative law firms aimed to rein in the environmental, health, and safety regulation of the early 1970s. They mounted a defense of private property rights and attacked government efforts to protect the air, land, and water in the American West. The Pacific Legal Foundation, for example, battled the California Coastal Commission to protect property owners from restrictive land use regulation. In the Rocky Mountain region, the Mountain States Legal Foundation, with support from brewing magnate Joseph Coors and led by James Watt, fought to preserve access to resources on federal public lands and to block air quality mandates emanating from Washington. The new conservative legal groups explicitly sought to push back against the liberal public interest movement. "They say they're out to tame environmental extremists and rabid regulators," reported the *Wall Street Journal*, "and to bring balance to a regulatory process that has tipped in favor of environmental and consumer activists." The emergence of the conservative law firms, which also claimed the "public interest" mantle, confirmed the shift underway in the American political economy. For many liberal public interest advocates, the evolution was supposed to stop with the establishment of a citizen voice to counter industry lawyers and lobbyists in the struggle over government policy. But the very success of the public interest movement created new arenas for conflict—in the courts, Congress, regulatory settings, and the media. Conservative legal activists rushed to join the fight.[35]

Chapter Eight

The Carter Administration's Struggle for Balance

IN AUGUST 1976, AT THE HEIGHT OF THE PRESIDEN-tial campaign, Ralph Nader flew to Georgia to meet with former governor Jimmy Carter, the Democratic nominee. In an extended private conversation, Nader lectured Carter on how government really worked, "distill[ing] into three hours the lessons of a dozen years." Nader warned Carter against falling prey to traditional Washington special interests. He also pressed Carter to create a federal consumer protection agency that would institutionalize public interest advocacy within the government. In Nader's mind, the consumer agency would serve as a kind of government ombudsman, an advocate for citizens within the bureaucratic system itself.

During his Georgia visit, Nader participated in a softball game with Jimmy Carter; the candidate's brother, Billy Carter; and assorted journalists, locals, and political guests. Nader, a lifelong Yankees fan, served as umpire, sweltering behind the plate in a suit and tie. The New York alternative weekly the *Village Voice* picked up on the sports metaphor to wonder what role Nader might play in a Carter administration: "Umpire or Player?" Would Nader join the Carter team?, the *Voice* wondered.[1]

But Nader wanted to continue in his role outside and above politics and governance. "Are you kidding?" Nader told the paper. A Carter administration would need a "civic backbone" on the outside.

Ralph Nader walks with Democratic presidential nominee Jimmy Carter in Plains, Georgia, in August 1976. While many public interest advocates joined the new Carter administration, Nader remained outside as a government critic and watchdog. AP Photo.

Nader wanted to "work on the government, not in it." A few days later, back in Washington, Nader enthusiastically introduced Carter at an event sponsored by Public Citizen, his primary nonprofit organization. In formal remarks, Carter endorsed many of Nader's ideas: stronger antitrust enforcement, an end to regulatory appointments from regulated industries, and an agency dedicated to consumer protection. Carter reportedly told the audience that he hoped to compete with Nader "for the role of top consumer advocate in the country." In a speech to the American Bar Association that same week, Carter promised to "take a new broom to Washington and . . . sweep the house of Government clean."[2]

Despite the friendliness between Nader and Carter on the campaign trail, Carter's victory in November 1976 raised existential questions for the liberal advocacy community. Tensions quickly emerged between liberals inside and outside of government during the Carter years, centering on the umpire-versus-player distinction. Did the nonprofit public interest movement have a continuing role when a sympathetic Democratic president occupied the White House? And could public interest advocates govern? Many advocates who launched new public interest organizations after 1968 had drawn energy and motivation from their passionate dislike of the Nixon administration. It was easy for public interest advocates to sue, and roundly denounce, the federal government when they despised the people in charge of running the government, with its continuing pursuit of an unpopular war in Vietnam and the political corruption represented by Watergate.

Carter's election raised questions about whether the public interest movement had been a temporary reaction to the Nixon presidency and the turmoil of the late 1960s and early 1970s, or if it would become a permanent part of the American political system. At a conference convened by Nader in early December 1976, Carter advisor Stuart Eizenstat assured the public interest community that it would have the administration's ear. "Advocates will become administrators and those on the outside will be inside," Eizenstat promised. Eizenstat's message was "at once pleasing and disturbing to the audience," the *Washington Post* observed. One attendee asked whether the administration's welcoming embrace meant public interest groups were no longer needed. Eizenstat assured them that they now did have a permanent place in the American political system. "All of those things on your agenda are not necessarily on ours," Eizenstat said. More bluntly, Nader urged public interest advocates to be "very, very aggressive. Don't take anything for granted." Good feelings from a potential alliance with the Carter administration were not to be relied upon, Nader suggested.[3]

While Nader chose to remain an outside umpire, many of his allies and followers did take positions in the administration. They wanted to play the game, not simply watch and judge it. Carter gave them hope that he could craft a new Democratic approach to government. James Fallows, who as a young Nader employee had coauthored an investigative report on water pollution and then helped write the best-selling exposé *Who Runs Congress?*, became Carter's chief speechwriter. Fallows later recalled his optimism that Carter might successfully navigate the "swirl of liberal and conservative sentiment then muddying the political orthodoxy." Fallows had sat in on the epic three-hour private meeting between Nader and Carter in Plains, Georgia, in August 1976, during which Nader had lectured the presidential nominee on the lessons from his many investigations of the federal government. Fallows told his friends that summer that Carter had the potential to transform the government, "not by expanding federal responsibilities, as Roosevelt had done, or by continuing the trend of the Great Society," but by following Nader's pragmatic advice and improving and better watching over the government's operations. Fallows believed that the 1970s public interest investigations and critiques showed that the Democratic Party had to build support for the government by improving the government's effectiveness, efficiency, and accountability.[4]

In addition to Fallows, many other public interest leaders and activists took top positions in the Carter administration. The administration "wanted to appoint people who were not from the corporate world," the public interest lawyer and lobbyist Joan Claybrook recalled. "And so the public interest world was a great place to look." The public interest community, *Fortune Magazine* noted, offered knowledgeable experts who were "untainted by any possible conflict of interest" and "were not retreads from earlier Democratic administrations." Claybrook, head of Nader's Congress Watch project, took charge at the National Highway Transportation Safety Administration. Dozens of others took prominent roles:

- Harrison Wellford, the first executive director of Nader's Center for Study of Responsive Law, joined the Office of Management and Budget as a deputy director in charge of the White House's government reorganization project.
- Barbara Blum, former public interest lobbyist with Save Amer-

ica's Vital Environment, became deputy administrator at the Environmental Protection Agency.

- James Moorman, founding executive director and staff attorney at the Sierra Club Legal Defense Fund, joined the Department of Justice to head the land and natural resources division.

- James Gustave Speth, cofounder and attorney at the Natural Resources Defense Council, was appointed member, and subsequently chair, of the Council on Environmental Quality.

- David Hawkins, an NRDC lawyer, became EPA's air quality chief.

- Carol Lee Tucker-Foreman, executive director of the Consumer Federation of America, joined the Carter administration as assistant secretary for food and consumer services.

- Michael Pertschuk, former chief counsel to the Senate Committee on Commerce and an ally of Nader and the public interest movement, became chair of the Federal Trade Commission.

The movement, *Fortune* reported in an article about nearly sixty public interest appointees, now had the "kind of access to departments and the White House once enjoyed only by national labor unions and large corporations working through highly paid Washington lobbyists." Approaching the federal agencies, one advocate said, was "like dealing with old drinking buddies now."[5]

Mark Green, who coauthored *Who Runs Congress?* with Fallows and would later go into New York politics, praised these public interest leaders joining the Carter administration. The new appointees had been "trained in the trenches of anti-government advocacy," Green wrote in the *Washington Post* in March 1977. For the previous eight years, they had been "pressuring government, suing government, working *on* government rather than in government," Green explained. "Now many are going in." Carol Lee Tucker-Foreman, who joined the Department of Agriculture after hounding the department while executive director of the Consumer Federation of America, explained, "You become critics of things you don't like, and if you're successful, somebody turns around and says, 'All right, by God, you do it.' Then you have to learn, by a very painful process, whether you can do it better than the people you criticized." Mark Green agreed that the public interest community had to try to govern. "It is as important to show how government *can* work as to demonstrate why it cannot," he wrote. But Green anticipated disillusionment, and he predicted frequent resignations to protest policy differences. Government is "an exercise in compromise," Green noted. "For some mavericks accustomed to advocating their own views unalloyed by political considerations, government service may prove uncomfortable, if not untenable."[6]

✦

DISILLUSIONMENT CAME EASILY and quickly to Ralph Nader, still on the outside. Just a month after the 1976 election, "The Public Citizen," as *Washington Post* columnist David Broder called Nader, complained about his limited access and clout in shaping Carter's cabinet appointments. "I want access. I want to be able to see him and talk to him," Nader said presumptuously about Carter. "I expect to be consulted, and I was told that I would be, particularly on regulatory and consumer matters." Despite Carter's many public interest appointees, Nader thought too many people entering the administration still reflected "the old-line entrenched interests of the big-business establishment." Nader's disappointment didn't keep him from being somewhat optimistic that things would improve. "Compared to Ford, it's got to get better. We've started from nothing," Nader said in December 1976. But Nader remained on edge about whether the Carter administration was a true ally.[7]

After Carter took office in January 1977, Nader's outlook continued to sour. Only months into Carter's presidency, Nader grew furious with Joan Claybrook, previously one of his closest friends and collaborators. Claybrook came from a politically active family in Baltimore and had started her career after college in 1959, working for the Social Security Administration. In 1965, Claybrook received a fellowship from the American Political Science Association that allowed her to work for a year in Congress on the new auto safety legislation that Nader was fighting to push through. After the legislation passed in 1966, Claybrook joined the Department of Transportation, where she worked as special assistant to William Haddon, the epidemiologist who served as the first administrator of the new highway safety bureau.

Claybrook decided to leave the federal government after Richard Nixon's election in 1968. In her view, the new Republican leadership was "not a government that was as focused on getting things done." Though the Nixon administration was exploring the possibility of an airbag regulation, one of Claybrook's top policy priorities, she "had no trust that Nixon was going to see this through." Claybrook started going to law school at night, and in the fall of 1970 she took a position in Nader's new Public Interest Research Group. Working alongside Nader, Claybrook continued to advocate for auto safety, watching over the Department of Transportation, where she had previously worked. She also oversaw the production of congressional member profiles for the 1972 Congress Project. Like Nader, she could be a "tough task-master," pushing herself as hard as those who worked for her. "She can work consistently until one o'clock in the morning, or until five if she has to, and never complain," a colleague told the *National Journal* in 1973. "Ralph likes this and trusts her." Claybrook herself recalled being fascinated by Nader's approach. "It was a whole different way of looking at what citizens had the authority to do," she recalled in a 2015 interview. "He had essentially enabled people to become citizen advocates and to critique the government."[8]

Just before joining the Carter administration in 1976, Claybrook had headed Nader's Congress Watch group, working on legislative issues, particularly related to her specialty, auto safety. Now Claybrook directed Carter's National Highway and Transportation Safety Administration, the agency created as a direct result of Nader's 1960s advocacy. Claybrook felt less conflicted than some other public interest advocates who entered the Carter administration. "I had been a previous insider, so for me it was much more natural, perhaps, than for others," she recalled. "And I went into an agency that I had worked in for four years and helped put together a lot of its early systems and standards, and ways of doing business. . . . I knew the things where the industry had been deficient, and what needed to be done. And I knew a lot of the people there, still." The automobile industry considered Claybrook's appointment a kind of hostile takeover. A Chrysler executive called her appointment "appalling," saying that Claybrook had "always been against the industry."[9]

Despite Claybrook's enthusiasm to make change from the inside, in June 1977 Nader released an eleven-page public letter criticizing her. He complained particularly about the Carter administration's decision to delay the airbag mandate from 1981 to 1982–84. Requiring airbags in automobiles to protect drivers and passengers was a top auto safety priority. The delay risked a policy reversal by the next administration, Nader said, as well as death and injury to thousands of motorists. The Carter administration's shortcomings, Nader declared in his letter, "etch a trail of averted or broken promises . . . this is more than a failure of leadership: it is a failure of nerve." Nader called on Claybrook to resign from her government post and return to the public interest movement.[10]

On the afternoon of the day that Nader released his call for her resignation, Claybrook called a press conference to respond to his charges. Shortly after she began talking, Nader himself entered the room. "An uneasy hush fell over the gathering," reported Henry Scarupa in the *Baltimore Sun*. "Eyes averted, the two friends exchanged icy hellos. When Mr. Nader raised a question, Mrs. Claybrook cut him down with, 'I came here to talk to the press, not you.' To a newsman's query on how she felt about the attack on her by a friend, she replied, flushing, 'Not good.'"[11]

Nader's attack on Claybrook was unusual in its harsh personal terms; few other public interest advocates joined in. Other highway safety advocates repudiated Nader's criticism, calling his behavior "outrageous." Writing in the *Washington Post*, David Cohen, the president of Common Cause, the organization founded by John Gardner, disagreed with Nader's tone and approach. Cohen embraced the

Ralph Nader presses his former close colleague, Joan Claybrook, at a news conference in November 1977. When Nader urged her to resign her position as National Highway Traffic Safety Administrator, Claybrook refused. AP Photo/JD.

duality between external advocacy and internal administration. "The public-interest movement must be hard-hitting," Cohen wrote. "It must criticize. It must demand. It must pressure. But it can't excommunicate." Cohen argued that the public interest constituency had achieved a significant place in US politics. The public interest advocates working in the Carter administration necessarily had to shift their perspective when they entered government. "As public-interest advocates," Cohen explained, "they represented solely the concerns of the public-interest constituencies. As public officials, they have a broader mandate. They must administer the law as written, not as they would like it to be; they must negotiate trade-offs between competing demands and engage in lively debates with all interested parties, including their present and former colleagues."[12]

Cohen's language underscored the slipperiness of the "public interest" idea. Public officials, following the technicalities of the law and navigating difficult politics, wouldn't always pursue the right course. Public interest advocates needed to focus on establishing accountability mechanisms within government and opening government to the public. Consequently, public interest advocacy needed to be a permanent and independent part of the political process. "No matter how many public-interest veterans serve in government, there has to be a thriving public-interest movement." The movement's job, Cohen argued, was to "stretch the art of the politically possible" by working outside government and having allies within government.[13]

In her role at the highway safety agency, Claybrook found herself caught between industry and the consumer movement. Industry groups derided her as "the dragon lady," while Nader complained that she had sold out and capitulated. Looking back on her relationship with Nader in a 1991 interview, Claybrook recalled that Nader sought to be a "counterforce" to industry by "criticizing us for not being tough enough." Nader was "probably more critical of me than of anybody else in the Administration because he felt that I should have known better. And he had to scold." Claybrook eventually figured out that she shouldn't take Nader's criticism personally, and she could even use it to her advantage. "When Ralph criticized me," Claybrook said in 1991, "my mother called me up and said, you must forgive him immediately because that's what he has to do. I felt that it was really helpful to have her say that to me. . . . I felt after that that I really took advantage of Ralph's criticism of me." Claybrook used Nader's criticism as a way to leverage the agency's position in relation to industry lobbying. This strategy reflected the newly emerging approach to governance that positioned the government not as the independent expert responsible for determining the public interest, but rather as a broker or mediator between industry and, increasingly, citizen advocates.[14]

Nader's inability to come to terms with the compromises inherent in running the executive branch illustrated how hard it was for many 1970s liberals to figure out a new way to govern. Nader, *Time* magazine noted in the fall of 1977, should have been at the "zenith of his power." He had a robust network of watchdog organizations and had "salted the Government with allies and former colleagues in regulatory posts." Yet Nader appeared to be "losing rather than gaining momentum." He struggled to get his vision translated into government policy. At the close of Carter's first year in office, six former public interest advocates attended a Nader-sponsored forum to report on what the administration had accomplished. Nader criticized them as overly cautious. "There are no friends in government," Nader said pointedly. There are "only people who use power properly or improperly." He again called on Claybrook to resign, and warned that bureaucrats shouldn't use "the credibility they gained in the consumer movement" to justify bad decisions in government. For Harrison Wellford, the former close ally now working at OMB on government reorganization plans, coming to Nader's forum felt like "the Washington equivalent of the Chinese sending their government cadres back out into the countryside to be re-educated by the people." Carter's public interest appointees, such as EPA deputy administrator Barbara Blum, largely defended the president and his compromises as the best attainable "within the framework of reality."[15]

✦

THE TENSION BETWEEN the pragmatic "reality" of governing and the idealistic aspirations of outside critics persisted throughout the Carter administration. "Ralph could propose things, and he didn't have to be around for the consequences," Harrison Wellford later recalled in an interview. "At some point you've got to convert that passion into a program." On issues such as water and energy policy, Carter struggled to realign federal programs with an environmental agenda. In the process of trying, Carter often paid a tremendous political price. Yet the public interest community faulted Carter for his lack of will more than it credited him for sacrificing his political position for the environmental cause. Environmental advocates described Carter as both "the best environmentalist we have ever had in the White House," and a "wishy-washy" leader who "fails to carry through." In their view, Carter was unwilling to expend his political capital sufficiently, and therefore he disappointed them, and their support for him weakened. The public interest movement's faith in the rightness of its cause could frequently outweigh the political precariousness of its position.[16]

During his first year in office, Carter stirred a hornet's nest of congressional opposition when he sided with environmentalists to try to cancel a set of proposed water projects. Carter's attack on the federal dam-building program was an explicit effort to implement the public interest critique of postwar infrastructure development. The move also reflected Carter's personal environmental commitments and his distaste for wasteful government spending. As governor of Georgia, Carter had blocked a dam planned for the Flint River, which he called "the most valuable stream in Georgia." During the 1976 presidential campaign, Carter called for cuts to pork-barrel construction projects such as dams to save money and protect the environment. "We ought to get the Army Corps of Engineers out of the dam-building business," Carter said as a candidate. "I personally believe that we have built enough dams in this country and will be extremely reluctant as President to build any more." Immediately after Carter took office, his administration had to develop its budget proposal for Congress. Carter sought to fulfill his campaign promises by eliminating funding for unnecessary dams. The administration quickly developed a list of questionable projects and, in February 1977, released a list of nineteen that would be eliminated.[17]

Carter's water project proposal landed in Congress as if the president were "declaring war on the West," recalled Stuart Eizenstat, Carter's domestic policy advisor. Brock Evans, a Sierra Club lobbyist at the time, later described Carter's strategy as "politically inept." The administration's "hit list" precipitated a "violent political counter-reaction," recalled Evans. The president had not laid adequate groundwork with congressional representatives from the affected states. Describing the president's proposal in June 1977, the *New York Times* wrote that Carter's "insistence on killing the projects has puzzled Washington officialdom, to whom the cost in poisoned relations with Congress does not seem worth the financial or environmental gain." Congress was particularly attuned to its power of the purse and rejected Carter's assertion of presidential authority. Congress reinstated the water projects and passed them back to the president.[18]

Environmental organizations and congressional reformers fought fiercely to block them, thinking they finally had a "president who might veto water projects." But Carter backed down. He did not veto the bill. After gaining commitments from congressional allies to support a veto, Carter then traded his support of nine of the targeted projects for a withdrawal of funding for another federal project that he opposed: the proposed Clinch River nuclear breeder reactor in Tennessee. Brock Evans declared that Carter had "betrayed" his environmental allies by not vetoing the water project bill. Although Carter expressed his continued desire to block wasteful dam projects that had received renewed funding, disappointed environmental advocates declared that "talk is cheap." Carter said, "'trust me' and we trusted him," lamented Allan Stocks, the head of Friends of the Savannah River, which was fighting the Richard B. Russell Dam on the border of South Carolina and Georgia.[19]

Carter had frustrated his environmental allies, while also antagonizing powerful congressmen from his own party. His fixation on the water projects brought "catastrophic results," according to Eizenstat, exposing "every weakness of the new administration." "Politically he lost in every way possible," Eizenstat later recalled. James Moorman, who had left the Sierra Club Legal Defense Fund to join Carter's Justice Department, concurred, later noting that Carter's handling of the water projects "was a political blunder of the first order . . . the whole thing was just a disaster." Carter himself later conceded that his opposition to the water projects "created one of the most difficult confrontations between me and members of Congress of anything I did while I was in office."[20]

Carter's fight with western and southern politicians over water projects continued through his presidency. The issue also lingered as a point of tension with his environmental allies, as Carter struggled to keep them on his side. In November 1977, Carter met with representatives of the Coalition for Water Project Review, a group uniting environmental critics of the dam program. "The President reiterated that he was with us," reported Audubon's representative. Carter encouraged the groups to campaign to "keep the issue before the public." But the following spring, the coalition accused Carter of "dancing to a different tune: the old politics of pork and of sacrificing rivers, streams and wetlands to the demands of narrow groups and powerful beneficiaries." The Carter administration had slipped into the patterns of administrative abuse that the public interest groups had been denouncing for the previous decade. In October 1980, just before the presidential election, the coordinator for the Coalition for Water Project Review would conclude that the president had not been disciplined enough in blocking projects. Carter had raised awareness about "Congressional pork barreling on water projects," the coordinator said. And Carter had given people some "hope that the reckless, single-minded pursuit of dam building is ending." In the midst of the 1980 presidential campaign, however, this lukewarm endorsement by dam critics did not credit Carter for the political capital that he had expended, with little return, on the effort to block dam construction.[21]

✦

A SIMILAR STORY of enthusiastic support, followed by disappointment and ambivalence, unfolded in the area of energy. President Carter took office determined to set a new policy direction after the shock of the 1973–74 oil embargo. In April 1977, three months after taking office, Carter delivered a major White House address, calling energy policy the "moral equivalent of war." The president warned that the United States faced a "national catastrophe" if it did not plan adequately for its energy future. Carter called for aggressive new conservation measures, increased production of renewable energy, such as solar power, and more domestic production of oil and coal to replace imported fuels.[22]

After Carter's April speech, public interest and environmental advocates worked to organize support for the president's proposals to boost renewable energy and energy conservation. NRDC's Richard Ayres and others hoped that partnering with a sympathetic president would enable advocates to "push for positive programs and not merely oppose bad programs." Many of Carter's proposals overlapped with those being made by NRDC and others. In contrast to earlier in the decade, Ayres and two colleagues wrote in a letter to more than thirty environmental and citizen organizations, administrative agencies were "generally in agreement with us." Environmental groups, Ayres and his colleagues concluded, needed to send the White House a "clear signal that when it is responsive to our concerns we will support it."[23]

Environmental advocates particularly favored Carter's emphasis on energy conservation. They believed, as one researcher explained, that "rampant energy waste" pervaded the US economy. Energy researchers, including those working at the nonprofit Energy Policy Project funded by the Ford Foundation, argued that the United States could grow economically without significantly expanding its energy consumption. A common refrain was the idea that it was "cheaper to save energy than to generate energy." Amory Lovins, author of the widely read book *Soft Energy Paths*, called for an embrace of "soft energy," meaning conservation and renewable energy, rather than fossil fuels and nuclear power.[24]

Yet despite this stated desire to join forces behind the new energy program, the environmental groups would not commit to giving the new administration their unqualified backing. Ayres and other public interest advocates were independent operators, providing a counterforce to industry in their efforts to advance what they saw as the public interest in energy policy. They aimed to show agencies how their new programs "can be made even better." When the government proved "unwilling to go as far as necessary," then they would "make our case to the White House." Suing the government also might be necessary, they said.[25]

As with the administration's position on water projects and dam construction, the initial honeymoon period on energy policy soon faded. High oil prices and continued concern over energy supply softened Carter's commitment to "soft energy paths" and led to greater openness to oil, coal, and nuclear power. In April 1978, twelve major organizations, including the Natural Resources Defense Council, Environmental Defense Fund, and Nader's energy group, accused Carter of having abandoned his campaign promises. "We have waited patiently and silently for most of this past year," the group said. "We have watched in surprise and with growing discouragement as the President abandoned one campaign commitment after another." Environmentalists particularly loathed Carter's growing enthusiasm for synthetic fuels as a potential strategy to address energy scarcity and security. The synthetic fuels, or "synfuels," would be produced from liquefied coal, oil shale, and other sources, requiring a tremendous amount of water, as well as toxic chemicals. Environmentalists called the synthetic-fuels program a "disastrous and irreparable mistake" and warned that Carter was being "stampeded by the same panic and ignorance which have driven Congress to impetuous folly."[26]

In the summer of 1979, when Carter proposed federal support and waivers of federal environmental rules to produce two million barrels per day of these synthetic fuels by 1990, environmentalists reacted with horror. William K. Reilly, president of the Conservation Foundation, said that the "only hard choice the President made in his energy message was to abandon his environmental supporters." Richard Ayres, the NRDC staff attorney, called Carter's energy proposals "terrible" and a "serious blow to the environmental movement." "The long honeymoon of the environmental movement with Jimmy Carter is over," Robert Cahn wrote in *Audubon* magazine about Carter's energy mobilization plans. "In the space of a few days last July, the President turned, in the eyes of environmental leaders, from staunch friend to potential enemy."[27]

Nuclear power was another polarizing energy issue that divided the environmental community from the Carter administration. By October 1977, environmental advocates outside the government and their allies within it feared an "about-face on nuclear power policy"—one that would shift from the campaign's neutral and cautionary position toward active encouragement of nuclear power development. For Carter, a former nuclear engineer in the navy, nuclear energy remained a promising and safe technology that the government should support as an alternative to oil. For antinuclear opponents like Ralph Nader, nuclear power was a chief example of technology run amok. The federal government, in Nader's view, could not be trusted to look out for the safety of its citizens. In March 1979, the Three Mile Island nuclear power plant in Pennsylvania experienced a partial meltdown of a reactor and a radiation leak. Jimmy Carter, who had worked on the nuclear submarine program in the navy, largely minimized the danger of the accident. Although the long-term impact was less than initially feared by many nuclear power critics, the incident fed doubts about whether the government could be trusted on nuclear safety questions. Nader called for an antinuclear march, saying that Carter had "lied to the American people" and "hitched his political future" to nuclear power. "Jimmy Carter has driven Ralph Nader into the streets," the columnist Mary McGrory wrote in the *Boston Globe*.[28]

In September 1979, Nader headlined an antinuclear rally of two hundred thousand people at Battery Park City in New York. Nader and other speakers, including actress Jane Fonda and activist Tom Hayden, were joined by musicians like Bonnie Raitt, Pete Seeger, and Jackson Browne. Nader told the crowd that "stopping atomic energy is practicing patriotism; stopping atomic energy is fighting cancer; stopping atomic energy is fighting inflation." At the rally, many of the speakers touted a new "Citizen's Party" that would back antinuclear candidates in the 1980 elections. Opposition to Carter's energy proposals was splitting environmentalists off from the Democratic Party and lending support to the idea that only outside the established parties could public interest advocates pursue their political objectives with integrity. To Nader and many other critics outside the government, the Democratic Party, with its tendency to compromise and its vulnerability to corporate influence, seemed hopelessly lost.[29]

✦

ANOTHER KEY SPLIT occurred around the Carter administration's efforts to simplify and reorganize the government, and to scrutinize federal regulation more closely. As with its water and energy initiatives, Carter's government reform efforts incorporated important insights from the public interest movement. Nader and other liberal critics had amply demonstrated the distorted, unintended, and often irrational outcomes of government regulation and agency operations. Informed by the public interest critique of government, Carter sought to reimagine the active administrative state as a flawed but still vital enterprise. Government reform, as imagined by liberals like Carter, aimed to reconcile the well-documented limitations of government with the positive possibilities for government action.

Government reorganization and regulatory reform were heartfelt priorities for Jimmy Carter. As governor of Georgia, Carter had worked to rationalize state government, abolishing and consolidating hundreds of state agencies. "The President has a damned intense interest in all this," Harrison Wellford declared in a January 1978 interview. Wellford helped lead Carter's reorganization initiative from his position in the Office of Management and Budget. Wellford also provided a direct link to Ralph Nader's public interest network, going back many years. After completing his doctoral degree in government at Harvard, Wellford had become the first director of Nader's Center for Study of Responsive Law. Wellford had written a 1972 Nader report, *Sowing the Wind*, on agricultural pesticides and food safety. Now in the Carter White House, Wellford expressed the administration's view that improving government performance could bring enormous benefits.[30]

From the perspective of the administration, the federal government had grown too tangled and sclerotic and needed to be refreshed and streamlined. On his suit coat, for the 1978 interview, Wellford wore a big button with red letters saying "SIMPLIFY." Soon after taking office, Carter eliminated nearly five hundred federal advisory committees—40 percent of the total. Carter also sought to consolidate programs into single units to increase effectiveness. He created the Department of Energy out of several bureaucratic units, for example, to focus the government's energy programs. Carter worked to introduce "merit" into the civil service system and to reorganize the civil service. Carter wanted to emphasize performance standards to improve incentives for government efficiency and effectiveness. To be sure, the political results from these kinds of internal government reforms were uncertain. "If there is no public perception of an improvement in government's performance," Wellford conceded in his 1978 interview, "we will have failed."[31]

During the years of the Carter presidency, a broad political coalition successfully joined forces to deregulate key industries, including airlines and trucking, which had been under a kind of managed government control since the 1930s. Rather than being led from the conservative right, deregulation tapped into the liberal critique of business's hold on government. "The cartel is the government," Ralph Nader explained at a congressional hearing about the interests of American consumers. Pointing to aviation, trucking, nuclear power, banking, and other industries, Nader said, "There is scarcely a major business interest which does not have a Federal agency or department designed to promote, subsidize, or advocate" for it. Senator Edward Kennedy, a leading liberal Democrat, agreed with Nader's view that too many agencies were dominated by the industries that they regulated. Kennedy's critical view of the agencies led him to explicitly question the administrative legacy of the New Deal. The "New Deal faith in the science of the regulatory art," Kennedy said, was "a delusion." "As a practical matter," agency independence "has come to mean independence from the public interest." Seeking to lower prices on consumer goods and air travel, Kennedy steered bills through Congress that increased competition in trucking and airlines. Jimmy Carter enthusiastically signed the measures. Carter's staff considered deregulation "one of the President's great domestic legacies" and a "major turning point . . . in the way our government approaches basic industries in our country."[32]

The surprising consensus that emerged around deregulating transportation in the late 1970s, however, did not extend to some of Carter's other reform projects. In addition to structural reorganization and changes to the civil service, Carter pushed for more cost-effective, market-based regulation. Here the sharp tension between pragmatic governance and external critique emerged again.

Carter's efforts to improve the efficiency of regulation were motivated by a critical insight that liberal critics had been articulating since the late 1960s: the federal government increasingly shaped the economy and the environment through mechanisms lying outside formal spending. This understanding of the growth of government power had resulted in a series of efforts to better review and manage federal activities, ensuring that they served the public interest. An important 1969 tax reform bill, for example, incorporated the novel idea that federal tax breaks constituted a form of government spending. Tax reformers argued that an effective and equitable tax system needed to budget more transparently for "tax expenditures," including tax deductions for mortgage interest, oil drilling, charitable gifts, and state and local tax payments. The National Environmental Policy Act, also passed by Congress in 1969, took aim at the unaccounted-for environmental costs of federal actions. The "environmental impact statements" mandated by NEPA forced federal agencies to assess the environmental consequences of their decisions. No longer would the federal government make decisions about building dams, airports, and highways as if they had no environmental costs.[33]

Now Carter wanted to tackle the often-unaccounted-for costs of regulation. According to regulatory reformers, regulations, just like tax deductions and infrastructure projects, also had costs that needed to be calculated. Regulation had such a "pervasive" impact, a Carter advisor argued in 1979, that it needed to be reconceptualized as a "planning and management tool," rather than a piecemeal solution to pollution, safety, or efficiency problems. Through its regulatory actions, "the government in a real sense is 'managing' the automobile industry, the steel industry, the chemicals industry, the electric power industry, etc. But it is 'managing' these industries in an uncoordinated and *ad hoc* way." Carter, an engineer by training and an enthusiastic planner, sought to subordinate individual regulations to government-wide systems for allocating limited public resources. "Society's resources are vast, but they are not infinite," Carter told Congress in 1979, explaining how his regulatory reform program would help manage resources effectively.[34]

Within the agencies and in the White House, Carter's appointees pursued their reform mission by pushing for more cost-effective, market-based regulatory tools. At the Environmental Protection Agency, Assistant Administrator William Drayton was known as the "reform guru" charged with advancing programs to allow industry to decide how best to cut pollution and meet legislative mandates. Drayton had graduated from Yale Law School in 1970 and then worked in Connecticut state government, where he had helped launch experiments with market-based regulatory strategies, such as imposing fines on polluting companies to encourage them to invest in pollution control. The Carter administration's chief challenge, Drayton now argued, was "giving those we regulate the flexibility and incentive to find new, more economic and effective ways of complying." EPA's emphasis on regulatory innovation fit well with a White House initiative to require all federal agencies to compare the likely costs and benefits of proposed new regulations. The Council of Economic Advisors and Office of Management and Budget sought to partner with agencies to help them improve regulatory performance with new rule-writing processes.[35]

Carter administration efforts to reform regulation, including increasing competition in major economic sectors such as transportation, thus partly incorporated the insights of Nader and other liberal critics. Government could be overbearing, inefficient, and counterproductive, captured by industry or led astray by largely unaccountable bureaucrats. Yet questioning regulatory costs and the design of government programs also paradoxically affected agencies that were cherished, and had been fought for, by the public interest movement. Nader and his colleagues generally rejected Carter's attempts to extend the reform spirit to the Environmental Protection Agency and the Occupational Safety and Health Administration. Flexibility and cost-effectiveness, Nader and others complained, were simply ways to undermine those agencies. The emphasis on regulatory flexibility ran counter to the command-and-control mandates that the public interest community had advocated in the early 1970s.

When White House policy advisors pushed for somewhat less costly regulations to address problems such as air quality (ozone), strip mining, and textile factory air pollution, the public interest movement erupted in anger. NRDC attorney Richard Ayres denounced "economic gunslingers" at the Office of Management and Budget and the Council of Economic Advisors, guilty of "bald faced speaking for special interests" and insensitive to "anything more subtle than narrow conservative economics." Nader's Corporate Accountability Research Group released *Business War on the Law*, a 1979 report that dismissed complaints about regulatory costs as simply a "power play by corporations." Inflated claims about regulatory costs, Nader testified to Congress, were "consumer fraud" and "ideological arithmetic."[36]

Nader's harsh comments showed how liberals demanding tougher regulation rejected Carter's efforts to make regulation more efficient, casting reform proponents as simply corporate shills. When Leon Billings and Karl Braithwaite from Senator Edmund Muskie's staff met with White House policy makers in February 1979, they expressed "profound hostility to the regulatory reform draft and to all the regulatory reform activities of the administration." Billings promised an all-out fight, reportedly saying, "There is nothing I prefer more than to kick the shit out of an administration." Muskie, Billings said, would brand Carter's regulatory reform legislation "an industry-oriented device to destroy the regulatory process." Billings himself thought that cost-benefit analysis was "at best witchcraft and at worse it simply does not exist." No one, Billings believed, had the right to pollute the environment "in the name of economics or technology or otherwise."[37]

True to his word, later that month Senator Muskie declared in a speech at the University of Michigan that the chief threat to the environment was not a new pollutant, an industry, or an interest group, but rather "the mood of the anti-regulators who claim it is too costly and burdensome to protect people from the hazards of pollution." Muskie publicly attacked White House economists for "trying to undo much of the environmental progress" resulting from environmental legislation. Carter's regulatory council, and the White House's formal review of proposed regulations, according to Muskie, had served as an "economic veto" of new policies. Muskie demanded detailed reports on contacts between Carter's economic advisors and EPA officials to document inappropriate White House influence. Warning of a White House "assault on regulations," Muskie called Carter's regulatory reform bill "a bone tossed to industry by bureaucratic economists." "This is the year of the anti-regulators," Muskie said. "They are cloaked in the language of narrow, academic, cost-benefit analysis."[38]

By contrast, Carter's domestic and economic policy advisors saw regulatory reform as the only way to craft a successful Democratic Party politics in the late 1970s. Effective, efficient government, they thought, would enable Democrats to preserve the progressive accomplishments of previous decades. "If we are to build on the record of the New Deal and the Great Society, and if we are to continue to have a constituency for social programs in this country," domestic policy advisor Stuart Eizenstat said in a speech at the National Press Club, "we are going to have to convince the American people that those social programs are going to be administered in a fair and efficient way, with a minimum of red tape and an absence of fraud and abuse." To sustain initiatives such as a federal energy policy, the Office of Management and Budget's Jim McIntyre concurred, Democrats needed to "restore public confidence in government action itself."

Carter's White House advisors thus took one side on a fundamental choice in Democratic Party politics: Was it better to acknowledge substantive critiques of government and build support for a moderate, sustainable progressive politics, or did it make more sense to offer a full-throated defense of government regulation and reject the fundamental premises that energized conservative critiques? Nader and his allies in government and outside of it, many of whom had spent the previous decade criticizing federal agencies, now took the latter, hard-line position, defending some of the federal agencies against Carter's reform efforts.[39]

✦

JIMMY CARTER ULTIMATELY failed in his attempt to craft a new liberalism that could champion federal action while also recognizing government's flaws and limitations. Carter sought to incorporate the public interest critique into government. He appointed many public interest advocates and sought to reorganize and reform federal agencies. Public interest advocates outside the administration sometimes supported and helped to channel Carter's reform effort. At other times they harshly criticized the administration. Criticizing government power was what they knew how to do, and it was the role that they had defined for themselves.

As Carter's term in office proceeded, his administration's compromises and inadequacies increasingly weakened the public interest movement's support for the president. Perhaps out of excessive confidence in the liberal control of the House and Senate, both of which had been controlled by Democrats for decades, the liberal public interest movement cared more about political purity than about maintaining or strengthening the liberal political coalition. In September 1979, after Carter signed a bill that authorized a controversial dam project despite litigation under the Endangered Species Act, Marion Edey, director of the League of Conservation Voters, announced that Carter "cannot feel assured of active support." Carter had tried unsuccessfully to appoint Edey to the Council on Envi-

ronmental Quality in 1977, only to have her nomination blocked by
Senate opposition. Edey now declared, "It is no longer easy to answer
if we will drop Carter. He had our strong support in 1976, but, at the
moment, there is no guarantee." Two months later, after a November
meeting at which Carter asked for the support of environmental
leaders, Edey reiterated, "I cannot say we will or will not support the
president for re-election." "If not Carter, who can environmentalists
back?" asked the *Christian Science Monitor*, which similarly reported
that environmentalists were "hinting that they may desert" Carter in
his reelection effort. Leaders of The Wilderness Society and Friends
of the Earth expressed interest in alternative candidates, including
potential Democratic challenger Ted Kennedy and Republican candidate John Anderson. The spokesperson for The Wilderness Society
said, "We've just been appalled with the President this past year."
Robert Alvarez, a representative of the Washington, DC–based
Environmental Policy Center, said, "Environmentalists now, given
where Carter and Kennedy are at, must be noncommittal." Carter
had raised oil prices, spoken out for nuclear power, and opened public lands for development. "What more could Ronald Reagan do?"
Nader asked that same year.[40]

Disappointment with the Carter administration fed a broad critique of both parties and the political establishment. Nader declared
in mid-1979 that the two-party system was "crumbling and bank-
rupt," and that the differences between the two major parties were
like those between "Tweedle Dum and Tweedle Dee." A new political party was needed in the United States, Nader said. "It's time
to replace the two-party system with new parties, new spirit, new
programs, new constituencies, new optimism." The overarching
political issue, Nader argued, was corporate power and the "expansion of citizen access to all branches of government, the mass media
and corporate decision-making." Nader contended that the previous eight months had revealed a "complete corporatization of Jimmy
Carter." The president, Nader said, did not "appreciate the dimen-
sions of national leadership. Simply to mumble your way through

two years is to suggest you're not comfortable with the role of presidential leadership."[41]

Nader particularly blamed Carter for not pushing hard enough on one of his personal priorities: congressional passage of consumer protection agency legislation. Nader hoped that a new consumer agency would represent the "public interest" before other federal departments and regulatory agencies, counterbalancing special-interest lobbyists. After a lengthy legislative battle, however, the proposal to create the agency failed to pass Congress in 1978. "The loss of the Consumer Protection Agency bill was a major blow and it had a big effect on Ralph personally," Joan Claybrook recalled in a 1991 interview. While the consumer movement and nonprofit sector continued to grow and establish itself institutionally, Claybrook recalled, "there was a real feeling that Ralph had peaked." In August 1979, Nader announced that consumers had been "very badly treated by the Carter Administration." Carter had promised to become the "leading consumer champion," Nader said, but instead he might be "the president who has done more damage to the consumer interest than any recent president." Carter deepened Nader's dismay by appointing Lloyd Cutler, Nader's legal nemesis, to be his presidential counsel in 1979. Cutler's decades of representing large corporations in Washington, including the automobile companies during the highway safety fight, Nader said, made Cutler an "institutionalized conflict of interest." "Carter is inviting corporate power, lock stock and barrel, to run the White House," Nader complained.[42]

Nader's name was soon linked to a new Citizens Party being organized for the 1980 election. Nader himself continued to disavow any intention to run for political office. He still saw a more fruitful path for himself outside the electoral arena. "I would like to have the power to give other people power," Nader said. The ecologist Barry Commoner, however, was willing to plunge into a third-party presidential campaign. Commoner described the two parties in a manner that echoed Nader's rhetoric, saying in February 1980 that Democrats and Republicans offered "a choice between Tweedle-dee and Tweedledum." Instead of backing Carter, Commoner called on the president to withdraw his bid for a second term.[43]

Commoner had risen to prominence as an activist scientist in the 1950s as part of the nuclear test ban movement. During the 1960s and 1970s, Commoner had become one of the nation's most eloquent and influential environmental writers and visionaries. Now at the close of the "environmental decade," Commoner saw little difference between Kennedy, Carter, and the Republican primary candidate George H. W. Bush. The two parties, he said, were similarly "dominated by very narrow interests." The "grip of the corporations on the country" was the fundamental problem facing the United States, and both Carter and Anderson were "incapable of even asking the right question." In October 1980, just weeks before the election that would bring Ronald Reagan to power, Commoner continued to lump the Democrats and Republicans together, explaining that "most people have turned their backs" on both parties "because they're unable to come to grips with the basic issue in the country, which is that the corporations run it." Like Nader in his 2000 Green Party presidential run, Commoner aimed to get 5 percent of the vote so that the Citizens Party would qualify for federal election funds in the 1982 and 1984 elections. "I am not running to be elected," said Commoner. "Our aim was to build a party during this campaign," he said.[44]

While Commoner ultimately received just a few hundred thousand votes on Election Day, his campaign was symptomatic of the lack of unity on the left that weakened Carter's reelection campaign, much as Nader's 2000 run contributed to a broader undercutting of Al Gore twenty years later. In addition to Commoner's third-party effort, disappointed liberals flirted first with Ted Kennedy's fierce primary challenge to Carter, and then with the independent candidacy of John Anderson. Kennedy's rousing speech at the Democratic Convention in Madison Square Garden in August 1980 suggested that Carter, the Democratic nominee, was not a standard-bearer for liberal values. "For all those whose cares have been our concern, the work goes on," Kennedy proclaimed to great applause. "The cause endures. The hope still lives. And the dream shall never die." In a symbolic rejection of the president, Kennedy took the stage with Carter but refused to join hands in a show of party unity. Kennedy's challenge in the primary, Joan Claybrook recalled, helped strip away "the traditional support that the left had and it left the reelection campaign somewhat without a theme. The public really didn't have anything to hang on to as sort of their reason in wanting to reelect this President."[45]

Liberal critics and the left, including public interest advocates like Nader, actively undermined Carter's bid for reelection. Nader unenthusiastically called Jimmy Carter the "least of the worst," and he complained that Carter's "consumer protection position is a shadow of what he gave the people of this country a right to expect in the 1976 election." According to Nader, Carter had "gone against consumer interests in his largest decisions on unemployment, energy, inflation and the budget." Shortly before the 1980 election, Nader appeared on Phil Donahue's talk show. Asked whose energy policies he favored, Nader declined to endorse Jimmy Carter's energy program, and instead pointed to Barry Commoner of the Citizens Party.[46]

With high inflation and unemployment, the Iran hostage crisis, and the Soviet invasion of Afghanistan, liberal disarray was hardly the only reason that Carter lost to Reagan in 1980, but it was an important factor. The public interest critique of government held those in power up against a model of what they might be, rather than what the push and pull of political compromise and struggle allowed. Could liberals and the left build political power and govern? Public interest advocates who joined the Carter administration insisted in December 1980 that, from the "perspective of environmental quality," Carter's presidency had been "historic." They cited protection of Alaskan lands, energy policy, water resources reform, and regulation of strip-mining, among other actions. "No President has done more." Yet many of their counterparts outside of government complained that Carter and the Democrats were not good enough and that they had squandered opportunities to do the right thing. Flaws in the Democratic political leadership were enough to lead some to question whether it even mattered whether Reagan or Carter were elected. Nader concluded in January 1981, shortly after Reagan's election, that public interest advocates who had gone to work for Carter had "tried to shield the government from the capricious interest groups, but it was more than they could handle." Carter's presidency, Nader said, had been "anesthetizing . . . for the whole citizen movement." After seeing their public interest allies go into the Carter administration, Nader said dispiritedly, "the outsiders were just waiting and watching, once in a while pricking them but just waiting and watching."[47]

Chapter Nine

Stalemate: The 1980 Election and Its Legacy

BY THE END OF THE 1970S, RALPH NADER AND HIS allies had made the nonprofit sector and issue-based advocacy a potent force in US politics. A robust network of citizen organizations, including dozens started by Nader himself, scrutinized government practices. Public interest law firms regularly sued the government to make it enforce more than a dozen new health, safety, and environmental laws that Nader and others had helped pass early in the decade. A strengthened Freedom of Information Act, bolstered through amendments and litigation, helped to force open the workings of the government, enabling investigative research by journalists, as well as by citizen groups.

These changes did not just add a new actor; they reconceptualized the policy process. James Moorman, the first executive director of the Sierra Club Legal Defense Fund, described the new situation as a "triangular 'public interest model' of government"—one that he considered "far better" than the earlier "regulated vs. regulator model." The triangular model pitted public interest groups against corporations and others in a contest to direct government policy. "In the 1950s," Moorman said, "it was assumed that government lawyers were public interest lawyers." But that assumption no longer held in 1980, Moorman explained. The public interest existed separate from the government. Citizens who wanted clean air and water, for example, needed outside lawyers of their own to represent them before the government. Policy advocacy and litigation by public interest groups proliferated across a range of issues during the 1970s, including women's rights, civil rights, mental health, poverty, and criminal justice.[1]

The public interest movement had established social change advocacy as an alternative career for college graduates. Nader's Center for Study of Responsive Law formalized this new path in 1980 when it published *Good Works: A Guide to Social Change Careers*. *Good Works* introduced hundreds of organizations and opportunities, many of which had been created during the rapid growth in nonprofit organizations over the previous decade. No longer would employment advice have to come in the form of "a few scattered addresses jotted on the backs of envelopes," Nader noted. The book showed young people that they could become "professional citizens" by working at places where they could "bring their consciences with them," Nader explained in a subsequent edition. In his characteristically moralizing tone, Nader disparaged careers in business as "trivial jobs chasing manipulated wants" and complained that government was "replete with drone-like sinecures." Young people, Nader commented, did not need to take jobs "marketing underarm deodorants, promoting a chemical food dye, or shuffling inconsequential papers around." Instead, social change organizations could nourish "the taproots of an ever deeper democratic society." In Nader's vision, a "whole new set of people, values, and needs can find expression if the citizen entrepreneurs are at work."[2]

In keeping with the triangular model of government described by James Moorman, Nader located this "deeper democratic society" in self-organizing groups of citizens outside of the government, rather than in traditional democratic institutions or public agencies. The public interest vision of citizenship reflected ideas of self-actualization and personal fulfillment prevalent in books such as Charles Reich's 1970 bestseller, *The Greening of America*. Reich's influential book celebrated how the emerging youth movement rejected the "consciousness" and structures of the "Corporate State" that had dominated American society since World War II. Nader's career advice echoed Reich's critique.

"Fulfilling one's talents and dreams," Nader said, "is the antithesis of jobs that, however well paid, make you feel that you are just putting your time in, that life begins after the nine-to-five drudgery is over." Venerating public interest work reflected a contempt for bureaucratic institutions, including government agencies and large corporations, considered slow-moving and ethically compromised, unable to sustain the creative individual. Increasingly, talented liberals thought that civic and political action took place through nonprofit advocacy organizations that offered purer expressions of their political sentiments.[3]

Even as individuals sought to escape the drudgery of business and government work, however, the "professional citizen" became more and more "professional." In the late 1960s and early 1970s, young people working for Nader on a task force report or employed by fledgling organizations like the Environmental Defense Fund often anticipated a stint in social change advocacy before moving on to other jobs. The short-term nature of the work frequently had justified the long hours, low pay, and chaotic, freewheeling organizational structure. A career in social change now started to imply something different. Nonprofit leaders seeking to create alternatives to business and government sought to build viable organizations that could become a permanent part of the American political landscape. In the process, highly educated public interest advocates developed into administrators balancing fundraising, planning, board development, and human resources management.

Nader had helped to create an institutionalized policy advocacy community that he himself was poorly suited to lead. At the start of the 1970s, Nader had seemed like a "Lone Ranger" riding to the rescue of the American public, accompanied by a team of youthful "Nader's Raiders"; by the end of the decade, however, he had become just one of many leading voices in a cacophony of public interest advocacy. Nader's personal quirks and dogmatic positions left him more frequently on the margins of an increasingly organized and politically savvy nonprofit community. Nader preferred to start new projects than to manage and raise money for a large, structured organization.

Two days before the 1980 election, in a symbol of this change, Nader resigned as the head of Public Citizen, the umbrella group overseeing several of his major projects. The extraordinary growth of the public interest movement over the course of the 1970s meant that Ralph Nader as an individual was no longer as central or important to it.[4]

✦

AT THE END OF 1980, the burgeoning and increasingly formalized public interest movement found itself in a newly challenging position. Ronald Reagan's election to president, along with the Republican Party's seizure of control of the US Senate for the first time since 1955, represented a colossal defeat. An emboldened and increasingly conservative Republican Party profoundly threatened the invigorated government that the public interest movement had pushed to protect health, safety, and the environment during the previous fifteen years. Reagan's election definitively marked the end of the New Deal liberal period, during which Americans had optimistically looked to the federal government for solutions.

Yet focusing on Reagan and the conservatives overlooks exactly how the post–World War II administrative state lost its footing during the 1970s. Blaming conservatives for the end of the New Deal era is far too simplistic. Liberal and left-leaning advocates amply and harshly documented the government's problems and campaigned aggressively to reform federal administration to serve the "public interest." To many liberals, the New Deal model was structurally flawed in the excessive power that it concentrated in executive agencies, and the system had betrayed its initial promises. "Our political and governmental processes have grown so unresponsive, so ill-designed for contemporary purposes that they waste the taxpayers' money, mangle good programs and smother every good man who gets into the system," John Gardner declared in 1970 when he founded Common Cause as a citizens' lobby.[5]

Gardner's rhetorical attack on the failure of public institutions contrasted strikingly with John F. Kennedy's call to young people in 1960 to serve the nation by working for the federal government in Washington. Public interest organizations like Common Cause existed because liberals like Gardner thought that the government was failing Americans. Gardner, Nader, and other public interest advocates urged Americans to question whether the government adequately represented their interests, or whether, in Nader's words, the government instead had been given over to "special interest groups, waste, insensitivity, ignorance, and bureaucracy."[6]

The attack on the New Deal state, culminating in Reagan's election and so often attributed to an ascendant conservative movement, thus also was driven by an ascendant liberal public interest movement. Having shown how federal regulatory institutions too often served corporate monopolies rather than American consumers, Nader had joined forces with liberals like Ted Kennedy and with conservatives to push for the deregulation of key industries. Nader criticized the "increasing interwovenness between large corporations and large governmental units," describing common business-government relationships as a "shared monopoly over the market mechanism." Government economic regulation was too often "corporate socialism." Economic deregulation in the late 1970s, carried out in the name of the American citizen and consumer, took aim directly at the tight alliance between industry, government, and labor that characterized much of the postwar period. Liberal Democrats celebrated these deregulatory accomplishments. "While others talked of free enterprise," Kennedy declared in his speech to the 1980 Democratic National Convention, "it was the Democratic Party that acted and we ended excessive regulation in the airline and trucking industry, and we restored competition to the marketplace." The late-1970s deregulatory push was thus a culmination of the public interest movement's long-standing critique of government agencies, and reports like those carried out by Nader's task forces. Jimmy Carter similarly embraced this critical analysis of the agencies. "Many regulatory agencies," President Carter said bluntly in 1980, "protect monopolies."[7]

Ralph Nader saw Ronald Reagan as his antithesis, but the two men sounded a surprising number of common themes. In the 1972 book *Who Runs Congress?* Nader, who wrote the introduction, and the book's coauthors attacked "big government, big business, and big labor—all combined into one giant coalition." Ronald Reagan criticized the same coalition. When Reagan announced his first presidential campaign in 1975, he couched his candidacy as an attack on the Washington, DC, "'buddy' system" that Nader denounced. Those responsible, Reagan said, included "Congress, the bureaucracy, the lobbyist, big business and big labor." The survival and progress of the American people, Reagan declared in Nader-esque language, depended on "a leadership that listens to them, relies on them and seeks to return government to them."[8]

The solution that Reagan advocated was, of course, radically different from the one touted by liberals and the left. Nader and his allies demanded *more aggressive* government action to serve the "public interest," instead of the interests of industry. In their tripartite model of government, public interest advocates wielded the power of the new, third pillar—a citizens' movement watching over government to prevent the private sector from corrupting and dominating it. Through government ombudsmen and a consumer protection agency, Nader even wanted to internalize the institutional oversight of government within the government itself. Public interest advocates complained that federal agencies used their planning and directive powers to nefarious and destructive purposes. But they still believed in government and wanted it to deploy expertise in the right way, by listening to the correct experts. In the view of people like Nader, planning was a worthy goal, but in the postwar period, planners had followed the wrong impulses and had been corrupted by industries that bent the government to serve their interests.

By contrast, Reagan and other market-oriented conservatives sought to liberate the private sector from regulation. Reagan acted to undermine, rather than invigorate, federal oversight. Rather than see a role for citizen activists pressing government to do more and do better, Reagan embraced the simple duality of state versus market. He sided with regulated industries against government regulators and also against labor unions. In his 1981 inaugural address, Reagan declared plainly, "Government is not the solution to our problem; government is the problem." Citizens, companies, and workers needed to be given the freedom to govern themselves. "From time to time we've been tempted to believe that society has become too complex to be managed by self-rule, that government by an elite group is superior to government for, by, and of the people," Reagan said. "Well, if no one among us is capable of governing himself, then who among us has the capacity to govern someone else?"[9]

During his presidential campaign, Reagan forcefully criticized environmental and public interest advocates, using them frequently as a rhetorical foil. Reagan justified his very candidacy on an explicit rejection of ideas that framed popular anxieties about resource scarcity and the prospects for future economic growth. In his 1979 campaign announcement, Reagan declared that the reason "why I'm running for president" was to counter the liberal idea that Americans "must learn to live with less." Reagan denounced "false estimates by unknown, unidentifiable experts" who suggested that the American standard of living was a "selfish extravagance which we must renounce as we join in sharing scarcity."[10]

Candidate Reagan wanted none of Jimmy Carter's sweaters, lowered thermostats, and gas station lines. He repudiated the research behind Carter's dour predictions of scarcity, such as the influential 1972 book *Limits to Growth*, which drew on computer models to warn of catastrophic societal collapse due to overpopulation and excessive resource consumption. Reagan rejected the idea that experts, whether in government or outside it in the public interest movement, could diagnose and solve societal problems. He called health, safety, and environmental regulations well-intentioned but misguided. "Too often," Reagan said, "regulations work against rather than for the interests of the people." He mocked "Utopian regulators" of the 1960s and 1970s for their naive belief that "we could attain a risk-free world if only they could plan it centrally and enforce the rules and regulations."[11]

As part of his attack on government and public interest experts, Reagan particularly blamed the environmental movement for high energy prices. According to his reasoning, public interest lawyers influenced agency policy and blocked energy companies from expanding production. In his July 1980 speech accepting the Republican nomination, Reagan explained that oil companies were "thwarted by a tiny minority opposed to economic growth which often finds friendly ears in regulatory agencies for its obstructionist campaigns." The United States could solve its energy problems, he said, if "the government would get out of the way and let the oil companies explore and drill and produce the oil we have." In a televised October debate, Reagan continued his call for "more domestic production of oil and gas," as well as for the expanded use of nuclear power. Reagan emphasized, "We do not have to go on sharing in scarcity."[12]

◆

REAGAN'S PRESIDENTIAL VICTORY simplified political conflict to a battle between advocates for government and antagonists to government. The two positions erased complexities and nuances that had emerged during the 1970s and had been formulated into policy during the Carter years. Liberals now assumed a largely defensive position. They decried proposals to alter regulatory programs as simply a sellout to industry and an assault on fundamental principles, much as they had done for elements of Carter's regulatory overhaul. Meanwhile, many Reagan Republicans articulated a simplistic antigovernment rhetoric, demanding to overturn or weaken 1970s regulations rather than address their flaws. While they offered starkly different solutions, in another sense the Reagan administration and its liberal antagonists shared a common theme: they both pitted government against market, rather than emphasizing challenges inherent to balancing government regulation and efficiency.

Jimmy Carter had aspired to something different. Carter's governing approach had acknowledged both the value of government and the limitations of government action. Carter tried to take account of the accumulating criticisms of government in order to craft a pragmatic approach to governing that might integrate these conflicting truths.

Carter's efforts to reform regulation while simultaneously expanding it were illustrated clearly on a Thursday morning in December 1980, when he signed into law two separate bills that stood for the multi-faceted legacy he wanted for his departing administration. One of the measures, the "Superfund" law, created a new funding mechanism to facilitate the cleanup of the nation's hazardous waste sites. The Superfund bill filled a "major gap in the existing laws of our country," Carter said that day, strengthening the hand of federal environmental regulators. The second bill, the Paperwork Reduction Act, appeared to point in the completely opposite direction. The Paperwork Reduction Act aimed to "eliminate unnecessary Federal regulations" as well as "wasteful and unnecessary" federal information requirements. The law, Carter declared, would "regulate the regulators" by giving the White House Office of Management and Budget "the final word" on regulations.[13]

In retrospect, Carter's double bill signing, which linked Superfund with the Paperwork Reduction Act, marked the end of the 1970s as the environmental decade and the end of most new environmental legislation. In the forty years following the passage of Superfund, Congress enacted few significant new environmental laws. Unable to agree on policy reforms, Washington politicians instead fought over the implementation and legitimacy of the environmental laws that had been passed in the 1970s. In a simplistic rendering of that December morning's events, liberals stood for Superfund and for environmental regulation, while conservatives stood for Paperwork Reduction and the power of the budget office. A national political stalemate followed.

Yet that stalemate—metaphorically, the pitting of Superfund against Paperwork Reduction—was decidedly not the legacy that Jimmy Carter intended. Carter envisioned something different from bitter strife between environmentalists and deregulators. Rather than force a choice between starkly different paths, the Paperwork Reduction Act and the Superfund bill represented, for Carter, two important developments of the 1970s that were compatible and should be merged.

Threats to public health, safety, and the environment had demanded a government response of the kind that Superfund represented. Ten years earlier, on New Year's Day 1970, Richard Nixon had signed the National Environmental Policy Act, declaring that it was "now or never" for Americans to "restore the cleanliness" of the nation's air and water. In the decade between NEPA and the Superfund bill, Congress, after much prodding by citizen advocates like Ralph Nader, passed the major environmental bills of the era, addressing air and water pollution, toxic chemicals, oil pollution, endangered species, forest and marine management, and energy efficiency. Federal agencies, including the new Environmental Protection Agency and Occupational Safety and Health Administration, sprang into action to write and enforce new rules and regulations. Superfund turned out to be the last major building block in this emerging federal environmental regulatory state.[14]

Yet as the federal government expanded its reach during the 1960s and 1970s, many critics also complained about the perverse impact of government regulations on Americans. Regulation and paperwork were not free goods, these critics argued. The government needed to manage the costs that it imposed on the American people. New York Republican Frank Horton, one of the paperwork bill's House sponsors, reported being "besieged" in his district with complaints of "strangulation by regulation."[15]

Carter himself embodied both of these impulses: he embraced government action to protect the environment and public health, and he also sought to make regulation less burdensome and costly. Both causes, in fact, were personal passions. Carter had spent childhood days roaming the woods and fields in rural Georgia. "Everyone who knows me," he said while signing the Superfund bill, "understands that one of my greatest pleasures has been to strengthen the protection of our environment." But government efficiency also animated the president. With a background in the navy's nuclear submarine program, Carter was used to calculating and balancing risks and benefits for strategic purposes. As governor of Georgia, Carter also had worked to rationalize state government, abolishing and consolidating hundreds of state agencies. Now in the closing days of his presidency, Carter spoke fondly of the utterly bureaucratic cause of information management and regulatory reform. One of the "high points of my presidency," Carter recalled, was a day in 1978 when more than nine hundred minor and outdated safety and health regulations "were stricken from the books." Carter characterized the Paperwork Reduction Act as a defining legacy. The law, Carter said at the signing ceremony, was "embedding my own philosophy . . . into the laws of our Nation."[16]

In striking contrast to the tactics of the incoming Reagan administration, Carter advanced deregulation and regulatory reform while *also* actively defending the critical importance of regulation and government. Carter believed strongly in active government regulation. He thought that by making regulation more efficient and effective, he could build public trust and support for the government's role. Looking back from the vantage point of the mid-1990s, Carter's EPA administrator Doug Costle concluded that Carter's regulatory review program sought to "create a cooperative environment among the regulators . . . without the kind of political tension that had existed and has now emerged again." In Costle's view, the key to this cooperative relationship—and a major distinction from subsequent Reagan budget office oversight—was that the White House economic staff "wasn't just a hit squad trying to throttle us." As EPA administrator, Costle had chaired Carter's interagency Regulatory Council and had made the Environmental Protection Agency a key site for innovation in market-based regulation and economic analysis.[17]

Despite similarities and a common institutional foundation, Ronald Reagan and his advisors vocally rejected, and distanced themselves from, Carter's nuanced approach to regulation. During the 1980 campaign, Reagan denounced the "regulatory web" that was "smothering" the economy. Reagan's first OMB director, David Stockman, raised hackles with calls for a "regulatory ventilation" that would block or reverse costly federal environmental standards. Business lobbyists, according to a *Washington Post* article in February 1981, were drawn to the Reagan administration "like a stocked candy store." Businesses had a "shopping list of regulations" that they wanted to eliminate, and some of the business interests were "reaching in with both hands." A letter from four major business organizations, including the Chamber of Commerce, National Association of Manufacturers, Business Council, and National Federation of Independent Business, proposed strengthening OMB's control of the regulatory agencies. They told Reagan aides that "an opportunity for decisive action exists now as never before."[18]

During his first month in office, Reagan took several dramatic public steps that Carter had deliberately eschewed at the end of his term. To his critics, Reagan appeared to be trying to shut down the government's regulatory apparatus. Reagan ordered hundreds of new regulations postponed, and asked agency heads to review and rescind other rules. He created a new cabinet-level task force on regulatory relief, led by Vice President George H. W. Bush, to identify and modify overly burdensome regulations. Reagan also issued a new executive order to further strengthen presidential power over federal regulation. The Carter administration had required OMB review only of regulations costing over $100 million. Carter's economic advisors had emphasized the importance of creating a deliberative learning process within the agencies to encourage improved regulatory techniques. Under Reagan, OMB would review *all* proposed regulations as a way to limit regulatory actions.

Reagan's new executive order also mandated that agencies use formal cost-benefit calculations to guide their regulatory decisions. Instead of simply considering a range of options, the agencies now were directed to undertake new regulatory actions *only* if their "potential benefits to society" outweighed the "potential costs." While the Carter administration had favored comparing the costs and benefits of new regulations, Carter's economic advisors had rejected a formulaic application of cost-benefit analysis. They argued that neither costs nor benefits could be calculated accurately enough to drive final policy decisions.[19]

Even though some of Reagan's actions to centralize power within the budget office were the "next logical steps" and built directly on Carter's efforts and experience, Reagan's purpose seemed "completely different." Reagan's call for "regulatory relief" sparked fears that the Office of Management and Budget planned to "eviscerate essential health, safety, and environmental protections for the benefit of big business," recalled Christopher DeMuth, who headed Reagan's Office of Information and Regulatory Affairs, the division within the budget office that was responsible for regulatory reform. The Reagan administration's antiregulatory rhetoric inflamed liberal opponents and mobilized conservative supporters, rather than building support for more effective government. Attempts to pass regulatory reform legislation in Congress, or to extend cost-benefit analysis within the government, were seen as retreats. They set off fierce partisan battles in the early 1980s.[20]

In retrospect, Reagan's more emphatic and explicit attack on government impeded, rather than advanced, regulatory reform. Reagan's combative approach prompted congressional Democrats and public interest advocates to denounce the White House budget office's expanded role. There was simply no trust in the Reagan administration's regulatory reform process. The House Committee on Energy and Commerce, chaired by Representative John Dingell, a Michigan Democrat, issued a report lambasting the Office of Management and Budget's "unfettered authority" as "unprecedented" and lacking essential controls or standards. The report questioned whether "secret, undisclosed, and unreviewable contacts" by businesses seeking to influence agency actions deprived the public of its right to "meaningful participation in the decisionmaking process." The focus on the Office of Management and Budget signaled how the internal structures of government became polarized in the Reagan years. A new nonprofit public interest group called OMB Watch was established in the early 1980s to monitor the budget office that, it said, was "secretly controlling public policy." Other critics argued that the Environmental Protection Agency was being reduced to simply a "rubber stamp for OMB-industry manipulations."[21]

The Reagan administration particularly targeted federal environmental and natural-resource policy in its efforts to cut and weaken regulations. Cultural clashes over abortion and feminism perhaps drew more public attention. But the businesses backing the Republican Party wanted relief from the environmental laws and natural-resource policies of the 1970s. The EPA was "the critical agency" for regulatory change, according to David Stockman, a Republican congressman from Michigan whom Reagan appointed as director of the Office of Management and Budget. "They've got rules that would practically shut down the economy if they were put into effect," Stockman complained shortly after the 1980 election. "You need a whole new mindset down at EPA or you're not going to [do] anything about regulation."[22]

The week before his inauguration, President-elect Reagan met with his transition team to discuss ways to immediately "relieve the regulatory burden in a number of sectors." Ten of fifteen proposed actions focused on the environment and energy. The administration wanted to weaken hazardous waste regulation and chemical labeling, appliance efficiency standards and building-temperature restrictions, and pollution standards for carbon monoxide, water effluent, diesel emissions, and noise. Former EPA administrator Douglas Costle, who had helped lead Carter's regulatory reform efforts, predicted a "struggle for the soul of this administration by the rape, pillage and burn crowd on the one hand and the moderate, conservative pragmatists who are building for the future on the other." His successor, Costle said, "has my total sympathy and empathy."[23]

Instead of Carter's phalanx of public interest appointees, Reagan named lawyers and lobbyists from regulated industries to run agencies like the Environmental Protection Agency. EPA administrator Anne Gorsuch Burford had previously worked as a lobbyist for the Mountain Bell Telephone Company. As a Colorado state legislator, Gorsuch had helped block a proposed measure to control toxic waste and had opposed air pollution regulation in the Denver area. Gorsuch's chief of staff came from the American Paper Institute and the Johns-Manville

Corporation, a major asbestos manufacturer. The new general counsel for EPA, Robert Perry, had worked as an attorney for Exxon. Rita Lavelle, the EPA assistant administrator for solid waste and emergency response, who was responsible for overseeing and implementing the new Superfund program, had worked previously for the Continental Chemical Corporation and Aerojet, a California defense contractor subject to the new law. An assistant administrator for air, noise, and radiation came from Crown Zellerbach, a pulp and paper conglomerate based in San Francisco; while another assistant administrator, in charge of pesticides and toxic substances, had previously worked at Hoffmann-La Roche, an international pharmaceutical and chemical company whose subsidiary had been involved in a major dioxin accident in 1976.[24]

This new EPA leadership team drawn from the ranks of industry oversaw a dramatic reduction in the EPA's budget and a significant reduction in legal enforcement. Russell Train, a Republican environmental leader who had served as the second EPA administrator, under Presidents Nixon and Ford, warned in 1982 that the agency was "rapidly being destroyed as an effective institution." Budget and personnel cuts, Train wrote in the *Washington Post*, threatened to "reduce the agency to a state of ineffectualness and demoralization from which it is unlikely to recover for at least 10 years, if ever." Douglas Costle similarly denounced the "assault on public health and safety programs." The "truth of the matter is that government is necessary," Costle said. "The free enterprise system does not automatically clean up the air and water."[25]

Many of Reagan's industry-oriented appointees used their intimate knowledge of the government in order to subdue the bureaucracy and accomplish reform. Appointing James Watt to serve as interior secretary flipped Jimmy Carter's strategy of hiring liberal public interest advocates. After a stint working in the federal government in the early 1970s, Watt had served as the founding president of the Colorado-based Mountain States Legal Foundation, a conservative, corporate-backed "public interest" law firm established in 1977. Watt had

Secretary of the Interior James Watt presents President Ronald Reagan
with a meat cleaver attached to a copy of the Code of Federal Regulations
split in two. The gift, presented in jest at a February 1981 cabinet
meeting, captured the new administration's open hostility to 1970s
federal environmental, health, and safety regulations. Ronald Reagan
Library.

dedicated the organization to battling against the "bureaucrats and
no-growth advocates," who he thought threatened economic freedom
and individual liberty. Watt was a devoutly religious man with a zeal
for conservative politics. In a 1978 speech in Dallas, Watt warned of "a
new political force in the land—a small group of extremists who don't
concern themselves with a balanced perspective or a concern about
improving the quality of life for mankind—they are called environmentalists." Watt asked rhetorically, "What is the real motive of these
extreme environmentalists? Is it to simply protect the environment? Is
it to delay and deny energy development? Is it to weaken America?"
Watt left little doubt that he thought the environmental movement
was out to destroy American private enterprise, particularly resource
extraction in the American West.[26]

For all his hostility toward federal regulation, Watt was a quintessential bureaucratic warrior. Watt knew the bureaucracy from prior experience working for the Federal Power Commission and the Department of the Interior. Many of the Interior staff would be "not responsive" to Reagan's programs, he believed, and Watt was determined to seize his opportunity to shake up the agency. "You have to strike fast in this business," Watt said about the controversial policy initiatives that he pursued in the first months in office. "Influence is a very perishable commodity. You can lose it practically overnight. You have to use what you've got when you've got it. For me that's right now."[27]

Watt campaigned to open wilderness-designated lands to coal and oil exploration, and to sell off large blocks of public lands. He sought to reopen federal waters off the California coast to offshore drilling. He aimed to block further expansion of the National Park System, and to shed the system's urban parks. Watt also sought to loosen policies in order to allow more grazing on public lands. Overall, Watt tried to reverse many of the more conservation-oriented policies that had been implemented in the Interior Department since the 1960s.[28]

◆

IN THIS SHARPLY POLARIZED climate, the nonprofit sector surged as an external force. The Reagan presidency was a demoralizing and seemingly existential threat to all that the public interest movement had worked for, and it provided a catalyzing enemy that clarified and mobilized support. "Reagan will help," Ralph Nader said in September 1981. "I think they are going to make bad errors, and it's up to the citizen movement to take off from that." Nader gestured toward the revolutionary idea that things had to get worse before they could get better. "That's not the proper way to forecast progress," Nader said, "to say there must be suffering before the reverse of any movement. But that's the way it's going to be."[29]

Mark Green, the Nader ally who coauthored the best-selling *Who Runs Congress?*, shared Nader's analysis in his own 1982 manifesto, *Winning Back America*. Reagan's election was "the worst of times for liberals," Green wrote, but at the same time it was "also the best of times." Being out of power gave liberal advocates the "freedom and energy" to criticize the ruling party and to develop more ambitious programs for the future. Green argued that the Reagan administration, ironically, would spur innovation more than if Jimmy Carter had been reelected. "Four more anesthetizing years of Carter could not have inspired a program of creative liberalism," he wrote. But the "Reagan Revolution" would "animate progressives in America."[30]

Membership in environmental organizations soared in the early 1980s. With the Reagan administration actively hostile toward the regulatory protections established during the 1970s, liberal public interest organizations seemed more important than ever. Watt at Interior and Gorsuch at the EPA provided easy targets against which the environmental organizations could run. "The degree to which Mr. Watt has caused our donations to go up is quite extraordinary," William Turnage, executive director of The Wilderness Society, said in an April 1981 interview. "Watt came in with guns blazing in ideological warfare, and we had no choice but to go into an adversarial relationship." The Sierra Club, which vigorously denounced Watt and Gorsuch, grew by 30 percent per year in the early 1980s, soon doubling in size. Fundraising appeals by the National Audubon Society directly attacking the Reagan administration resulted in donation levels ten times those of their previous efforts.[31]

Unlike the uncertainty of the Carter years, when advocates had to decide whether to go in or stay out, and whether to hold pure or pursue pragmatic change, public interest organizations now had few doubts about their purpose or mandate. "Our mission will be primarily to hold the line," Nader said in January 1981. The leading environmental policy groups formed a "Group of 10" coalition to meet regularly in Washington, DC, to strategize about ways to counter the Reagan administration. "We are going to maximize our grassroots clout," declared Russell Peterson, president of the Audubon Society. Many former Carter hands sought to join the fight, moving out of government back into public interest organizations to watch over the agencies that they had left. Joan Claybrook, the former administrator of the National Highway Traffic Safety Administration, became president of Public Citizen, a position that she would go on to hold for twenty-seven years, from 1982 to 2009. David Hawkins returned to the Natural Resources Defense Council from the EPA; he would remain at NRDC for decades. Gus Speth left the Council on Environmental Quality and launched the World Resources Institute, a new nonprofit organization focused on global sustainability. The former Justice Department lawyer Tony Roisman established "Trial Lawyers for Public Justice."[32]

As public interest advocates sought to invigorate the left and to counter the Reagan administration, they also searched for answers to what had gone wrong. One recurring question was, What was the relationship between the growing nonprofit sector and the political parties and electoral politics? In *Winning Back America*, Mark Green revealed a broadly felt ambivalence toward the Democratic Party and its relationship to the citizens' movement. Public interest activists saw themselves sometimes as allies with the Democratic Party, dependent on its political success, but often as an independent and separate force, developing their own campaigns and strategies.

Green himself embraced the idea of building political power in partnership with the Democratic Party. Green thought that a liberal resurgence depended on the "revival of the one national party that could conceivably adopt in its national platform the progressive alternatives" that liberals believed in. Green ran unsuccessfully for Congress as a Democrat in New York City in 1980, and for Senate in 1986, losing to a Republican incumbent in the general election each time. In the 1990s, Green was elected to the public advocate position in New York City, and he subsequently lost the 2001 mayoral election to Michael Bloomberg. In *Winning Back America*, Green argued that progressives could not afford to impose a litmus test on the Democrats. "Ideological self-cannibalism is an unaffordable luxury." Third parties, such as the Citizens Party, Green wrote, were inevitably just "a fringe exercise" in a two-party system. Progressives, Green argued, had to reconcile themselves to the Democratic Party as "an essential vehicle for change."[33]

Yet Green acknowledged the dilemma facing liberals and the left. Many of his like-minded activists viewed deeper engagement with the Democratic Party skeptically and saw the party as unpalatable and unsalvageable. "Pristine progressives," Green wrote, "may well object to working through such a stodgy structure as the Democratic Party. To be sure, at times it is barely distinguishable from the Republican Party." The "traditional role of the two-party system has declined," Green said. Though supportive of the Democratic Party, Green pointed to the public interest movement as the best representative of progressive causes. "If there is to be a progressive revival, it will be led by the issue politics of citizen groups," Green said. After their years pursuing elite legal strategies and working closely with the Carter administration, Green described a kind of rediscovery of grassroots politics by citizen groups, who were "beginning to apply their organizing skills to campaigns."[34]

The public interest organizations anticipated a turn toward more outside strategies, including grassroots organizing and politics. The insider approaches that they had pursued during the Carter years were no longer available to them. "We're going to have to revert to some of the tools of advocacy used in the past," Gregory Thomas, an NRDC attorney, told the *Los Angeles Times*. "It's time we started working with outsiders again instead of insiders." A lawyer at the Environmental Defense Fund concurred, saying that the environmental groups had "focused too exclusively on Washington." State and local organizing seemed particularly appealing in light of the unfriendly appointees in federal agencies. "We're going to do some of the field work that the Democratic Party stopped doing," Marion Edey of the League of Conservation Voters said.[35]

Ralph Nader sided with those who located progressive politics outside the Democratic Party. During the 1980s, Nader grew increasingly interested in alternative strategies for building citizen and consumer power. He championed buyer cooperatives, citizen boards to monitor state utilities, and state and local organizing efforts. In Wisconsin, for example, Nader helped create a Citizen Utility Board funded by utilities but acting in the interest of consumers to oppose rate increases and represent consumer interests. Nader remained as active as ever, but his public profile also diminished as other advocacy groups and leaders took the fore. "Nearly two decades after Nader became the king of consumers and environmentalists," Juan Williams wrote in the *Washington Post* in 1982, "he finds people calling him a has-been." Nader still had "an empire" of public interest organizations, but increasingly he was "largely out of view of the front pages." As he lost power and audience, Nader's frustration grew. His discontent would lead him in the 1990s to enter the political arena that he had eschewed for so long.[36]

◆

RONALD REAGAN'S ELECTION to president in 1980 is often characterized as the start of a new conservative age. When it came to environmental policy, however, neither liberals nor conservatives prevailed. Although the Reagan administration aggressively attacked federal environmental and natural-resource policies, its effort to roll back the regulatory advances of the 1970s proved unsuccessful. The environmental laws of the 1970s survived largely intact. At the Environmental Protection Agency, controversial efforts to undermine the new Superfund law prompted EPA administrator Anne Gorsuch's resignation in 1983 and led to the perjury conviction of Rita Lavelle, the assistant administrator in charge of the toxic waste program. James Watt, Reagan's firebrand appointee at Interior, also resigned in late 1983. Looking ahead to the 1984 election, Reagan appointed moderate caretakers to steer his administration's environmental and natural-resource policy. William Ruckelshaus, the first EPA administrator under Richard Nixon and a trusted environmentalist, returned to take charge at the environmental agency. William Clark, a Reagan loyalist, went to the Interior Department to, in his words, put "oil on the water" and calm relations with Interior's various constituencies.

At the same time, little new legislation passed. Enforcement stalled. Stalemate became the status quo for the next three decades. Major legislative breakthroughs, such as the 1990 Clean Air Act Amendments, would prove the exception to the rule.[37]

Many public interest advocates found themselves in a peculiar position. Their efforts to safeguard the government's regulatory role after Reagan's election pushed many liberal activists into a stance that ran counter to their own robust critique of the administrative state before 1980. How could they acknowledge the perverse outcomes of the postwar federal role—all the ways that government agencies had wielded power against communities and the environment—while still making a strong case for the government as an essential solution to societal problems? Jimmy Carter had tried to reconcile regulatory reform with regulatory action, but he had struggled to sell this complicated political position. The stalemate after 1980 was in many ways easier for both sides, even if it failed to yield new legislation or address long-standing issues. Reagan conservatives attacking the administrative state, and liberal activists forced to defend it, were increasingly each other's foils. It was an effective advocacy position for both sides, but not one that wrestled effectively with the inherent tensions of governing.[38]

Epilogue

IN THE SUMMER OF 1963, BILL CLINTON TRAVELED from Arkansas to Washington, DC, at the age of sixteen for a week-long politics program organized by the American Legion. The highlight of the trip was a visit to the White House Rose Garden, where Clinton elbowed his way to the front of the crowd and shook hands with his childhood hero, President John F. Kennedy. Kennedy's call to public service would prove a lasting inspiration for Clinton. But the future president also was deeply influenced by the era's struggle for civil rights, the Vietnam War, and the broader liberal and leftist critique of the government's flaws and failures. Clinton studied at Yale Law School in the early 1970s, when the school was a hotbed of public interest legal advocacy. Looking back in 1993, one of Clinton's law school classmates recalled, "We had an inappropriately large sense of our ability to affect the world." Students went to the law school, recalled another, "because they wanted to change the world for the better. They wanted to use the law in ways that would help people." In Yale's legal services clinic, students and clinical law faculty pursued public interest litigation involving prisons, mental health institutions, and other causes. In their coursework, they studied how law could serve as a tool for social change. After graduation, some graduates helped launch public interest law firms, including the Natural Resources Defense Council, the Center for Law and Social Policy, and other groups.[1]

Bill Clinton gravitated toward politics and government service as his method of change, but he married into the public interest movement. Hillary Rodham, whom he met at Yale, worked during and then after law school for the Children's Defense Fund, a new public interest organization focused on low-income families and children's rights. Rodham also was a staff member for the Judiciary Committee of the House of Representatives during the Watergate scandal, giving her a close look at Nixon administration political corruption. After her marriage to Bill and her move to Arkansas, Rodham cofounded a state-level children's advocacy organization. Together, in their work inside and outside of government, the Clintons took to heart the idea that the traditional Democratic Party was flawed, political leaders could be corrupted at the highest level, and the New Deal governing model, with powerful bureaucratic agencies partnering with business and labor to control major economic sectors, was deeply problematic.[2]

Entering the White House after the 1992 election, Bill Clinton sought to remake and invigorate the Democratic Party following twelve years of Republican rule. Along with Vice President Al Gore, Clinton hoped to answer the still-lingering question raised by Jimmy Carter's presidency and by the 1970s public interest movement: How could liberals both acknowledge the government's flaws and limitations and still persuasively call for vigorous government action?

Jimmy Carter had sought to incorporate 1970s critiques of government into a positive vision for government reform. Carter promoted regulatory approaches that "cut cost and red tape without sacrificing legitimate regulatory goals." He sacrificed valuable political capital by clashing with powerful congressional Democrats over wasteful and environmentally destructive federal projects, including the construction of big dams. Carter supported the breakup of cartel-like regulatory arrangements in major industries, including airlines, telecommunications, and trucking. He sought to introduce more flexible regulatory strategies that could achieve environmental and health protection goals at lesser economic cost. He hired dozens of public interest lawyers to important government positions where they could shape the agencies that they had been suing and pressuring.[3]

Now in the 1990s, Clinton and Gore renewed Carter's fight, with its complex duality: support for government action paired with a campaign for government reform. "I believe Government must do more," Clinton said in 1993, as he outlined an ambitious agenda for government intervention on health care, energy, and economic development. But the federal government would gain the ability to make these transformative investments only if it regained the confidence of American citizens. Improving government performance needed to become a "permanent part of how government works," Clinton argued. "The American people deserve a Government that is both honest and efficient, and for too long they haven't gotten it."[4]

Shortly after his inauguration in 1993, Clinton asked Vice President Gore to chair a new initiative on government reform. "Our goal is to make the entire Federal Government both less expensive and more efficient, and to change the culture of our national bureaucracy away from complacency and entitlement toward initiative and empowerment. We intend to redesign, to reinvent, to reinvigorate the entire National Government." Clinton proposed a consumer orientation that emphasized the "services" that the government provided to "Government's customers, the American people." The National Performance Review, which Gore led, aimed to do more than simply cut costs; it aspired to close "the *trust* deficit." Building trust in the government was central to how Clinton and Gore hoped to build support for a greater role on the part of the government.[5]

Clinton and Gore's government reform project explicitly repudiated the "top-down, centralized bureaucracies" that had defined the federal government from the 1930s to the 1960s—the very agencies that Nader and the public interest movement also had railed against. Federal agencies often were "monopolies" with "few incentives to innovate or improve," Gore wrote in a 1993 report entitled *From Red Tape to Results: Creating a Government That Works Better & Costs Less.* "With their rigid preoccupation with standard operating procedure, their vertical chains of command, and their standardized services, these bureaucracies were steady—but slow and cumbersome." The Clinton administration planned to make government more flexible, accountable, cost conscious, and customer focused. Ultimately, Gore argued, the performance review was about "values such as equal opportunity, justice, diversity, and democracy." Transforming the federal government was imperative because the bureaucracies, too often, "failed to nurture these values."[6]

To further his mission of reinventing government, Clinton appointed administrators willing to experiment with more flexible strategies for pursuing progressive goals. These were people who believed strongly in federal environmental regulation, but also felt that more flexible rules could bring equal or better results at lower cost. Interior secretary Bruce Babbitt, former governor of Arizona, sought to protect endangered species by using habitat conservation plans instead of rigid development moratoriums. Habitat conservation plans overseen by the Department of the Interior permitted trade-offs between increased private development in one location and heightened species protection in another. EPA administrator Carol Browner, a former Gore legislative aide who had headed Florida's environmental agency, introduced programs to give companies greater flexibility in exchange for more stringent pollution control. The Clinton administration also enthusiastically implemented the 1993 Government Performance and Results Act, which required agencies to experiment with performance plans to track progress on specific and measurable goals.[7]

In his 1996 State of the Union address, Bill Clinton memorably conceded, "The era of big government is over." To many observers, Clinton's statement seemed like just a Democratic capitulation following the Republican Party takeover of Congress in 1994. But Clinton's declaration had deeper roots in liberal Democratic politics, going back to the 1970s and to the public interest attack on "big government." In the sentence after he declared the end of big government, Clinton insisted, "We cannot go back to the time when our citizens were left to fend for themselves." He promised to develop a "smaller, less bureaucratic government" that would better serve the public interest. Clinton still believed that efficient and effective government operations would bolster public trust and make possible a more active liberal government.[8]

An active but more efficient and effective government seemed like it could be a winning political package. Yet Clinton's attempts to craft such an approach, like Carter's before him, met with only modest success. Liberal advocates outside of government saw Clinton's reform moves as insufficiently ambitious and dangerous compromises, while many Republicans simply opposed his attempts to expand government's role. To be sure, Clinton ultimately achieved a second presidential term during a period of strong economic growth. Yet his administration often found itself in the same defensive crouch that had become typical for Democrats. Following the 1994 midterms, the Clinton administration was forced once again to fight to protect 1970s regulations against frontal attacks by emboldened congressional Republicans. Clinton's efforts to make government more flexible were undercut, and the rearguard action he had to fight left little room for innovation and deeper reform. The result was a continuing stalemate over the role of government.

◆

RALPH NADER, NOW in his sixties, viewed Clinton's pragmatic liberal politics with disdain. Nader's political frustration led him to run, half-heartedly, as the Green Party's nominee for president in 1996. "You can't tell Democrats from Republicans anymore," Nader complained. As a Harvard law student in the 1950s, Nader had praised minor parties for expressing dissent and framing vital issues, but over decades of activism he had always shied away from pursuing a third-party candidacy. Now he jumped in to criticize Bill Clinton as "a complete two-face" and to describe the Democratic Party as ruled by corporations. Clinton's effort to loosen the controlling yoke of government and become more open to market efficiencies and private-sector initiative seemed to Nader like a complete sellout. "We have government by the Exxons, of the Du Ponts and for the General Motors!" Nader exclaimed to an audience at UCLA. While Nader was right about the pervasive influence of corporations in both the Democratic Party and the government, his sweeping accusations missed the balancing act that Clinton sought to achieve with his government reform efforts. Nader did not try hard to influence the outcome of the 1996 election. He acted the part of an unwilling draftee, refusing to actually join the Green Party, endorse its platform, or raise any money for his own campaign. Still, he enjoyed the attention. Joan Claybrook, his old ally and the president of Public Citizen, described the Green Party's nomination of Nader in 1996 as a "gift from heaven to give him a greater voice."[9]

Four years later, in the 2000 election, Nader got far more attention by campaigning aggressively as the Green Party's presidential candidate. Nader was particularly agitated by corporate influence over free trade agreements and campaign finance. He felt he had spent the previous two decades trying "every way to get Democrats to pick up on issues" and trying to enlist the "least worse" of the two parties in his cause. Now, like Barry Commoner and the Citizens Party in 1980, Nader aimed to create a viable third-party alternative by garnering 5 percent of the national vote and qualifying the Green Party for future federal election funds. Asked why he was qualified to run the government's "vast bureaucracy," Nader played up his decades of experience tangling with federal government agencies. "I don't know anybody who studied more of them," he told PBS's Jim Lehrer. "I don't know anybody who has sued more of them."[10]

Nader expressed politically damaging vitriol for Gore and the Democrats by equating them with Republicans. "Our two parties are basically one corporate party wearing two heads and different makeup," Nader said dismissively in April 2000. "There is a difference between Tweedledum and Tweedledee, but not that much." Nader had always found insufficiently pure Democrats a particularly attractive and effective target. There was "no end to his betrayal," Nader said of Gore. "All I can see is this Pinocchio nose coming." In language reminiscent of his criticism of Carter's presidency before the 1980 election, Nader declared that the country might be better off having the Republican George W. Bush fire up the progressive movement. "If it were a choice between a provocateur and an 'anesthetizer,' I'd rather have a provocateur," Nader said. "It would mobilize us."[11]

Many of Nader's former allies and associates watched with dismay as Nader lumped Al Gore and George Bush together. Nader threatened to dampen voter enthusiasm for the Democratic candidate, they thought, and to tip the balance in one of the swing states. In October, twelve former Nader's Raiders urged Nader to stop conflating Democrats and Republicans. Nader risked putting Bush in the White House, they said, setting back "the social progress to which you have devoted your entire, astonishing career." Others organized an effort to persuade Nader to abandon his "kamikaze" strategy and endorse Gore. But Nader refused their entreaties, vigorously campaigning in the swing state of Florida. And of course, liberal fears came true: the ninety-seven thousand votes Nader won in Florida far exceeded Bush's tiny and contested margin of victory in the swing state that decided the election.[12]

To his supporters, Nader had spoken truth to power, rightfully denounced compromises made by the Democratic Party, and charted a progressive political agenda that could mobilize disengaged and disempowered voters. But to mainstream Democrats, the 2000 election was a debacle. Nader became one of the most polarizing figures in US politics. Nader himself remained unapologetic in the face of Bush's narrow victory. "Gore beat Gore," he said. His critics, he complained, were "willing to settle for a stagnant, indentured corporate Democratic Party."[13]

Nader's campaign and his uncompromising stance were the culmination of tensions that had existed within the left and liberalism for decades. The public interest movement, since its founding in the late 1960s, related awkwardly to the Democratic Party and to the liberal establishment. In the very first task force report that Nader and his researchers produced on the Federal Trade Commission, they had demanded the resignation of Paul Rand Dixon—the agency's Democratic chairman—and had exposed widespread Democratic political patronage. Subsequent reports criticized party luminaries like Maine senator Edmund Muskie and urged an overhaul of the congressional structure that had bolstered Democratic power since the 1950s. In the 2000 election, Nader took this lifelong criticism of establishment liberalism to its logical extreme. Many of Nader's former allies saw things differently, of course. They embraced compromise and pragmatic action through the Democratic Party. The journalist and former Nader's Raider James Fallows later called it "here-and-now incrementalism," in contrast to Nader's push for "root-and-branch fundamental change."[14]

Nader and other public interest advocates particularly thrived in an opposition role calling for fundamental change. Starting with the 1960s publication of agenda-setting books like *Silent Spring*, *The Death and Life of Great American Cities*, and Nader's *Unsafe at Any Speed*, the public interest movement sometimes clashed with, and sometimes allied with, the Democratic Party and the liberal establishment. The moral clarity of Carson, Jacobs, Nader, and the broader public interest movement countered the reckless disregard for the environment and individual citizens that was exhibited by powerful institutions—including the government—in the postwar period. Nader and his allies helped open government to greater public participation and transparency, and undercut government's role as the expert and authority defining the public interest, often in partnership with business and labor. In the process, the public interest movement did nothing less than refashion the relationship between citizens, state, and the private sector. By 1980, the legislation that Nader and others helped advance, the institutions they built, and the leaders they launched had become a permanent part of the American political landscape.

Public interest advocates showed how both markets and government are inherently limited and flawed. Yet so, too, is the strategy that Nader and others helped to pioneer. Public interest advocacy did not solve the problems of regulatory capture by industry or the bureaucracy's tendency toward bullheadedness and indifference. The movement's emphasis on purity and its frequent disdain for traditional institutions, including political parties and unions, turned a generation of liberals away from local and state politics, and from the pursuit of the institutional power necessary to make political change. Pragmatic and slow-moving compromise compared poorly to the creativity, independence, and ideological righteousness of the public interest organizations. The emphasis on professional expertise and policy influence also failed to inspire a broader social justice movement bridging gaps across class and race. The movement's litigation strategies, while initially wildly successful in the 1970s, were soon easily adopted by conservative antagonists backed by corporate donors and private philanthropists, and proved to be overly dependent on sympathetic judges appointed by liberal politicians. With a conservative majority now entrenched in the federal courts, litigation offers fewer transformative opportunities. In more recent years, the protective strategies used to prevent overdevelopment and protect the environment also have been blamed for making it impossible to do big things and respond to major societal problems by building housing, transportation, or energy infrastructure, such as the electrical grid or offshore wind power. Empowering citizen activism and amplifying citizen voices, seen from another vantage point, also could shift power from broadly representative government bodies to narrow, self-organized groups protecting a private interest, such as the value of private property.

By primarily playing the role of uncompromising outside critic, the public interest movement neglected to build support for government in a way that could facilitate policy-making in a politically divided nation or that could support internal reforms that might improve government operations. Americans continue to struggle to craft an approach to governance that acknowledges, and strives to balance, the inherent limitations of government, markets, and citizen action. A half century later, the regulatory accomplishments of the early 1970s have continued to provide a legal framework that somewhat binds and constrains US capitalism. The nation's air and water are cleaner and its workplaces are safer. At the same time, government itself is unpopular and often incapable of action to address new threats, especially climate change. We need to invigorate government and also continue fighting to improve it. The challenge is to marshal the efficiency of markets, the accountability provided by citizen activism, and the collective power of government action. The struggle to remake liberalism for a new age endures.

Acknowledgments

My friends, family, students, and colleagues in New Haven and beyond have been a constant support and intellectual stimulation in the time I spent working on this book. At Yale, I have been fortunate to work with so many exceptional people in the Department of History, the Environmental Humanities program, and at the campus as a whole. Thank you for being terrific colleagues.

Beverly Gage, Edward Ball, and Claire Potter helped shape the manuscript through our lively writers' group, and David Engerman influenced it on walks and with a close reading. I've benefited particularly from conversations about legal history, public interest law, and the administrative state with Lincoln Caplan, Dennis Curtis, E. Donald Elliott, Daniel Esty, Robert Gordon, Jacob Hacker, Douglas Kysar, Naomi Lamoreaux, Zach Liscow, Nicholas Parrillo, Robert Post, Judith Resnik, Susan Rose-Ackerman, James Scott, Kalyanakrishnan Sivaramakrishnan, John Wargo, and John Witt. I also appreciate the constructive scholarly insights of Adam Arenson, Donald Critchlow, Elizabeth Dale, William Deverell, Susan Ferber, Gary Gerstle, Karl Jacoby, Laura Kalman, Matthew Klingle, Nancy Langston, Nelson Lichtenstein, Neil Maher, John McNeill, Alice O'Connor, Adam Rome, Travis Ross, Eric Rutkow, and Richard White, and participants in the Beyond the New Deal Order conference, New York Writing History Seminar, New York Metro Environmental History

Workshop, and Yale Legal History Workshop. I also appreciate the helpful comments of anonymous reviewers for the *Journal of Policy History* and the *Law and History Review*. Frances Beinecke, Christopher Elliman, Donald Chen, Errol Mazursky, and myriad other participants in the Environmental Leadership Program informed my understanding of the changing nature of environmental advocacy and institutional leadership. This book also bears the special influence of several mentors, especially William Cronon, Robin Einhorn, and Harry Scheiber.

I am particularly grateful to the people who talked about their work in oral history interviews that informed the project, including Marcy Benstock, Barry Bosworth, Ralph Cavanagh, Joan Claybrook, Geoffrey Cowan, Christopher DeMuth, James Fallows, Charles Halpern, John Harte, Thomas Hopkins, Sanford Jaffe, Anthony Kline, Alan Morrison, Laura Nader, Ralph Nader, William Nordhaus, Charles Reich, William Reilly, David Rosen, Peter Shelley, James Gustave Speth, James Tozzi, Thomas Troyer, Harrison Wellford, and David Zwick. I was also lucky to have the assistance of many librarians and archivists at Yale and across the country, including at the National Archives, presidential libraries, Library of Congress, and numerous other special collections.

At W. W. Norton, my editor Matt Weiland provided crucial guidance. Lily Gellman, Huneeya Siddiqui, Stephanie Hiebert, and others steered the book to completion. My agent, David McCormick, enthusiastically supported the project and helped me frame it. I'm deeply grateful to the many Yale students who provided research assistance, including Jamie Cooper, Carolyn Forrester, Lisa Furchtgott, Michelle Kim, Ben Kline, Helen Li, Carolee Klimchock, Kelly O'Donnell, Joya Sonnenfeldt, Christopher Sung, Catherine Tarleton, Michael Wysolmerski, and Ben Zdencanovic.

I particularly appreciate the friendship and good humor of Dirk Bergemann, Ned Blackhawk, Dani Botsman, Mark Chung, Deborah Coen, Nicky Dawidoff, David and Joanne Goldblum, Jake Halpern, Caleb Kleppner, Anthony Leiserowitz, Pericles Lewis, Daniel Maga-

ziner, Jennifer Marlon, Kishwar Rizvi, David Simon, and many others in New Haven. From afar, Seth Goldman, Steven Moss, Steven
Mufson, Ethan Pollock, Rachel Gross, and James Sturm have been
supportive and helpful.

Thank you to my extended family. My parents, Margery and Jim
Sabin, continue to inspire me with their devotion to teaching and
learning. My love and gratitude to Michael and Debbie Sabin, and
Zach, Matt and Elena, and the Bazelons, including Rick and Eileen,
Lara, Carter and Ella, Jill, Jackson and Trevor, Dana, David, Leo and
Maya. My wife, Emily, offered love—and edits—all along the way.
Now we can move on to new adventures! My sons, Eli and Simon,
influenced my thinking with their views on politics, helping me see
how the issues I study look to the next generation. I dedicate the book
to you, with love and admiration. I can't wait to see your paths as citizens of the world.

Notes

BEYOND THE SOURCES abbreviated here, additional materials came from the archived collections of Henry Brandon, Stuart Eizenstat, Jane Jacobs, Patsy T. Mink, Edmund Muskie, Michael Pertschuk, James Gustave Speth, James G. Watt, and Harrison Wellford as specified, as well as the Gerald Ford and Jimmy Carter presidential libraries and the National Archives.

Adams Records	NRDC Records, Accession 2012-M-055 Administrative, Executive Director John H. Adams Records, MS 1965
Carson Papers	Rachel Carson Papers, Yale Collection of American Literature, Beinecke Rare Book and Manuscript Library, Yale University, New Haven, CT
CCGF	Carnegie Corporation Grant Files, Columbia University, Collection IIIA
EDFA	Environmental Defense Fund Archive, Stony Brook University, Special Collections and University Archives, Stony Brook, NY

FFA	Ford Foundation Archive, Rockefeller Archive Center, Sleepy Hollow, NY
JC-CEA Collection	Jimmy Carter Council of Economic Advisers Collection, US National Archives and Records Administration, Washington, DC
LAT	*Los Angeles Times*
McIntyre Collection	James T. McIntyre Collection, Jimmy Carter Library, Atlanta, GA
Moynihan Papers	Daniel P. Moynihan Papers, Manuscript Division, Library of Congress, Washington, DC
NAS Papers	National Audubon Society Papers, New York Public Library
NRDC Records	Natural Resources Defense Council Records, Manuscripts and Archives, Yale University Library, New Haven, CT
NYT	*New York Times*
Taft Papers	William H. Taft Papers, Manuscript Division, Library of Congress, Washington, DC
TAPP	The American Presidency Project, http://www.presidency.ucsb.edu
WP	*Washington Post*
WSJ	*Wall Street Journal*

Introduction

1. "Texts of Remarks by Johnson and Nader on Safety," *NYT*, September 10, 1966, 12. The *Washington Post* credited Nader as the "gadfly" responsible for "arousing public demand for safer automobile design" and similarly put a picture of LBJ shaking hands with Nader on the front page of the paper after the bill signing. Carroll Kilpatrick, "LBJ Signs Two Highway Safety Bills," *WP*, September 10, 1966, A1.
2. Ronald Reagan, "Inaugural Address," January 20, 1981, TAPP. The consumer movement, one historian has written, "was closely aligned with liberalism" and "allied itself with almost all of the tendencies of the New Frontier and Great Society liberalism." Lawrence B. Glickman, *Buying Power: A History of Consumer Activism in America* (Chicago: University of Chicago Press, 2009), 284, 288. For recent surveys of the history of conservatism, see Kim Phillips-

Fein, "Conservatism: A State of the Field," *Journal of American History* 98, no. 3 (December 2011): 723–43, and the accompanying forum; and Julian E. Zelizer, "Reflections: Rethinking the History of American Conservatism," *Reviews in American History* 38, no. 2 (2010): 367–92. For select monographs, see Kim Phillips-Fein, *Invisible Hands: The Making of the Conservative Movement from the New Deal to Reagan* (New York: W. W. Norton, 2009); Bethany Moreton, *To Serve God and Wal-Mart: The Making of Christian Enterprise* (Cambridge, MA: Harvard University Press, 2009); Darren Dochuk, *From Bible Belt to Sunbelt: Plain-Folk Religion, Grassroots Politics, and the Rise of Evangelical Conservatism* (New York: W. W. Norton, 2011); Lisa McGirr, *Suburban Warriors: The Origins of the New American Right* (Princeton, NJ: Princeton University Press, 2001); Matthew D. Lassiter, *The Silent Majority: Suburban Politics in the Sunbelt South* (Princeton, NJ: Princeton University Press, 2006); Jason Morgan Ward, *Defending White Democracy: The Making of a Segregationist Movement and the Remaking of Racial Politics, 1936–1965* (Chapel Hill: University of North Carolina Press, 2011); Rick Perlstein, *The Invisible Bridge: The Fall of Nixon and the Rise of Reagan* (New York: Simon & Schuster, 2014); Perlstein, *Reaganland: America's Right Turn, 1976–1980* (New York: Simon & Schuster, 2020); and Michelle M. Nickerson, *Mothers of Conservatism: Women and the Postwar Right* (Princeton, NJ: Princeton University Press, 2012). For the disintegration of the New Deal coalition, see, for example, Robert O. Self, *American Babylon: Race and the Struggle for Postwar Oakland* (Princeton, NJ: Princeton University Press, 2003); and Robert O. Self, *All in the Family: The Realignment of American Democracy since the 1960s* (New York: Hill and Wang, 2012); Thomas J. Sugrue, *The Origins of the Urban Crisis: Race and Inequality in Postwar Detroit* (Princeton, NJ: Princeton University Press, 1996); Jefferson Cowie, *Stayin' Alive: The 1970s and the Last Days of the Working Class* (New York: New Press, 2010); Jefferson Cowie and Nick Salvatore, "The Long Exception: Rethinking the Place of the New Deal in American History," *International Labor and Working-Class History* 74 (October 2008): 3–32; and Jennifer Klein, "A New Deal Restoration: Individuals, Communities, and the Long Struggle for the Collective Good," *International Labor and Working-Class History* 74 (October 2008): 42–48. See also Todd Holmes, "Political Backlash: The Corporate West, the United Farm Workers' Movement, and the Rise of Reaganism in American Politics" (PhD diss., Yale University, 2013); and Todd Holmes, "The Economic Roots of Reaganism: Corporate Conservatives, Political Economy, and the United Farm Workers Movement, 1965–1970," *Western Historical Quarterly* 41, no. 1 (April 1, 2010): 55–80. For environmental legislation as extension of an activist state, see Steven M. Teles, "Conservative Mobilization against Entrenched Liberalism," in *The Transformation of American Politics: Activist Government and the Rise of Conservatism*, ed. Paul Pierson and Theda Skocpol (Princeton, NJ: Princeton University Press, 2007), 160–88; Steven M. Teles, *The Rise of the Conservative Legal Movement: The Battle for Control of the Law* (Princeton, NJ: Princeton University Press, 2010); Bruce Schulman and Julian Zelizer, eds., *Rightward Bound: Making America Conservative in the 1970s* (Cambridge, MA: Harvard

University Press, 2008), 7; and Thomas O. McGarity, "Regulatory Reform in the Reagan Era," *Maryland Law Review* 45, no. 2 (1986): 253–73, 253. For conservative public interest law, see also Ann Southworth, *Lawyers of the Right: Professionalizing the Conservative Coalition* (Chicago: University of Chicago Press, 2008); Jefferson Decker, *The Other Rights Revolution: Conservative Lawyers and the Remaking of American Government* (New York: Oxford University Press, 2016); and Arthur F. McEvoy, "Environmental Law and the Collapse of New Deal Constitutionalism," *Akron Law Review* 46, no. 4 (2013): 881–908.

3. Ralph Nader, *Unsafe at Any Speed: The Designed-in Dangers of the American Automobile* (New York: Grossman, 1965), ix.

4. G. Christian Hill, "Stepping on Toes: Public-Interest Firm on a Winning Streak Shakes Up California," *WSJ*, October 16, 1975, 1; and "Statement of David R. Zwick," in House Committee on Public Works, *Water Pollution Control Legislation—1971 (Proposed Amendments to Existing Legislation). Hearings, Ninety-Second Congress, First Session*, Committee on Public Works, no. 92-16 (Washington, DC: US Government Printing Office, 1971), 1149.

5. Judith Stein, *Pivotal Decade: How the United States Traded Factories for Finance in the Seventies* (New Haven, CT: Yale University Press, 2010), 55–56, 152.

Chapter 1: THE POSTWAR PARTNERSHIP OF BUSINESS, LABOR, AND GOVERNMENT

1. John F. Kennedy, "Annual Message to the Congress on the State of the Union," January 30, 1961, TAPP.

2. For discussion of the New Deal Order, see Steve Fraser and Gary Gerstle, eds., *The Rise and Fall of the New Deal Order, 1930–1980* (Princeton, NJ: Princeton University Press, 1989); Gary Gerstle, Nelson Lichtenstein, and Alice O'Connor, eds., *Beyond the New Deal Order: U.S. Politics from the Great Depression to the Great Recession* (Philadelphia: University of Pennsylvania Press, 2019). For a critique of the idea of a New Deal Order based on uneven political development in a federalist system, see Margaret Weir, "States, Race, and the Decline of New Deal Liberalism," *Studies in American Political Development* 19, no. 2 (October 2005): 157–72.

3. Franklin D. Roosevelt, "Acceptance Speech for the Renomination for the Presidency, Philadelphia, Pa.," June 27, 1936, TAPP; and Franklin D. Roosevelt, "Address at Marietta, Ohio," July 8, 1938, TAPP.

4. David C. Engerman, *Modernization from the Other Shore: American Intellectuals and the Romance of Russian Development* (Cambridge, MA: Harvard University Press, 2003); Thomas K. McCraw, *Prophets of Regulation: Charles Francis Adams, Louis D. Brandeis, James M. Landis, Alfred E. Kahn* (Cambridge, MA: Belknap Press of Harvard University Press, 1984), 152; Donald A. Ritchie, "Reforming the Regulatory Process: Why James Landis Changed His Mind," *Business History Review* 54, no. 3 (1980): 283–302; Peter H. Irons, *The New Deal Lawyers* (Princeton, NJ: Princeton University Press, 1982); James McCauley Landis,

The Administrative Process (New Haven, CT: Yale University Press, 1938); Morton J. Horwitz, *Transformation of American Law, 1870–1960: The Crisis of Legal Orthodoxy* (New York: Oxford University Press, 1992), 220; Robert L. Rabin, "Federal Regulation in Historical Perspective," *Stanford Law Review* 38, no. 5 (May 1986): 1189–326; Reuel E. Schiller, "The Era of Deference: Courts, Expertise, and the Emergence of New Deal Administrative Law," *Michigan Law Review* 106, no. 3 (December 1, 2007): 399–441; and John M. Jordan, *Machine-Age Ideology: Social Engineering and American Liberalism, 1911–1939* (Chapel Hill: University of North Carolina Press, 1994). For the variety of meanings of the New Deal, see, for example, Ira Katznelson, *Fear Itself: The New Deal and the Origins of Our Time* (New York: W. W. Norton, 2013); Colin Gordon, *New Deals: Business, Labor, and Politics in America, 1920–1935* (Cambridge: Cambridge University Press, 1994); Alan Brinkley, *The End of Reform: New Deal Liberalism in Recession and War* (New York: Knopf, 1995); Fraser and Gerstle, *Rise and Fall of the New Deal Order*; Jennifer Klein, *For All These Rights: Business, Labor, and the Shaping of America's Public-Private Welfare State* (Princeton, NJ: Princeton University Press, 2006); Jason Scott Smith, *Building New Deal Liberalism: The Political Economy of Public Works, 1933–1956* (New York: Cambridge University Press, 2006); and Sarah T. Phillips, *This Land, This Nation: Conservation, Rural America, and the New Deal* (New York: Cambridge University Press, 2007).

5.   Smith, *Building New Deal Liberalism*; Phillips, *This Land, This Nation*; David Eli Lilienthal, *TVA; Democracy on the March* (New York: Harper and Brothers, 1944), 8, 48, 223; Finis Dunaway, *Natural Visions: The Power of Images in American Environmental Reform* (Chicago: University of Chicago Press, 2005), 77–86; David Ekbladh, "'Mr. TVA': Grass-Roots Development, David Lilienthal, and the Rise and Fall of the Tennessee Valley Authority as a Symbol for U.S. Overseas Development, 1933–1973," *Diplomatic History* 26, no. 3 (2002): 335–74, 347; and Henry Steele Commager, *The American Mind: An Interpretation of American Thought and Character since the 1880's* (New Haven, CT: Yale University Press, 1950), 344–45. For an influential early critique of Robert Moses–style urban development, see Jane Jacobs, *The Death and Life of Great American Cities* (New York: Random House, 1961). For the classic account of Moses's deployment of agency power, see Robert A. Caro, *The Power Broker: Robert Moses and the Fall of New York* (New York: Knopf, 1974). For a more recent revisionist account of Moses's contributions to New York's development, see Hilary Ballon and Kenneth T. Jackson, eds., *Robert Moses and the Modern City: The Transformation of New York* (New York: W. W. Norton, 2007). For a compelling account of the shift away from publicly financed and planned urban development strategies, see Lizabeth Cohen, *Saving America's Cities: Ed Logue and the Struggle to Renew Urban America in the Suburban Age* (New York: Farrar, Straus and Giroux, 2019).

6.   See, for example, Joanna L. Grisinger, *The Unwieldy American State: Administrative Politics since the New Deal* (Cambridge: Cambridge University Press, 2012).

7.   George B. Shepherd, "Fierce Compromise: The Administrative Procedure Act

Emerges from New Deal Politics," *Northwestern University Law Review* 90, no. 4 (1995–96): 1557–683, 1678.

8.   John Kenneth Galbraith, *American Capitalism: The Concept of Countervailing Power* (Boston: Houghton Mifflin, 1952), 142. For a more contemporary application of these ideas, see Ezra Klein, "Countervailing Powers: The Forgotten Economic Idea Democrats Need to Rediscover," *Vox*, May 17, 2019. For a discussion of Galbraith and Arthur Schlesinger's "qualitative liberalism," see Adam Rome, "'Give Earth a Chance': The Environmental Movement and the Sixties," *Journal of American History* 90, no. 2 (September 2003): 525–54.

9.   David P. Billington, Donald C. Jackson, and Martin V. Melosi, *The History of Large Federal Dams: Planning, Design, and Construction in the Era of Big Dams* (Denver: US Department of the Interior, Bureau of Reclamation, 2005); Ekbladh, "'Mr. TVA'"; Dan O'Neill, *The Firecracker Boys* (New York: St. Martin's Press, 1994); Dwight D. Eisenhower, "Special Message to the Congress Regarding a National Highway Program," February 22, 1955, TAPP; and Francesca Ammon, *Bulldozer: Demolition and Clearance of the Postwar Landscape* (New Haven, CT: Yale University Press, 2016).

10.   James M. Landis, *Report on Regulatory Agencies to the President-Elect* (Washington, DC: US Government Printing Office, 1960), 71.

11.   Ritchie, "Reforming the Regulatory Process," 300.

12.   Landis, *Report on Regulatory Agencies*, 71; see also Henry J. Friendly, *The Federal Administrative Agencies: The Need for Better Definition of Standards* (Cambridge, MA: Harvard University Press, 1962); Louis L. Jaffe, "The Effective Limits of the Administrative Process: A Reevaluation," *Harvard Law Review* 67, no. 7 (May 1954): 1105–35; and Louis L. Jaffe, "The Independent Agency. A New Scapegoat," *Yale Law Journal* 65, no. 7 (June 1956): 1068–76. For references to Landis's report by pioneers in public interest law, see Charles R. Halpern and John M. Cunningham, "Reflections on the New Public Interest Law: Theory and Practice at the Center for Law and Social Policy," *Georgetown Law Journal* 59 (1970–71): 1095–126, 1097; Edward Berlin, Anthony Z. Roisman, and Gladys Kessler, "Public Interest Law," *George Washington Law Review* 38, no. 4 (May 1970): 675–93, 677; and Simon Lazarus and Joseph Onek, "The Regulators and the People," *Virginia Law Review* 57, no. 6 (September 1971): 1069–108, 1094. For an earlier discussion of how regulatory agencies could be "ripe for capture by the regulated groups," see Marver H. Bernstein, *Regulating Business by Independent Commission* (Princeton, NJ: Princeton University Press, 1955), 285–96. For the growing liberal embrace of consumer rights in the 1960s, see Lawrence B. Glickman, *Buying Power: A History of Consumer Activism in America* (Chicago: University of Chicago Press, 2009), 15; and Michael R. Lemov, *People's Warrior: John Moss and the Fight for Freedom of Information and Consumer Rights* (Madison, NJ: Fairleigh Dickinson University Press, 2011).

13.   John F. Kennedy, "Special Message to the Congress on Protecting the Consumer Interest," March 15, 1962, TAPP.

14.   Kennedy, "Special Message to the Congress on Protecting the Consumer

Interest." For an earlier statement on the need to "defend and advance the interests of consumers," see efforts by New York governor Averell Harriman to establish a consumer counsel in his gubernatorial cabinet, as described in Lizabeth Cohen, *A Consumers' Republic: The Politics of Mass Consumption in Postwar America* (New York: Knopf, 2003), 446; and Daniel P. Moynihan, "Consumer Politics in Action: A Case Study of Consumer Representation, State of New York," draft manuscript, n.d., Moynihan Papers, box I:22, folder 11. For a discussion of how the Senate commerce committee took up Kennedy's call, see Edward A. Merlis, "Consumerism: A View from the Hill," in *SV—Proceedings of the Second Annual Conference of the Association for Consumer Research*, ed. David M. Gardner (College Park, MD: Association for Consumer Research, 1971), 10–14. See also Lyndon B. Johnson, "Special Message to the Congress on Consumer Interests," February 5, 1964, TAPP.

15. Robert Alan Dahl, *Who Governs? Democracy and Power in an American City* (New Haven, CT: Yale University Press, 1961); Grant McConnell, *Private Power & American Democracy* (New York: Knopf, 1966), 338–39; Henry S. Kariel, *The Decline of American Pluralism* (Stanford, CA: Stanford University Press, 1961); Gabriel Kolko, *Railroads and Regulation, 1877–1916* (Princeton, NJ: Princeton University Press, 1965); and Gabriel Kolko, *The Triumph of Conservatism; a Re-interpretation of American History, 1900–1916* (New York: Free Press of Glencoe, 1963). For a recent review of "capture" theory pointing to its pre-twentieth-century antecedents, see William Novak, "A Revisionist History of Regulatory Capture," in *Preventing Regulatory Capture: Special Interest Influence and How to Limit It*, ed. Daniel Carpenter and David Moss (New York: Cambridge University Press, 2013), 25–48.

16. Charles A. Reich, "The New Property," *Yale Law Journal* 73, no. 5 (April 1964): 733–87; Charles A. Reich, *The Greening of America: How the Youth Revolution Is Trying to Make America Livable* (New York: Random House, 1970), 18; and Roger Citron, "Charles Reich's Journey from the Yale Law Journal to the NYT Best-Seller List," *New York Law School Law Review* 52, no. 3 (January 2007): 387–416. For Reich's influence on Charles Halpern, James Gustave Speth, and Anthony Kline, see Charles Halpern, *Making Waves and Riding the Currents: Activism and the Practice of Wisdom* (San Francisco: Berrett-Koehler, 2008), 58–59; James Gustave Speth, *Angels by the River: A Memoir* (White River Junction, VT: Chelsea Green, 2014), 154–55; James Gustave Speth, interview by the author, October 2, 2014; Anthony Kline, interview by the author, October 24, 2014; and "NRDC Oral History Interview: Gus Speth, Yale University, New Haven, CT, August 13, 2003," in James Gustave Speth Papers, Manuscripts and Archives, Yale University Library, New Haven, CT, box 3, folder 20. For the turn toward judicial oversight of administrative law, see Reuel E. Schiller, "Enlarging the Administrative Polity: Administrative Law and the Changing Definition of Pluralism, 1945–1970," *Vanderbilt Law Review* 53 (October 2000): 1389–453; several of Reich's students jointly authored a student note discussing the emergence of the field and its connection to developments in

political science: "The New Public Interest Lawyers," *Yale Law Journal* 79, no. 6 (May 1970): 1069–152, 1070n1, n3.

17. Students for a Democratic Society, *The Port Huron Statement* (New York: Students for a Democratic Society, the Student Department of the League for Industrial Democracy, 1964).

18. John F. Kennedy, "Special Message to the Congress on the Regulatory Agencies," April 13, 1961, TAPP; and John F. Kennedy, "Executive Order 10934—Establishing the Administrative Conference of the United States," April 13, 1961, TAPP.

Chapter 2: RETHINKING THE LIBERAL EMBRACE OF GOVERNMENT AGENCIES

1. Mrs. R. H. Jacobs to Miss Talmey, November 22, 1961, Jane Jacobs Papers, Boston College, MS1995-29, box 5, folder 3 (Misc. Correspondence); Jane Jacobs, *The Death and Life of Great American Cities* (New York: Random House, 1961), 3, 7, 131; "Deplanning the Planners," *Time*, November 10, 1961; and Book advertisement for *The Death and Life of Great American Cities*, n.d., Jane Jacobs Papers, MS1995-29, box 23, Scrapbook no. 2. See also Robert A. Caro, *The Power Broker: Robert Moses and the Fall of New York* (New York: Knopf, 1974).

2. Rachel Carson, *Silent Spring* (Boston: Houghton Mifflin, 1962).

3. Linda J. Lear, *Rachel Carson: Witness for Nature* (New York: Henry Holt, 1997).

4. In Carson Papers, Series I: Rachel Carson, Speech to the National Parks Association, October 2, 1962 (box 101, folder 1889); Rachel Carson to William Shawn, February 14, 1959 (box 43, folder 814); Harold S. Peters to Rachel Carson, December 14, 1959 (box 43, folder 812); and Carl W. Buchheister to Rachel L. Carson, November 21, 1958 (box 43, folder 812).

5. In Carson Papers, Series I: Harold S. Peters to Rachel Carson, June 2, 1959 (box 43, folder 812); Rachel Carson to J. Lloyd Abbot, October 6, 1961 (box 90, folder 1586); and Harold S. Peters to Rachel L. Carson, August 7, 1959 (box 43, folder 812). Also Joshua Blu Buhs, *The Fire Ant Wars: Nature, Science, and Public Policy in Twentieth-Century America* (Chicago: University of Chicago Press, 2004).

6. In Carson Papers, Series I: John H. Baker to Rachel Carson, June 27, 1962 (box 85, folder 1493), which includes the "demon" quote; Peters to Carson, August 7, 1959; Harold S. Peters to Rachel L. Carson, July 28, 1959 (box 43, folder 812); and Peters to Carson, June 2, 1959.

7. Carson, *Silent Spring*, 162–67; and Rachel Carson, "A Sense of Values in Today's World" (speech, New England Wildflower Preservation Society, January 17, 1963), Carson Papers, Series I, box 101, folder 1889.

8. Carson, "Sense of Values"; and "What's the Reason Why: A Symposium by Best-Selling Authors," *NYT*, December 2, 1962, 435.

9. In Carson Papers, Series I: Carson, Speech to the National Parks Association,

October 2, 1962; and Rachel Carson, "A New Chapter to 'Silent Spring,'" *Bulletin of the Garden Club of America*, May 1963 (box 99, folder 1868).

10. In Carson Papers, Series I, box 86, folder 1516: Paul Knight to Rachel Carson, May 29, 1962; and see Paul Knight to Rachel Carson, June 5, 1963.
11. In Carson Papers, Series I, box 42, folder 771: C. Girard Davidson to John F. Kennedy, September 30, 1960; "Resources for the People: A Report of the Natural Resources Committee of Democratic Advisory Council, For Release, October 10, 1960"; Guest list for "Women's Committee for New Frontiers" meeting, October 10, 1960; and Margaret Price (vice chairman of the Democratic National Committee) to Rachel Carson, October 14, 1960. In Carson Papers, Series I, box 86, folder 1615: Stewart Udall to Rachel Carson, May 2, 1963; "Remarks by Stewart Udall" (Patuxent Wildlife Research Center, Patuxent, MD, April 25, 1963); Rachel Carson to Stewart Udall, November 12, 1963; and Stewart Udall, Statement before Senate Subcommittee on Reorganization and International Organizations, April 8, 1964.
12. Brian Balogh, *Chain Reaction: Expert Debate and Public Participation in American Commercial Nuclear Power, 1945–1975* (Cambridge: Cambridge University Press, 1991). For a study of how the issue of thermal pollution emerged from a conflict between the Atomic Energy Commission and the Fish and Wildlife Service, see J. Samuel Walker, "Nuclear Power and the Environment: The Atomic Energy Commission and Thermal Pollution, 1965–1971," *Technology and Culture* 30, no. 4 (October 1, 1989): 964–92. Harrison Wellford, interview by the author, June 23, 2015.
13. Lear, *Rachel Carson*, 428–56.
14. Elinor Langer, "Auto Safety: New Study Criticizes Manufacturers and Universities," *Science* 150, no. 3700 (November 26, 1965): 1136; Ronald Ostrow, "He Wrestles the Technological, Faceless System . . . and Wins," *Boston Globe*, May 8, 1966, 22; Ralph Nader, "Profits in Pollution," *Progressive*, 34 (April 1970): 19–22; Ralph Nader, *Unsafe at Any Speed: The Designed-in Dangers of the American Automobile* (New York: Grossman, 1965), ix; and Rachel Carson, "Environmental Hazards: Control of Pesticides and Other Chemical Poisons," June 4, 1963, Statement before the Subcommittee on Reorganization and International Organizations, Carson Papers, Series I, box 74, folder 1301. For quality-of-life issues and the rise of the environmental movement, see Adam Rome, "'Give Earth a Chance': The Environmental Movement and the Sixties," *Journal of American History* 90, no. 2 (September 2003): 525–54; and Samuel P. Hays, *Beauty, Health, and Permanence: Environmental Politics in the United States, 1955–1985* (Cambridge: Cambridge University Press, 1987).
15. Nader, *Unsafe at Any Speed*.
16. Anita Hecht, "An Oral History Interview with Ralph Nader," April 2, 2010, Senator William Proxmire Collection, Wisconsin Historical Society; Ralph Nader, interview by the author, May 30, 2018.
17. Hecht, "Oral History Interview with Ralph Nader."
18. Ralph Nader, "Automobile Design Liability," April 1958 (unpublished third-year paper in Harvard Law School Library, Cambridge, MA); and Ralph

Nader, "The American Automobile: Designed for Death?" *Harvard Law Record*, December 11, 1958, 1.

19. See, for example, Ralph Nader, "Auto Safety Considered: Pressures Build," *Christian Science Monitor*, April 15, 1963, 12; Ralph Nader, "Auto Tire Debate Spins: Legislation Pushed," *Christian Science Monitor*, October 19, 1964, 10; Ralph Nader, "Auto Tires: Are They Safe?" *Christian Science Monitor*, January 16, 1965, 11; Ralph Nader to Roscoe Pound, February 26, 1960, and "Automobile Design for Living Project" attachments, Roscoe Pound Papers, Part III, Series V, folder 001768-007-0356, ProQuest History Vault, https://congressional.proquest.com/historyvault; Ralph Nader, "The Governor Could Help His Safety Crusade by Insisting on Better Engineered Cars," *Hartford Courant*, October 16, 1959, 22; and Ralph Nader, "Cars Are Killers," *Hartford Courant*, May 1, 1963, 16. See also Ralph Nader, "A Safer Car Will Help to Reduce Casualties," *Hartford Courant*, November 7, 1962, 22.

20. Ralph Nader, "Connecticut First," *NYT*, November 28, 1965, sec. 10, p. 7; Ralph Nader, "Ombudsman, Anyone?" *Hartford Courant*, April 7, 1963, 2B; Ralph Nader, "An Ombudsman for the U.S.?" *Christian Science Monitor*, April 1, 1963, 18; Ralph Nader, "Ombudsmen for State Governments," in *The Ombudsman: Citizen's Defender*, ed. Donald C. Rowat (London: Allen & Unwin, 1965), 240–46; and Lawrence J. Denardis, "An Umpire for Government," *NYT*, April 16, 1978, CN16.

21. "State Motor Vehicle Registrations, by Years, 1900–1995," US Department of Transportation, Federal Highway Administration, April 1997, https://www.fhwa.dot.gov/ohim/summary95/mv200.pdf; "Public Road Mileage, Lane-Miles, and VMT, 1900–2016, Chart VMT-421C," US Department of Transportation, Federal Highway Administration, 2016, https://www.fhwa.dot.gov/policyinformation/statistics/2016/vmt421c.cfm; and William Safire, *Safire's Political Dictionary* (New York: Oxford University Press, 2008), 803.

22. Daniel P. Moynihan, "Epidemic on the Highways," *Reporter* 20, no. 9 (April 30, 1959): 16–23; Hecht, "Oral History Interview with Ralph Nader"; and Daniel P. Moynihan, "A Proposal for the Preparation of a Book on Traffic Safety," n.d., Moynihan Papers, box I:22, folder 10. For Haddon's extensive influence on Moynihan's "Epidemic" article, see Daniel P. Moynihan to Irving, March 19, 1959, Moynihan Papers, box I:22, folder 10; and Daniel P. Moynihan, *Traffic Safety and the Health of the Body Politic*, Monday Evening Papers 10 (Middletown, CT: Center for Advanced Studies, Wesleyan University, 1966), 25, 28. For the book contract, see, in Moynihan Papers, box I:15, folder 8: Daniel P. Moynihan to Henry Robbins, May 14, 1959; and Henry Robbins to Daniel P. Moynihan, May 7, 1959.

23. Christopher Jensen, "50 Years Ago, 'Unsafe at Any Speed' Shook the Auto World," *NYT*, November 27, 2015, B3; Douglas Martin, "Richard Grossman, Crusading Publisher of 1960s, Dies at 92," *NYT*, February 1, 2014. Grossman would eventually publish more than two dozen Nader-sponsored books. Patrick Anderson, "Ralph Nader, Crusader; Or, the Rise of a Self-Appointed Lobbyist," *NYT Magazine*, October 29, 1967, 25; and Michael Pertschuk,

When the Senate Worked for Us: The Invisible Role of Staffers in Countering Corporate Lobbies (Nashville, TN: Vanderbilt University Press, 2017), 62–63.

24. Anderson, "Ralph Nader, Crusader," 25; and Pertschuk, *When the Senate Worked for Us*, 49, 55, 65.

25. Carroll Kilpatrick, "LBJ Signs Two Highway Safety Bills," *WP*, September 10, 1966, A1; "Motor Vehicle Traffic Fatalities and Fatality Rates, 1899–2018," in *Traffic Safety Facts Annual Report*, National Highway Traffic Safety Administration, June 30, 2020; and "Congress Acts on Traffic and Auto Safety," in *CQ Almanac 1966*, 22nd ed. (Washington, DC: Congressional Quarterly, 1967), 266–68.

26. Jerry L. Mashaw and David L. Harfst, *Regulation and Legal Culture: The Case of Motor Vehicle Safety*, Faculty Scholarship Series 1147 (New Haven, CT: Yale Law School, 1987).

27. "Meet Ralph Nader: Everyman's Lobbyist and His Consumer Crusade," *Newsweek*, January 22, 1968, 65–73; "Youth: Nader's Neophytes," *Time*, September 13, 1968; Harry H. Stein, "The Muckraking Book in America, 1946–1973," *Journalism Quarterly* 52, no. 2 (Summer 1975): 297–303; and Lyndon B. Johnson, "Remarks upon Signing Bill Amending the Meat Inspection Act," December 15, 1967, TAPP.

Chapter 3: CREATING PUBLIC INTEREST FIRMS

1. William Greider, "Institutional Lone Ranger," *WP*, December 5, 1971, A1.

2. Greider, "Institutional Lone Ranger"; and "Consumerism: Nader on Nader," *Time*, May 10, 1971.

3. Fred L. Zimmerman, "Ralph Nader Plans to Expand His Crusade by Opening a Firm to Lobby for the Public," *WSJ*, October 31, 1967, 34; and Morton Mintz, "The Thundering Silence of Drug Consumers," *WP*, November 26, 1967, B2. For television radiation, see "Nader Raps GE, PHS on Roles in TV Ray Case," *WP*, July 13, 1967, A30.

4. In CCGF, box 478, folder 6: Irving Machiz to Center for Study of Responsive Law, September 20, 1968; and Form 1023 Exemption Application: Center for Study of Responsive Law, June 28, 1968.

5. Ralph Nader, interview by the author, April 30, 2018; and Eli Evans to Ralph Nader, November 15, 1967, CCGF, box 478, folder 5.

6. Edward F. Cox, Robert C. Fellmeth, and John E. Schulz, *The Nader Report on the Federal Trade Commission* (New York: R. W. Baron, 1969), vii, 17.

7. D. Lloyd Macdonald to Willie, October 17, 1968, Taft Papers, box 1, folder 5; "The Groom: Ed's Suitable Consort," *Boca Raton News*, June 11, 1971, 7; Harrison Wellford, interview by the author, June 25, 2015; and Edward F. Cox, "Reinvigorating the FTC: The Nader Report and the Rise of Consumer Advocacy," *Antitrust Law Journal* 72, no. 3 (January 1, 2005): 899–910.

8. Cox et al., *Nader Report on the Federal Trade Commission*, 169–70.

9. Cox, "Reinvigorating the FTC," 901, 904; Jerry Landauer, "Judge Geer's

Job—A Peculiar Tale," *WSJ*, November 15, 1968; and Cox et al., *Nader Report on the Federal Trade Commission*, 169–70.

10. "FTC Chairman Denounces Study of Agency by Nader," *Baltimore Sun*, January 10, 1969, A1; Robert Waters, "Dixon Answers Nader Criticism," *Hartford Courant*, April 25, 1969, 2; and John Chamberlain, "What Philosophy for a Regulatory Agency?" *Cumberland News*, January 16, 1969, 16.

11. Richard L. Strout, "'Nader's Raiders' Zero in on FTC," *Christian Science Monitor*, January 9, 1969, 3; William Greider, "Law Students, FTC Tangle over Apathy," *WP*, November 13, 1968, A3; Jack Newfield, "Nader's Raiders: The Lone Ranger Gets a Posse," *Life*, October 3, 1969, 56; and Cox et al., *Nader Report on the Federal Trade Commission*, xi–xii. For use of the "Raiders" term by Nader's own staff, see, for example, Ted Jacobs to Eli Evans, October 9, 1969, CCGF, box 478, folder 5.

12. "A Proposal for an Investigative Program," October 9, 1969, CCGF, box 478, folder 5; and John Kenneth Galbraith, *A Life in Our Times: Memoirs* (New York: Houghton Mifflin, 1981), 284.

13. "Proposal for an Investigative Program," October 9, 1969.

14. In CCGF, box 478: Evans to Nader, November 15, 1967 (folder 5); and Eli Evans to Staff, "Proposed Center for the Study of Responsive Law, Ralph Nader, Trustee," November 12, 1968 (folder 6). For the struggle to complete what became a 950-page manual, see, also in CCGF, box 478, folder 6: Erwin Glikes, Basic Books, and AR, January 14, 1972; Erwin A. Glikes to Eli Evans, December 21, 1972; Paul D. Neuthaler to Avery Russell, April 4, 1974; Avery Russell to AP, EE, and FA, "Dissemination Fund," April 22, 1974; Evans to Staff, "Proposed Center"; "Center for the Study of Responsive Law: Grant of $55,000 for Research on Citizen Access to the Federal Regulatory System"; and Carnegie Corporation of New York, Press Release, May 8, 1969.

15. In NAS Papers, box 171 (Environmental Defense Fund): Robert A. Barron, "Environmental Defense Fund," November 10, 1967; Conservation Law Society of America, "Cumulative Report: October 1966"; Donald C. Hays to Gene W. Setzer, "Re: Environmental Defense Fund," November 13, 1967; and Frank M. Potter Jr., "The Center for Environmental Protection: A Proposal for Action," October 1967. For an example of the perceived need to keep Audubon separate from the new legal group, see Roland C. Clement to Victor Yannacone Jr., May 26, 1967, EDFA, RG 1, SG 1.3, Robert Smolker Papers, Series 1: EDF Documents, box 1, folder 1 (General Correspondence 1967–69).

16. "Audubon Unit Votes for Funds to Back Conservation Suits," *NYT*, October 2, 1967, 49; Elvis J. Stahr to Mrs. Preston Davis, May 3, 1973, NAS Papers, box B-349 (Environmental Defense Fund); and Charles F. Wurster, *DDT Wars: Rescuing Our National Bird, Preventing Cancer, and Creating the Environmental Defense Fund* (Oxford: Oxford University Press, 2015), 13–28. For the NAACP and ACLU model, see also "Environmental Defense Fund, Inc," June 1968, EDFA, loose briefing book "Environmental Defense Fund, Inc. June 1968"; and *Alan Morrison, Esquire* (interviews conducted by Daniel Marcus in 2007 and 2008), Oral History Project, Historical Society of the District

of Columbia Circuit (Washington, DC: Historical Society of the District of Columbia Circuit, 2009), 15.

17. "EDF Bulletin: No 7," July 21, 1970, NAS Papers, box B-349 (Environmental Defense Fund); "Environment Group Takes Fight to Court," *WP*, December 27, 1970, A42; Charles R. Halpern, "Public Interest Law: Its Past and Future," *Judicature* 58, no. 3 (October 1974): 120; and Charles Halpern, *Making Waves and Riding the Currents: Activism and the Practice of Wisdom* (San Francisco: Berrett-Koehler, 2008), 105–6.

18. In Adams Records, box 24, folder 8: Gus Speth to Messrs. Reich, Lefcoe, Simon and Trubek, November 2, 1968; and "The Environmental Legal Defense Fund, Speth, First Draft, 11/6/68."

19. Gordon Harrison, "Resources and Environment: An Accounting," National Affairs Program, Ford Foundation, December 1972, 22, in Gordon A. Harrison, interview, March 21, 1972, FFA, Ford Foundation Oral History Project, box 2, folder 41, appendix I, 45; Steven M. Teles, *The Rise of the Conservative Legal Movement: The Battle for Control of the Law* (Princeton, NJ: Princeton University Press), 48–51; and George M. Woodwell to Dennis Puleston, January 4, 1968, EDFA, RG 1, SG1, Dennis Puleston Series 1: Environmental Defense Fund Documents, box 1, folder 1 (Correspondence 1968–69).

20. In FFA, Ford Foundation Oral History Project: McGeorge Bundy, interview, March 5, 1974 (box 1, folder 19); and Harrison, interview, March 21, 1972 (box 2, folder 41), 35. For defense of the Ford Foundation's support for the Environmental Defense Fund, see McGeorge Bundy to Congressman W. R. Poage, Chairman, Committee on Agriculture, April 12, 1971, EDFA, loose folder SG III.2, S1, box 2, folder 9 (Ford Foundation 1970–1971); Harrison, interview, 35, 38; Gordon Harrison and Sanford M. Jaffe, "Public Interest Law Firms: New Voices for New Constituencies," *ABA Journal* 58 (May 1972): 459–67; and Sanford Jaffe, interview by the author, October 28, 2013.

21. In NRDC Records, Accession 2013-M-056, MS 1965, box 18: "Address by Stephen P. Duggan, Chairman," Princeton, NJ, March 20, 1970 (folder 14); Stephen P. Duggan Jr. et al. to Mr. Ruth, December 17, 1970 (folder 4); and Senator Clifford P. Case to David M. Kennedy (Secretary of the Treasury), October 15, 1970 (folder 9). Also Gilbert Rogin, "All He Wants to Save Is the World," *Sports Illustrated* 30 (February 3, 1969): 24–29; and "IRS and the Public Interest," *WP*, November 14, 1970, A16.

22. In Adams Records, box 24, folder 8: Speth to Daum, Bryson, Ayres, Strohbehn, and Rosen, "Re: Call from Frank Barry," November 22, 1968; and for the Yale group's self-confidence, Gus Speth to Whitney North Seymour Jr., January 12, 1970; and Speth, Stoel, and Strohbehn to Ayres, Bryson, Daum, and Rosen, "Re: Natural Resources Defense Council," February 1970. Also for the self-confidence question, see Harrison, interview, March 21, 1972, 57; Jennifer Adams Martin, "'Do They Practice Law in Washington?': The Foundation of Natural Resources Defense Council as a Non-profit Environmental Law Organization" (master's thesis, University of Wisconsin–Madison, 2004); and "Address by Stephen P. Duggan," March 20, 1970. Adams described their

credentials in John H. Adams, *Responsible Militancy: The Anatomy of a Public Interest Law Firm* (New York: Record of the Association of the Bar of the City of New York, 1974), 633–34. See also David Rosen, interview by the author, November 20, 2013; CLASP, "Proposal to the Ford Foundation," April 24, 1970, FFA, Grants, reel 4683; and, in FFA, CLASP Correspondence, reel 4684: William Pincus to Charles R. Halpern, November 27, 1968; and Arthur Goldberg to McGeorge Bundy, October 3, 1969.

23. "Louis Cowan. Killed with Wife in a Fire; Created Quiz Shows," *NYT*, November 19, 1976, 1; Holly Cowan Shulman, "Wednesdays in Mississippi," *Lilith* 38, no. 4 (Winter 2013–14): 13–16; Geoffrey Cowan, interview by the author, November 1, 2019; Paul Cowan and Geoffrey Cowan, "Letters from Mississippi," *Esquire*, September 1, 1964, 105*ff*; and Geoffrey Cowan, "Montgomery's First Year of School Integration," *Southern Courier* 1, no. 4 (August 6, 1965): 4.

24. Katie Reilly, "Calls to Reform Democratic Nomination Process Have Roots in 1968 Convention," *Time*, July 25, 2016; Cowan, interview, November 1, 2019; Byron E. Shafer, *Quiet Revolution: Struggle for the Democratic Party & Shaping of Post-reform Politics* (New York: Russell Sage Foundation, 1983); and Jaime Sánchez Jr., "Revisiting McGovern-Fraser: Party Nationalization and the Rhetoric of Reform," *Journal of Policy History* 32, no. 1 (January 2020): 1–24. See also Geoffrey Cowan, *Let the People Rule: Theodore Roosevelt and the Birth of the Presidential Primary* (New York: W. W. Norton, 2016).

25. Judith Coburn and Geoffrey Cowan, "The War Criminals Hedge Their Bets," *Village Voice*, December 4, 1969, 4*ff*; and Judith Coburn and Geoffrey Cowan, "Training for Terror: A Deliberate Policy?" *Village Voice*, December 11, 1969, 5*ff*.

26. Judith Coburn and Geoffrey Cowan, "The Fourth Estate as the Fourth Branch," *Village Voice*, January 1, 1970, 18*ff*; and Seymour Hersh, "Looking for Calley," *Harper's Magazine*, June 2018.

27. "Nader's Raiders 20 Years Later," *LAT*, October 27, 1989, E1; Stephen Schlesinger, "The Young Good Guys," *Vogue*, August 1, 1971, 112–15.

28. Halpern, *Making Waves and Riding the Currents*, 31–32.

29. Michael E. Tigar and Robert J. Zweben, "Selective Service: Some Certain Problems and Some Tentative Answers," *George Washington Law Review* 37, no. 3 (March 1969): 510–35, 535. Zweben later would participate as a Nader task force member on *Vanishing Air*. Tony Leonard, "On Verge of Retirement, City Attorney Reflects on 33 Years (Part II)," Patch.com, December 16, 2011. Tigar's clerkship story is noted in Shelby Coffey III, "Attorney to the Angry Young: . . . and Bobby Baker," *WP*, June 22, 1969, 9; J. Skelly Wright, "Review: *Selective Service Law Reporter*, Michael E. Tigar," *Yale Law Journal* 78, no. 2 (1968): 338–42. Charles Halpern, interview by the author, February 15, 2010.

30. Harrison Wellford, interviews by the author, June 23 and 25, 2015; and Harrison Wellford to Editor, *Memphis Commercial-Appeal*, April 27, 1968, personal papers shared by Harrison Wellford with the author.

31. Wellford, interviews, June 23 and 25, 2015. See also James Fallows, "What Did You Do in the Class War, Daddy?" *Washington Monthly*, October 1975, 5–7.

32. Speth to Seymour, January 12, 1970; Harrison, interview, March 21, 1972, 57; Speth et al. to Ayres et al., "Re: Natural Resources Defense Council"; "Address by Stephen P. Duggan," March 20, 1970; CLASP, "Proposal to the Ford Foundation"; Halpern, interview, February 15, 2010; Halpern, *Making Waves and Riding the Currents*, 41–43, 56, 61; Rosen, interview, November 20, 2013; and Pincus to Halpern, November 27, 1968.

33. Richard E. Ayres, memo, June 29, 1971, Adams Records, box 24, folder 9; Harrison, interview, March 21, 1972, 58; McGeorge Bundy to Whitney North Seymour, November 30, 1970, FFA, National Affairs Sanford M. Jaffe, Series I: Select Correspondence, box 1, folder 6; Thomas A. Troyer, "The 1969 Private Foundation Law: Historical Perspective on Its Origins and Underpinnings," *Exempt Organization Tax Review* 27, no. 1 (January 2000): 52–65; Julian Zelizer, *Taxing America: Wilber D. Mills, Congress, and the State, 1945–1975* (Cambridge: Cambridge University Press, 1998), 301; Philip Warden, "Ford Grants Aid Travels of Congressmen: Bundy Admits Trying to Sway Policy," *Chicago Tribune*, February 21, 1969, sec. 3; "Bundy Defends before House Ford Grants to Aides of RFK," *Hartford Courant*, February 21, 1969, 4; "Ford Foundation to Trim Equity in Ford Motor Co," *WSJ*, February 21, 1969, 10; Bruce Galphin, "5 RFK Aides Defend Grants," *WP*, February 27, 1969, G1; and, in FFA, Svirdidoff, Admin Subject Files "H," box 9: Wilbur Mills to McGeorge Bundy, April 23, 1969 (folder 7); and McGeorge Bundy to Wilbur Mills, April 28, 1969, Wilbur Mills to McGeorge Bundy, May 9, 1969, and McGeorge Bundy to Wilbur Mills, May 9, 1969 (folder 8). For expression of foundation concern about the "attitude of Congress and other Feds," see Whitney North Seymour Jr. and Stephen Duggan, "Notes," December 23, 1969, Adams Records, box 24, folder 9; and James Gustave Speth to Charles Reich, October 3, 1969, in James Gustave Speth Papers, Manuscripts and Archives, Yale University Library, New Haven, CT, box 1, folder 2.

34. Eileen Shanahan, "Nixon Aide Fails to Dissuade I.R.S.," *NYT*, October 10, 1970, 1. For the struggle over NRDC's tax exemption ruling, see *Law and the Environment: Selected Materials on Tax Exempt Status and Public Interest Litigation*, prepared for the Committee on Interior and Insular Affairs, US Senate (Washington, DC: US Government Printing Office, 1970); White House Special Files, Richard Nixon Presidential Library and Museum, National Archives and Records Administration, Washington, DC, John Dean, box 61, folder "Public Interest Law Firms"; Tom Charles Huston to President Richard Nixon, June 18, 1969, in James Gustave Speth Papers, Manuscripts and Archives, Yale University Library, New Haven, CT, box 1, folder 3; "IRS Modifies Its Warning on Donations to Aid Some Public Interest Law Firms," *WSJ*, October 16, 1970, 5; Morton Mintz, "Rep. Ford Hits IRS Tax Stand," *WP*, October 29, 1970, A2; Bayard Webster, "IRS Move Stays Ford Fund Grant," *NYT*, November 9, 1970, 27; John H. Adams and Patricia Adams, *A Force for Nature: The Story of NRDC and the Fight to Save Our Planet* (San

Francisco: Chronicle Books, 2010), 22–30; Martin, "'Do They Practice Law in Washington?'"; Sanford Jaffe, interview, October 28, 2013; and Thomas Troyer, interview by the author, November 22, 2013.

35. For Ford's internal review, see, for example, in FFA, National Affairs Sanford M. Jaffe, Series I: Select Correspondence, box 1, folder 6: Ginsburg, Feldman, and Bress to Howard Dressner, "Draft," November 1971; Ginsburg, Feldman and Bress to Sanford M. Jaffe, May 24, 1973; Fred Bohen to Christopher Edley, December 1, 1970; Bundy to Seymour, November 30, 1970; Sanford M. Jaffe to Orison S. Marden, November 2, 1972; and William Gossett, Orison Marden, Whitney North Seymour, and Bernard Segal to Sanford M. Jaffe, December 12, 1972. Also McGeorge Bundy to David F. Cavers and Mitchell Rogovin, July 10, 1970, FFA, CLASP Grants, reel 4684; Harrison, interview, March 21, 1972, 59; and Sanford M. Jaffe, "Public Interest Law Advisory Committee Meeting of March 22, 1971," April 14, 1971, FFA, National Affairs Sanford M. Jaffe, Series II: Chronological Files, 1970, 1971–1973, box 3. Ford's active oversight continued through the 1970s; see, for example, SMJ and Edward Ames, "Memo to Public Interest Law Firms," February 10, 1977, FFA, National Affairs Sanford M. Jaffe, Series I: Select Correspondence, box 1, folder 6; and Sanford Jaffe, interview, October 28, 2013. See also Theodore Voorhees to Christopher Edley, September 22, 1969, FFA, CLASP Correspondence, reel 4684; and Luther J. Carter, "Environmental Defense Fund: Yannacone Out as Ringmaster," *Science* 166, no. 3913 (December 26, 1969): 1603. For the Ford staff's distrust of Yannacone as someone who "could not be advised, guided or controlled," see "Notes December 23, 1969: Meeting at Ford Foundation," in Adams Records, box 24, folder 9; Halpern, interview, February 15, 2010; CLASP to Sanford Jaffe, April 24, 1970, FFA, CLASP Correspondence, reel 4684; Sanford M. Jaffe to McGeorge Bundy, May 22, 1970, "Public Interest Advocacy: Executive Committee Meeting," FFA, CLASP Grants, reel 4684; SMJ to Mitchell Sviridoff, November 19, 1971, FFA, National Affairs Sanford M. Jaffe, Series II: Chronological Files, 1970, 1971–1973, box 3; and Harrison, interview, March 21, 1972. For sample monitoring reports, see Joel H. Sterns to Gordon Harrison, May 6, 1971, FFA, reel 3572, Grant 70-0643, sec. 4; and Joel Handler to Sanford Jaffe, March 31, 1977, FFA, CLASP Grants, reel 4683, Grant 70-477.

36. In CCGF, box 478, folder 6: Eli Evans to Staff, "Proposed Center"; FA to Ralph Nader, December 23, 1968; Eli Evans telephone conversation with Ralph Nader, February 13, 1969; Ralph Nader to Eli Evans, March 24, 1969; Eli Evans and Lou Pollak, Record of Interview: Layman Allen, April 15, 1969; Eli Evans and Bevis Longstreth, Record of Interview: Edmund Shaker, April 15, 1969; Eli Evans and William Hubbard, Record of Interview: Paul Gikas, April 17, 1969; Eli Evans and Morton Fried, Record of Interview: Laura Nader, April 22, 1969; Eli Evans and Travis Cross, Record of Interview: Laura Nader, April 23, 1969; Eli Evans and Paul Gikas, Record of Interview: Paul Gikas, April 28, 1969; Ralph Nader to Eli Evans, May 5, 1969; FA to Ralph Nader, May 12, 1969; and Carnegie Corporation, Press

Release, May 8, 1969. For continuing concern about the IRS, see FA to Ralph Nader, February 12, 1970, CCGF, box 478, folder 6; and Wellford, interviews, June 23 and June 25, 2015.

Chapter 4: "INSECURE" POWER AND THE NONPROFIT RATIONALE

1. Saul David Alinsky, *Reveille for Radicals* (New York: Random House, 1969), x; and Thomas J. Sugrue, "Saul Alinsky: The Activist Who Terrifies the Right," *Salon*, February 7, 2012.

2. Eileen Shanahan, "Reformer: Urging Business Change: Nader Interview," *NYT*, January 24, 1971, F1; and Ralph Nader, interview by the author, April 30, 2018.

3. Shanahan, "Reformer: Urging Business Change"; and Joe Klein, "Ralph Nader: The Man in the Class Action Suit," *Rolling Stone*, November 20, 1975.

4. Ralph Nader and Donald Ross, *Action for A Change: A Student's Manual for Public Interest Organizing* (New York: Grossman, 1971), 4–5.

5. Clayton Fritchey, "New Title for Nader: National Ombudsman," *Chicago Tribune*, January 10, 1971, A5.

6. Les Leopold, *The Man Who Hated Work and Loved Labor* (White River Junction, VT: Chelsea Green, 2007), 235–36.

7. Ralph Nader, "They're Still Breathing," *New Republic* 158, no. 5 (February 3, 1968): 15; and Ralph Nader to Stewart L. Udall, March 23, 1968, reprinted in *Hearings on the Occupational Safety and Health Act of 1968, before the Senate Committee on Labor and Public Welfare*, 90th Cong. 526 (1968). Also, as reprinted in *Congressional Record*, February 5, 1969, 2875, 2891: Jeanne Rasmussen, "Black Lung: What Is It? Malingering or Black Death," *Charleston Gazette*; and Ray Martin, "No Hearings Held on Bill: President Proposed Tough Mine Safety Law," *Morgantown Dominion-News*.

8. George H. Siehl, *Federal Role in Coal Mine Safety* (Washington, DC: Library of Congress, Legislative Reference Service, 1969), 9–12. Also, as reprinted in *Congressional Record*, February 5, 1969, 2868, 2900, 2911: George Lawless, "Bleak Prospects for Change," *Charleston Gazette*, February 2, 1969; Ray Martin, "Udall Confirms Accuracy of Nader's Mine Safety Charges," *Morgantown Dominion-News*; Ray Martin, "Miners Rap WVU Faculty and (Tony) Boyle," *Morgantown Dominion-News*.

9. "Miners Organize to Reduce Risks," *NYT*, January 27, 1969.

10. Ray Martin, "Hechler, Nader Attack Coal Safety Inertia," *Morgantown Dominion-News*, reprinted in *Congressional Record*, February 5, 1969, 2902; Nader, testimony, 90th Cong. 515 (1968); and "Nader Charges Miners' Union with Nepotism and Corruption," *NYT*, April 28, 1969, 23.

11. Nader, interview, April 30, 2018; Brit Hume, *Death and the Mines; Rebellion and Murder in the United Mine Workers* (New York: Grossman, 1971); John Gaventa, *Power and Powerlessness: Quiescence and Rebellion in an Appalachian*

Valley (Urbana: University of Illinois Press, 1980); Jefferson Cowie, *Stayin' Alive: The 1970s and the Last Days of the Working Class* (New York: New Press, 2010), 23–38; Mark A. Bradley, *Blood Runs Coal: The Yablonski Murders and the Battle for the United Mine Workers of America* (New York: W. W. Norton, 2020), 17–49, 79–80; and Nader and Ross, *Action for a Change*, 16.

12. *Alan Morrison, Esquire* (interviews conducted by Daniel Marcus in 2007 and 2008), Oral History Project, Historical Society of the District of Columbia Circuit (Washington, DC: Historical Society of the District of Columbia Circuit, 2009), 218–23.

13. *Alan Morrison, Esquire*, 218–23.

14. Susan L. Flader, "Citizenry and the State in the Shaping of Environmental Policy," *Environmental History* 3, no. 1 (January 1, 1998): 8–24. Nader traced his own conception of public citizenship back to ancient Athens; see, for example, Shanahan, "Reformer: Urging Business Change"; Richard Weintraub, "Commencements: Emmanuel," *Boston Globe*, May 28, 1973, 25. See also Gary Kulik, "Dams, Fish, and Farmers: Defense of Public Rights in Eighteenth-Century Rhode Island," in *The Countryside in the Age of Capitalist Transformation: Essays in the Social History of Rural America*, ed. Steven Hahn and Jonathan Prude (Chapel Hill: University of North Carolina Press, 1985), 25–50; Jennifer Price, *Flight Maps: Adventures with Nature in Modern America* (New York: Basic Books, 1999), 56–109; Carolyn Merchant, "Women of the Progressive Conservation Movement, 1900–1916," *Environmental Review* 8, no. 1 (Spring 1984): 57–85; and Karl Boyd Brooks, *Before Earth Day: The Origins of American Environmental Law, 1945–1970* (Lawrence: University Press of Kansas, 2009).

15. Terrianne K. Schulte, "Citizen Experts: The League of Women Voters and Environmental Conservation," *Frontiers: A Journal of Women Studies* 30, no. 3 (2009): 1–29, 20–21; League of Women Voters, *The Big Water Fight; Trials and Triumphs in Citizen Action on Problems of Supply, Pollution, Floods, and Planning across the U.S.A.* (Brattleboro, VT: S. Greene, 1966). For an account of mid-twentieth-century environmental activism in Salt Lake City, see Ted Moore, "Democratizing the Air: The Salt Lake Women's Chamber of Commerce and Air Pollution, 1936–1945," *Environmental History* 12, no. 1 (January 2007): 80–106. For a study that broadens the context for environmental action in the twentieth century to include a range of citizen interventions and particularly highlights women's leadership, see Robert Gottlieb, *Forcing the Spring: The Transformation of the American Environmental Movement*, rev. and updated ed. (Washington, DC: Island Press, 2005). For grassroots organizing particularly led by women, see also James Lewis Longhurst, *Citizen Environmentalists* (Medford, MA: Tufts University Press, 2010), 86–87.

16. Burton Allen Weisbrod, *The Nonprofit Economy* (Cambridge, MA: Harvard University Press, 1988), 170, table A.2. Weisbrod's statistics do not include the period 1968–76, for which data were not available. Individual donations to these nonprofit organizations more than tripled, from $16 billion in 1970 to $40.7 billion in 1980. Foundation donations, already much lower, increased

less than 50 percent, from $1.9 billion to $2.8 billion. Weisbrod, *Nonprofit Economy*, appendix C, 184; and "Giving in America: Toward a Stronger Voluntary Sector," Commission on Private Philanthropy and Public Needs, 1975, 47–48. For a survey of post–World War II citizen activism, see Samuel P. Hays, *Beauty, Health, and Permanence: Environmental Politics in the United States, 1955–1985* (Cambridge: Cambridge University Press, 1987).

17. Burton Allen Weisbrod, Joel F. Handler, and Neil K. Komesar, eds., *Public Interest Law: An Economic and Institutional Analysis* (Berkeley: University of California Press, 1978), 553.

18. In FFA, National Affairs Sanford M. Jaffe, Series I: Select Correspondence, box 1: Burton A. Weisbrod and Joel F. Handler to Robert Goldmann, "Proposal—An Evaluation of the Role of Public Interest Law Activities," May 31, 1972; and Burton A. Weisbrod and Joel F. Handler, "Public Interest Law Project: Progress Report," March 15, 1973.

19. Weisbrod, *Nonprofit Economy*, 5, 41–42.

20. Peter Dobkin Hall and Colin B. Burke, *Historical Statistics of the United States Chapter on Voluntary, Nonprofit, and Religious Entities and Activities: Underlying Concepts, Concerns, and Opportunities* (Rochester, NY: Social Science Research Network, 2002), 24; and Robert D. Putnam, "Bowling Alone: America's Declining Social Capital," *Journal of Democracy* 6, no. 1 (January 1995): 65–78, 70–71. For a critique of Putnam that emphasizes the growth of other forms of social engagement, such as youth soccer, see Nicholas Lemann, "Kicking in Groups," *Atlantic Monthly*, April 1996, 22–26.

21. Charles Halpern, *Making Waves and Riding the Currents: Activism and the Practice of Wisdom* (San Francisco: Berrett-Koehler, 2008), 50; Charles A. Reich, "Toward the Humanistic Study of Law," *Yale Law Journal* 74 (1965): 1408; Charles Reich, interview by the author, March 14, 2018; Ralph Nader, "Law Schools and Law Firms," *New Republic*, October 11, 1969, 20–23; Anthony Lewis, "Robert Kennedy Bids the Bar Join Fight against Social Ills," *NYT*, May 2, 1964, 22; Hilary Rodham Clinton, *Living History* (New York: Scribner, 2003), 44; and "The Role of the Law and Courts," summary of panel on environmental law at the Princeton conference, March 1970, NRDC Records, Accession 2013-M-056, box 18, folder 16.

22. Patrick Anderson, "Ralph Nader, Crusader; or, the Rise of a Self-Appointed Lobbyist," *NYT Magazine*, October 29, 1967, 25.

23. Robert J. Donovan, "Capital Lawyers: A Power Center of Government," *LAT*, February 9, 1969, 1; and Morton Mintz, "Top Lawyers Deny Lobbying Charge," *WP*, September 20, 1969, A7.

24. Ralph Nader, "The Great American Gyp," *New York Review of Books*, November 21, 1968, 27–34; William M. Blair, "Law Students Trade Charges with Leading Capital Lawyer," *NYT*, October 10, 1969, 30; "Nader Unit Clashes with Auto Lawyers," *Chicago Tribune*, October 10, 1969, C6; "Lawyer Hits 'Extremism' of Pickets," *WP*, October 10, 1969, C6; David Wise, "Washington, D.C.: Off with the Old! On with the New!" *LAT*, January 19, 1969, W8; Stuart Taylor Jr., "Lloyd Cutler: The Last Superlawyer," *Atlantic Monthly*, May

2005; and Michael T. Kaufman, "Lloyd N. Cutler, Counselor to Presidents, Is Dead at 87," *NYT*, May 9, 2005.

25. Ralph Nader, "Crumbling of the Old Order: Law Schools and Law Firms," *New Republic*, October 11, 1969, 20–23; and John P. MacKenzie, "Watergate Heightens Confusion over Lawyer's Proper Role," *WP*, August 5, 1973, A2.

26. Shanahan, "Reformer: Urging Business Change"; "Top Law Firms React to Pressure by Youths," *LAT*, December 25, 1969, G6; and Nader and Ross, *Action for a Change*, 6–7.

27. Nader and Ross, *Action for a Change*, 8–10; and Ralph Nader, Peter J. Petkas, and Kate Blackwell, eds., *Whistle Blowing; the Report of the Conference on Professional Responsibility* (New York: Grossman, 1972).

28. Saul David Alinsky, *Rules for Radicals: A Practical Primer for Realistic Radicals* (New York: Random House, 1971); and Adrian W. Sybor, "Missing: A Hero with All the Answers," *Baltimore Sun*, July 19, 1970, SD7.

Chapter 5: MAKING REGULATION "GOVERNMENT-PROOF"

1. Jack Tate, "Nader Slams Harvard Law School," *Harvard Law Record*, November 7, 1968, 1.

2. "Ralph Nader . . . ," *Harvard Law Record* 47, no. 7 (November 7, 1968): 8; Advertisement, *Harvard Crimson*, February 10, 1969; and Ronald Patterson, "Nader's 'Raiders' Plan Greater Invasion," *Harvard Law Record* 48, no. 2 (February 6, 1969): 2.

3. Ronald G. Shafer, "'Nader's Raiders' Stir Bureaucratic Concern in Washington Again," *WSJ*, July 22, 1969, 1.

4. Shafer, "'Nader's Raiders' Stir Bureaucratic Concern"; "Consumerism: Nader's Raider's Strike Again," *Time*, March 30, 1970; William Greider, "Nader Marshals 5 Attorneys as Raiders," *WP*, July 6, 1969, 7; Harrison Wellford, *Sowing the Wind; a Report from Ralph Nader's Center for Study of Responsive Law on Food Safety and the Chemical Harvest* (New York: Grossman, 1972); David Zwick and Marcy Benstock, *Water Wasteland; Ralph Nader's Study Group Report on Water Pollution* (New York: Grossman, 1971); Claire Townsend, *Old Age: The Last Segregation* (New York: Grossman, 1971); James S. Turner, *The Chemical Feast; the Ralph Nader Study Group Report on Food Protection and the Food and Drug Administration* (New York: Grossman, 1970); John C. Esposito, *Vanishing Air; the Ralph Nader Study Group Report on Air Pollution* (New York: Grossman, 1970); and Robert C. Fellmeth, *The Interstate Commerce Omission, the Public Interest and the ICC; The Ralph Nader Study Group Report on the Interstate Commerce Commission and Transportation* (New York: Grossman, 1970).

5. Ralph Nader, "The Violence of Omission," *Nation* 208, no. 6 (February 10, 1969): 166–68; James Macnees, "Mobilize against Pollution, Nader Tells 'New' Lawyers," *Baltimore Sun*, November 9, 1969; Ralph Nader, "Profits in Pollution," *Progressive* 34 (April 1970): 19–22; Ralph Nader, "Crime in the Corporate Offices," in *Earth Day—The Beginning: A Guide for Survival*, ed.

Environmental Action staff (New York: Arno, 1970), 133; and Ralph Nader, foreword to *Vanishing Air*, by John C. Esposito, viii.

6. Esposito, *Vanishing Air*; Greider, "Nader Marshals 5 Attorneys"; and Julius Duscha, "Stop! In the Public Interest!" *NYT Magazine*, March 21, 1971, 4.

7. Robert Martin and Lloyd Symington, "A Guide to the Air Quality Act of 1967," *Law and Contemporary Problems* 33, no. 2 (April 1, 1968): 239–74; and Doyle J. Borchers, "The Practice of Regional Regulation under the Clean Air Act," *Natural Resources Lawyer* 3, no. 1 (January 1, 1970): 59–65.

8. Esposito, *Vanishing Air*, 152, 190; "Nader Team Questions Muskie's Sincerity in Sharp Attack on U.S. Clean-Air Efforts," *WSJ*, May 13, 1970, 13; Nader, foreword to *Vanishing Air*, vii, ix; and E. W. Kenworthy, "Muskie Criticized by Nader Group," *NYT*, May 13, 1970, 6.

9. Esposito, *Vanishing Air*, 289; *Earth Days*, directed by Robert Stone (2009; PBS).

10. Esposito, *Vanishing Air*, 289–304; Nader, foreword to *Vanishing Air*, iix; Kenworthy, "Muskie Criticized"; Matthew Storin, "Nader Says Muskie Undeserving of Image as Pollution Crusader," *Boston Globe*, May 13, 1970, 1; and "Nader Team Questions Muskie's Sincerity," *WSJ*.

11. Storin, "Nader Says Muskie Undeserving"; George Lardner Jr., "Muskie Defends His Record as Fighter against Pollution," *WP*, May 14, 1970, A2; Kenworthy, "Muskie Criticized"; "Senator Edmund Muskie, Leader and Fighter for Environmental Quality," *Congressional Record—House*, 91st Cong., 2nd Sess., May 14, 1970, 15607–9; and John MacLean, "Muskie Defends Pollution Work," *Chicago Tribune*, May 14, 1970, 15.

12. "Senator Randolph Comments on Ralph Nader Task Force Air Pollution Report," *Congressional Record—Senate*, May 12, 1970, 15066; and David Stout, "Senator Jennings Randolph of West Virginia Dies at 96," *NYT*, May 9, 1998. For Nader's conflict with Randolph over UMWA leadership, see Ray Martin, "Miners Rap WVU Faculty and (Tony) Boyle," *Morgantown Dominion-News*, reprinted in *Congressional Record*, February 5, 1969, 2911.

13. Justin Martin, *Nader: Crusader, Spoiler, Icon* (Cambridge, MA: Perseus, 2002), 117; and "Senator Edmund Muskie," *Congressional Record*.

14. Leon Billings, remarks in "The Earth Institute—Columbia University—Origins of Environmental Law (Class 4; Fall 2014)," Vimeo, accessed May 22, 2018, https://vimeo.com/122376085; and Leon G. Billings, "Eagleton and the Environment: Promises Made; Promises Kept," *Saint Louis University Law Journal* 52, no. 1 (Fall 2007): 91–96. For the broader rivalry between leading Democrats and Nixon over environmental leadership, see J. Brooks Flippen, *Nixon and the Environment* (Albuquerque: University of New Mexico Press, 2000); and LGB–Ralph Nader Conversation, December 16, 1970, 2:00 p.m., in Edmund S. Muskie Archives and Special Collections Library, Bates College, Lewiston, ME, Edmund S. Muskie Papers, 1826–2005, Series V.C.: U.S. Senate, Senate Office and Committee Staff, box 73A (Ralph Nader), folder 1.

15. Emily Yehle, "Recalling the Long, Hard Slog to a 'Historic Piece of Legislation,'" *E&E News*, January 20, 2014, https://www.eenews.net/stories/1059993175/print; Sam Roberts, "Leon G. Billings, Architect of Clean

Air and Clean Water Acts, Dies at 78," *NYT*, November 17, 2016; Nader, "Profits in Pollution"; and Martin Melosi, "Lyndon Johnson and Environmental Policy," in *The Johnson Years*, ed. Robert A. Divine, vol. 2, *Vietnam, the Environment, and Science* (Lawrence: University Press of Kansas, 1987), 113–49. For a discussion contrasting Great Society and early 1970s regulation, see Thomas Jundt, *Greening the Red, White, and Blue: The Bomb, Big Business, and Consumer Resistance in Postwar America* (Oxford: Oxford University Press, 2014), 167–73; and Robert Rabin, "Federal Regulation in Historical Perspective," *Stanford Law Review* 38, no. 5 (May 1986): 1189–1326.

16. Billings, "Eagleton and the Environment."

17. David Zwick, interview by the author, July 31, 2015.

18. Zwick, interview, July 31, 2015.

19. Zwick, interview, July 31, 2015.

20. David Cocke, "Phantom 3L Attacks Pollution, Congress," *Harvard Law Record* 55, no. 6 (November 10, 1972): 4; Zwick, interview, July 31, 2015; and Richard Nixon, "Remarks on Signing the Clean Air Amendments of 1970," December 31, 1970, TAPP. Apparently, Nixon didn't invite Muskie to the signing or mention his name; see Meir Rinde, "Richard Nixon and the Rise of American Environmentalism," Science History Institute, June 2, 2017, https://www.sciencehistory.org/distillations/magazine/richard-nixon-and-the-rise-of-american-environmentalism.

21. Marcy Benstock, interview by the author, April 13, 2018; Zwick and Benstock, *Water Wasteland*, xi–xii; and "Environment: Nader on Water," *Time*, April 26, 1971.

22. "Environment: Nader on Water," *Time*; and "Statement of David R. Zwick," in House Committee on Public Works, *Water Pollution Control Legislation—1971 (Proposed Amendments to Existing Legislation). Hearings, Ninety-Second Congress, First Session*, Committee on Public Works, no. 92-16 (Washington, DC: US Government Printing Office, 1971), 1149.

23. "Statement of David R. Zwick," 1149.

24. Zwick, interview, July 31, 2015; and E. W. Kenworthy, "Nader Is Seeking to Unite Anglers," *NYT*, July 25, 1971.

25. Leonard Ross, "Who Regulates the Regulator? The Regulated," *NYT*, August 8, 1971, BR1; Simon Lazarus and Leonard Ross, "Rating Nader," *New York Review of Books*, June 28, 1973, 31–33; David Seckler, "Book Review: Water Wasteland: Ralph Nader's Study Group Report on Water Pollution," *American Journal of Agricultural Economics* 55, no. 1 (February 1973), 134; and Adrian W. Sybor, "Missing: A Hero with All the Answers," *Baltimore Sun*, July 19, 1970, SD7.

26. William Greider, "Institutional Lone Ranger," *WP*, December 5, 1971, A1; Colman McCarthy, "How the 'Raiders' Work," *WP*, July 30, 1970, D10; and William L. Clairborne, "Tedious Study Is Key Tool of Nader's Raiders," *WP*, August 26, 1971, A3.

27. For an account of one fight over PIRG activity fees, see Paul G. E. Clemens and Carla Yanni, *Rutgers since 1945: A History of the State University of New*

Jersey (New Brunswick, NJ: Rutgers University Press, 2015), 181–86. See also Ralph Nader and Donald Ross, *Action for a Change: A Student's Manual for Public Interest Organizing* (New York: Grossman, 1971); and Donald K. Ross, *A Public Citizen's Action Manual* (New York: Grossman, 1973).

28. Rudy Abramson, "Nader's Raiders: A Bigger Team, More Targets," *LAT*, September 24, 1970, 1; Greider, "Institutional Lone Ranger"; Ronald Shafer, "Empire of the Consumer Crusader Blossoms," *WSJ*, November 19, 1970, 40; and John D. Morris, "A New Nader Group Aids Consumer," *NYT*, June 29, 1969, 24.

29. Duscha, "Stop! In the Public Interest!"

30. Duscha, "Stop! In the Public Interest!"; Shafer, "Empire of the Consumer Crusader Blossoms"; "Campaign GM," *Harvard Crimson*, September 20, 1971; Richard Halloran, "Nader to Press for G.M. Reform," *NYT*, February 8, 1970, 44; Jerry M. Flint, "G.M. Will Win Proxy Battle with Nader, but the War May Just Be Starting," *NYT*, May 22, 1970, 18; and William W. Buzbee, *Fighting Westway: Environmental Law, Citizen Activism, and the Regulatory War That Transformed New York City* (Ithaca, NY: Cornell University Press, 2014).

31. Michael Kinsley, *Outer Space and Inner Sanctums: Governments, Business and Satellite Communication* (New York: John Wiley, 1976); and Phil Freshman, "Nader Intern: Inexperienced Self-Starter," *WP*, August 16, 1971, A3.

32. Greider, "Institutional Lone Ranger"; and Abramson, "Nader's Raiders."

Chapter 6: "SUE THE BASTARDS"

1. Natural Resources Defense Council, "Attendees," Princeton Conference, Princeton Inn, March 20–21, 1970, NRDC Records, Accession 2013-M-056, MS 1965, box 18, folder 8.

2. David Sive, "The Role of the Natural Resources Defense Council," Princeton Conference, Princeton Inn, March 21, 1970, NRDC Records, Accession 2013-M-056, MS 1965, box 18, folder 19. For a similar complaint that the government was "extraordinarily vulnerable to the accrual of political power" by "narrow but powerful economic interests," see Roderick Cameron, "Demonstrate" (SUNY Stony Brook, April 22, 1970), in *Earth Day—The Beginning: A Guide for Survival*, ed. Environmental Action staff (New York: Arno, 1970), 194. See also, Paul Sabin, "Environmental Law and the End of the New Deal Order," *Law and History Review* 33, no. 4 (November 2015): 965–1003.

3. "S.3575: Introduction of the Environmental Protection Act of 1970," Congressional Record—Senate, March 10, 1970, 3321–25.

4. "S.3575: Introduction," Congressional Record.

5. "S.3575: Introduction," Congressional Record; Cameron, "Demonstrate," 193; James Moorman, remarks, "The Role of the Law and Courts," summary of panel on environmental law at the Princeton conference, March 1970, NRDC Records, Accession 2013-M-056, MS 1965, box 18, folder 16; and Victor J. Yannacone, "Sue the Bastards," in *Earth Day—The Beginning*, 210.

6. *Office of Communication of the United Church of Christ et al. v. Federal Communications Commission*, 359 F.2d 994 (D.C. Cir. 1966), 1003, 1005.

7. *United Church of Christ v. FCC*, 1006; Kay Mills, *Changing Channels: The Civil Rights Case That Transformed Television* (Jackson: University Press of Mississippi, 2004); Sidney A. Shapiro, "*United Church of Christ v. FCC*: Private Attorneys General and the Rule of Law," *Administrative Law Review* 58, no. 4 (Fall 2006): 939–60; Charles Halpern, interview with the author, February 15, 2010; and CLASP, "Proposal to the Ford Foundation," April 24, 1970, FFA, Grants, reel 4683, 3.

8. John Kenneth Galbraith, *The Affluent Society* (Boston: Houghton Mifflin, 1958), 209. For the courts as leaders in an effort to reform agency practices, see R. Shep Melnick, *Regulation and the Courts: The Case of the Clean Air Act* (Washington, DC: Brookings Institution, 1983), 3–4; R. B. Stewart, "The Reformation of American Administrative Law," *Harvard Law Review* 88, no. 8 (June 1975): 1667–813; and Thomas W. Merrill, "Capture Theory and the Courts: 1967–1983," *Chicago-Kent Law Review* 72 (January 1997): 1039–117. Adam Rome discusses Galbraith and Arthur Schlesinger's impact on environmental politics in Adam Rome, " 'Give Earth a Chance': The Environmental Movement and the Sixties," *Journal of American History* 90, no. 2 (September 2003): 525–54; see also Samuel P. Hays, *Beauty, Health, and Permanence: Environmental Politics in the United States, 1955–1985* (Cambridge: Cambridge University Press, 1987). For the classic article arguing for standing for nonhuman elements of nature, which the courts did not embrace, see Christopher Stone, "Should Trees Have Standing?—Toward Legal Rights for Natural Objects," *Southern California Law Review* 45 (1972): 450–501.

9. *Scenic Hudson Pres. Conf. v. Federal Power Commission*, 354 F.2d 608 (1965), 616; David Sive, "Pioneering Environmental Lawyer and Atlantic Chapter Leader, 1961–1982," in *Sierra Club Leaders II, 1960s–1970s*, by Ann Lage et al. (Berkeley: Regional Oral History Office, Bancroft Library, University of California, 1985); Leonard S. Rubinowitz, "Of Birds, Bees, and the FPC," *Yale Law Journal* 77, no. 1 (November 1967): 117–38; and John E. Bonine, "Private Public Interest Environmental Law: History, Hard Work, and Hope," *Pace Environmental Law Review* 26 (2009): 465–91, 466. For an in-depth account of the Storm King fight and its broader implications for environmental law and politics, see Robert Lifset, *Power on the Hudson: Storm King Mountain and the Emergence of Modern American Environmentalism* (Pittsburgh, PA: University of Pittsburgh Press, 2014).

10. *Udall vs. FPC*, 387 U.S. 428 (1967), 450, 444, 451; Karl Boyd Brooks, *Before Earth Day: The Origins of American Environmental Law, 1945–1970* (Lawrence: University Press of Kansas, 2009), 149–57; *Sierra Club v. Morton*, 405 U.S. 727 (1972), 746–47; and James M. Landis, *Report on Regulatory Agencies to the President-Elect* (Washington, DC: US Government Printing Office, 1960).

11. CLASP, "Proposal to the Ford Foundation"; "The New Public Interest Lawyers," *Yale Law Journal* 79, no. 6 (May 1970): 1069; Louis Jaffe, remarks, "The Role of the Law and Courts," summary of panel on environmental law at the

Princeton conference, March 1970, in NRDC Records, Accession 2013-M-056, MS 1965, box 18, folder 16; John H. Adams, *Responsible Militancy: The Anatomy of a Public Interest Law Firm* (New York: Record of the Association of the Bar of the City of New York, 1974), 634. See also Simon Lazarus and Joseph Onek, "The Regulators and the People," *Virginia Law Review* 57, no. 6 (September 1, 1971): 1069–108.

12. In NRDC Records, Accession 2013-M-064, MS 1965, box 4, folder 1: Harry M. Caudill to Mr. and Mrs. Dudley, June 8, 1971; and Laurance Rockefeller to Mr. and Ms. Picker, January 10, 1972.

13. For an insider account of EPA's early enforcement efforts, see John Quarles, *Cleaning Up America: An Insider's View of the Environmental Protection Agency* (Boston: Houghton Mifflin, 1976). For an overview of EPA's evolution, see Richard N. L. Andrews, "The EPA at 40: An Historical Perspective," *Duke Environmental Law & Policy Forum* 21 (Spring 2011): 223–58.

14. In FFA, reel 1359, Grant 68-906: Joseph L. Sax to Gordon Harrison, August 28, 1968 (sec. 1); Joseph L. Sax to Frank J. Barry, July 15, 1968 (sec. 4). Also Denis Hayes, "The Beginning" (Sylvan Theater, Washington, DC, April 22, 1970), in *Earth Day—The Beginning*, preface; and CLASP, "Proposal to the Ford Foundation."

15. Harry N. Scheiber, "The Road to *Munn*: Eminent Domain and the Concept of Public Purpose in the State Courts," *Perspectives in American History* 5 (1971): 327–402; and Harry N. Scheiber, "Affected with a Public Interest," in *Encyclopedia of the American Constitution*, ed. Leonard W. Levy and Kenneth L. Karst, 2nd ed., vol. 1 (New York: Macmillan Reference USA, 2000), 52–53.

16. Ralph Cavanagh, interview by the author, September 26, 2013. For a survey of TVA's evolution as a power company and increasing litigation against the agency, see Wilmon H. Droze, "The TVA, 1945–80: The Power Company," and Dean Hill Rivkin, "TVA, the Courts, and the Public Interest," in *TVA, Fifty Years of Grass-Roots Bureaucracy*, ed. Erwin C. Hargrove and Paul Keith Conkin (Urbana: University of Illinois Press, 1983), 66–85, 194–229. For the shift of TVA into an agent of southern industrialization and military development, see Bruce J. Schulman, *From Cotton Belt to Sunbelt: Federal Policy, Economic Development, and the Transformation of the South, 1938–1980* (New York: Oxford University Press, 1991), 91–93; see also Erwin C. Hargrove, *Prisoners of Myth: The Leadership of the Tennessee Valley Authority, 1933–1990* (Princeton, NJ: Princeton University Press, 1994), 155–94; and William U. Chandler, *The Myth of TVA: Conservation and Development in the Tennessee Valley, 1933–1983* (Cambridge, MA: Ballinger, 1984), 115–54. See also James C. Scott, *Seeing like a State: How Certain Schemes to Improve the Human Condition Have Failed* (New Haven, CT: Yale University Press, 1998).

17. Sierra Club Legal Defense Fund, Inc. and Sierra Club, "Legal Program Accomplishments during Period August 1, 1971–August 1, 1973," FFA, SCLDF reel 2154; Environmental Defense Fund, "A Proposal to the Ford Foundation: October 5, 1972, Attachment 1," FFA, EDF reel 2587, grant files;

and Ed Strohbehn to Executive Committee, "Analysis of NRDC Legal Action Initiatives," July 28, 1971, Adams Records, box 23, folder 1.

18. Helen Leavitt, *Superhighway—Superhoax* (Garden City, NY: Doubleday, 1970); Bob Simmons, "The Freeway Establishment," *Cry California* 3, no. 2 (Spring 1968): 31–38; and Raymond A. Mohl, "The Interstates and the Cities: The U.S. Department of Transportation and the Freeway Revolt, 1966–1973," *Journal of Policy History* 20, no. 2 (2008): 193–226, 197. For the decades-long struggle to insulate California highway user funds from competing state demands, see Paul Sabin, *Crude Politics: The California Oil Market, 1900–1940* (Berkeley: University of California Press, 2005), 159–201; and Conservation Foundation, "What Is the Role of the Highway in Society and the Environment?" *CF Letter*, June 1970, 1.

19. In NAS Papers, box 171 (Environmental Defense Fund): "EDF: One Anti-pollution Device That Works!" n.d. [presumably 1969 or 1970]; and Roderick A. Cameron to Friends, April 10, 1970.

20. James W. Moorman, "Attorney for the Environment, 1966–1981: Center for Law and Social Policy, Sierra Club Legal Defense Fund, Department of Justice Division of Lands and Natural Resources" (oral history conducted in 1984 by Ted Hudson), Sierra Club History Committee, 1994, 48. Also, in Sierra Club Legal Defense Fund, Inc. and Sierra Club, "Legal Program Accomplishments during Period August 1, 1971–August 1, 1973," FFA, SCLDF reel 2154, 5, 11, 30: *Sierra Club v. California Coastal Zone Conservation Commission, Deane & Deane, et al.* (country club); *Sierra Club et al. v. Morton et al.* (Jim Bridger power plant); and *Sierra Club et al. v. Edward P. Cliff et al.* (ski lifts). For the pipeline case, see *Wilderness Society v. Hickel, 325 F. Supp. 422* (1970) (citing NEPA as well as the Mineral Leasing Act of 1920's pipeline right-of-way provisions); subsequent litigation included *Wilderness Society v. Morton*, 479 F.2d 842 (D.C. Cir., 1973); and *Alyeska Pipeline Svc. Co. v. Wilderness Society 421 U.S. 240* (1975) (denying attorney fees to the environmental litigants for more than four thousand hours of attorney time).

21. "A Proposal to the Ford Foundation, October 5, 1972," EDFA, loose folder SG III.2, S1, box 2, folder 10 (Ford Foundation 1974–1975); John H. Adams to Friend of NRDC, October 1972, NAS Papers, box B-379 (Natural Resources Defense Council, 1972–73); Minutes of Executive Committee, Meetings March 18, August 10, and December 8, 1970, EDFA, RG 2, SG 1, Governing Committees Series 2: Executive Committee Subseries 2: Meetings, box 1 (Meeting Minutes 1967–1977).

22. In NAS Papers, box 171 (Environmental Defense Fund): Environmental Defense Fund, "Press Release: Leading Environmentalists Petition U.S.D.A. to Ban DDT," October 31, 1969; and "Banning Cancer-Producing Chemicals," *WP*, October 25, 1969, A12. Also Mark Dowie, *Losing Ground: American Environmentalism at the Close of the Twentieth Century* (Cambridge, MA: MIT Press, 1995); and Robert Gottlieb, *Forcing the Spring: The Transformation of the American Environmental Movement*, rev. and updated ed. (Washington, DC:

Island Press, 2005). See also Harrison Wellford, interview by the author, June 25, 2015; and Anthony Kline, interview by the author, October 23, 2014.

23. "New Public Interest Lawyers," *Yale Law Journal*, 1112–13. Edelman sought to help CLASP navigate Ford's demands when Ford tried to merge CLASP with the National Legal Aid & Defender Association; see Marian Wright Edelman to Christopher Edley, July 8, 1969, FFA, CLASP Correspondence, reel 4684; Charles Halpern, interview, February 15, 2010; Charles Halpern, "The Public Interest Bar," in *Verdicts on Lawyers*, ed. Ralph Nader and Mark Green (New York: Crowell, 1976), 158; and Simon Lazarus, *The Genteel Populists* (New York: Holt, Rinehart and Winston, 1974), 142. For early criticism of CLASP as insufficiently focused on litigation directly serving the poor, see Theodore Voorhees to Christopher Edley, September 22, 1969, FFA, CLASP Correspondence, reel 4684. For an early critique of unaccountable and elitist public interest law, particularly focused on environmental issues, see Edgar S. Cahn and Jean Camper Cahn, "Power to the People or the Profession? The Public Interest in Public Interest Law," *Yale Law Journal* 79 (1970): 1005–48.

24. Adams, *Responsible Militancy*, 632; Gordon Harrison, "Resources and Environment: An Accounting," National Affairs Program, Ford Foundation, December 1972, 22, in Gordon A. Harrison, interview, March 21, 1972, FFA, Ford Foundation Oral History Project, box 2, folder 41, appendix I; and Harrison, interview, 39.

25. James Gustave Speth, *Angels by the River: A Memoir* (White River Junction, VT: Chelsea Green, 2014), 154, 152.

Chapter 7: INSTITUTIONALIZING THE PUBLIC INTEREST MOVEMENT

1. John W. Gardner, "Uncritical Lovers, Unloving Critics," *Journal of Educational Research* 62, no. 9 (1969): 396–99; and "Johnson Team Loses Another Star: Cost of War Made Apparent Part in Campaign Seen," *Christian Science Monitor*, January 27, 1968.

2. John W. Gardner, "Common Cause: A Forum for Responsible Citizen Action," *Parents' Magazine & Better Family Living*, March 1972; and Warren Weaver Jr., "Gardner Organizing a Lobby of Citizens," *NYT*, July 31, 1970, A1.

3. Jeffrey M. Berry, *Lobbying for the People* (Princeton, NJ: Princeton University Press, 1977), 29; Alexander M. Bickel, "What Is John Gardner Up To?" *NYT*, December 21, 1970; Robert D. McFadden, "John W. Gardner, 89, Founder of Common Cause and Adviser to Presidents, Dies," *NYT*, February 18, 2002; "Birthday for Common Cause," *Time* 98, no. 7 (August 16, 1971): 14; and "Gardner's Common Cause," *Time* 96, no. 6 (August 10, 1970): 10.

4. Henry Brandon Interview with Ralph Nader, 1970, Henry Brandon Papers, Manuscript Division, Library of Congress, Washington, DC, box 29, folder 3; "Gardner's Common Cause," *Time*, 10; Justin Martin, *Nader: Crusader, Spoiler,*

Icon (Cambridge, MA: Perseus, 2002), 159; and Peter Barnes, "Toward '72 and Beyond: Starting a Fourth Party," *New Republic*, July 24–31, 1971, 19.

5. "The Congress: Nader's Biggest Raid," *Time*, July 31, 1972. For "citizen's army," see the back cover of Mark J. Green, James M. Fallows, and David Zwick, *Who Runs Congress?* (Toronto: Bantam, 1972).

6. "Nader's Aides Probe Congress," *Hartford Courant*, July 16, 1972, 5; "Congress: Nader's Biggest Raid," *Time*; Joan Claybrook, interview by the author, August 26, 2015; and David Bollier, *Citizen Action and Other Big Ideas: A History of Ralph Nader and the Modern Consumer Movement* (Washington, DC: Center for Study of Responsive Law, 1991), 26–29. For a copy of the Congress Project questionnaire, see Patsy T. Mink Papers, Manuscript Division, Library of Congress, Washington, DC, box 686, folder 7.

7. Claybrook, interview, August 26, 2015.

8. Green et al., *Who Runs Congress?*, 2, 6; and Mary Russell, "Nader Report Sees Congress 'Abdicating,'" *WP*, October 4, 1972, A2.

9. Ralph Nader Congress Project, *The Environment Committees: A Study of the House and Senate Interior, Agriculture, and Science Committees* (New York: Grossman, 1975), 9, 20; Green et al., *Who Runs Congress?*, 21, 46–47; and Martin, *Nader: Crusader, Spoiler, Icon*, 152–66.

10. Steven C. Schulte, *Wayne Aspinall and the Shaping of the American West* (Boulder: University Press of Colorado, 2002); Jonathan Martin, "Alan Merson Tried to Make a Difference," *Seattle Times*, October 21, 2005, B6; Colorado's Republican legislature had redistricted Aspinall's constituency to include a more liberal Democratic base and a more Republican constituency overall. "Aspinall Is Loser in Colorado Race," *NYT*, September 13, 1972, 1; Stephen C. Sturgeon, *The Politics of Western Water: The Congressional Career of Wayne Aspinall* (Tucson: University of Arizona Press, 2002), 133–44; and Jennifer Yachnin, "Still 'Electing the Best, Defeating the Worst'—but with Far Greater Resources Than Before," E&E News, December 11, 2013, https://www .eenews.net/stories/1059991640.

11. Ralph Nader Congress Project, *Environment Committees*, 4–5; and Green et al., *Who Runs Congress?*, 52, 250.

12. *Alan Morrison, Esquire*, interviews conducted by Daniel Marcus in 2007 and 2008, Oral History Project, Historical Society of the District of Columbia Circuit (Washington, DC: Historical Society of the District of Columbia Circuit, 2009), 160, 188; and Myrna Oliver, "John Gardner; and Common Cause Founder Was 89," *LAT*, February 18, 2002.

13. John A. Lawrence, "How the 'Watergate Babies' Broke American Politics," *Politico*, May 26, 2018, https://www.politico.com/magazine/story/2018/05/26 /congress-broke-american-politics-218544.

14. Kenneth Lasson, *Proudly We Hail: Profiles of Public Citizens in Action* (New York: Grossman, 1975), 77, 3.

15. *Alan Morrison, Esquire*, 50–53.

16. *Executive Privilege, Secrecy in Government, Freedom of Information. Hearings before the Subcommittee on Intergovernmental Relations of the Committee on Gov-*

ernment Operations and the Subcommittees on Separation of Powers and Administrative Practice and Procedure of the Committee on the Judiciary, United States Senate, Ninety-Third Congress, First Session, April 10, 11, 12, May 8, 9, 10, 16, 1973, vol. 1 (Washington, DC: US Government Printing Office, 1973), 214–15; and Michael Halberstam, "Beyond Transparency: Rethinking Election Reform from an Open Government Perspective," *Seattle University Law Review* 38 (2015): 1018.

17. Charles R. Halpern, "Public Interest Law: Its Past and Future," *Judicature* 58, no. 3 (October 1974): 118–27; and Art Cooley to Board of Trustees, October 17, 1973, EDFA, RG 1, SG 1.3, Robert Smolker Papers, Series 1: EDF Documents, box 1, folder 13 (Board of Trustees Memos 1972–73).

18. In EDFA, RG 1, SG 1, Dennis Puleston Series 1: Environmental Defense Fund Documents, box 1, folder 2 (Memoranda—Executive Committee 1971–1972): Executive Committee to Edward Lee Rogers, July 14, 1972; and Rod Cameron to Executive Committee, "Executive Director Job Description," November 2, 1972. Also Executive Director to Board of Trustees, "Overvew of 1973," n.d. [approximately November 1973], EDFA, RG 1, SG 1.3, Robert Smolker Papers, Series 1: EDF Documents, box 1, folder 13 (Board of Trustees Memos 1972–73).

19. Rod Cameron to Board of Trustees and EDF Professional Staff, January 10, 1973, EDFA, RG 1, SG 1.3 Robert Smolker Papers, Series 1: EDF Documents, box 1, folder 14 (Board of Trustees 1972–73).

20. Executive Director to Board of Trustees, "Overview of 1973."

21. Halpern, "Public Interest Law: Its Past and Future," 122; and Elvis J. Stahr to Mrs. Thomas M. Waller, April 23, 1973, NAS Papers, box B-405 (Tax Exemption for Public Charities).

22. Roderick A. Cameron to Gordon Harrison, November 1971, EDFA, loose folder SG III.2, S1, box 2, folder 9 (Ford Foundation 1970–1971); Sidney W. Green to Rod Cameron, "Perspectives for EDF," May 13, 1970, EDFA, RG 1, SG 1.4, Charles F. Wurster Papers Series 3: EDF-Board of Trustees ss2: Meeting Minutes and Agendas, box 3, folder 5 (Board Meeting Agendas 1970).

23. Roderick A. Cameron to Gordon Harrison, October 5, 1972, EDFA, loose folder SG III.2, S1, box 2, folder 10 (Ford Foundation 1974–1975); and Cathe Wolhowe, "Environmental Groups Face Fund Cut," *WP*, 28 September 1973, A6.

24. Sanford M. Jaffe, "Public Interest Law—Five Years Later," *American Bar Association Journal* 62, no. 8 (August 1976), 985; and Halpern, "Public Interest Law: Its Past and Future."

25. In CCGF, box 528, folder 2: Joseph Onek to Eli Evans, "Grant Application for the Council for the Advancement of Public Interest Law," August 7, 1974; and Eli Evans, "Possible Establishment of the Council for the Advancement of Public Interest Law," May 24, 1974. Also Sanford M. Jaffe, "Public Interest Law—Five Years Later," 986–87; Frederick R. Anderson and Armin Rosencranz, "The Future of Environmental Defense," *American Bar Association Journal* 61, no. 3 (March 1975): 316–21; and Joseph Lelyveld, "Nader Undaunted

by Setbacks to Consumer Drive in the Congress, Press, Universities and White House," *NYT*, November 24, 1975, 73. On the value of funding public participation in FTC proceedings, see Michael Pertschuk, "Listening to the Little Guy," *WP*, June 26, 1979, A19.

26. EDF depended heavily on its membership; half of its $1.2 million annual budget came from about forty-five thousand members. Alfred L. Webre to William Felling and Edward Ames, "Environmental Defense Fund, Monitor Report No. 1," October 15, 1973, EDFA, RG 1, SG 1.3, Robert Smolker Papers, Series 1: EDF Documents, box 1, folder 13; and Arlie W. Schardt and Robert Joe Pierpont, "Second Year Report to the Ford Foundation from the Environmental Defense Fund," EDFA, loose folder SG III.2, S1, box 2, folder 11 (Ford Foundation 1976–1977).

27. Arlie Schardt, "Statement on the Relocation of EDF's National Headquarters to New York City," October 27, 1977, EDFA, RG 1, SG 1.3, Robert Smolker Papers, Series 1: EDF Documents, box 1, folder 3 (General Correspondence 1974–84).

28. For examples of union-based environmental action, see, for example, Josiah Rector, "Environmental Justice at Work: The UAW, the War on Cancer, and the Right to Equal Protection from Toxic Hazards in Postwar America," *Journal of American History* 101, no. 2 (2014): 480–502; Robert Gordon, "'Shell No!': OCAW and the Labor-Environmental Alliance," *Environmental History* 3, no. 4 (1998): 460–87; Robert Gordon, "Poisons in the Fields: The United Farm Workers, Pesticides, and Environmental Politics," *Pacific Historical Review* 68, no. 1 (February 1999): 51–77; and Anderson and Rosencranz, "Future of Environmental Defense." For a sample of the ongoing struggle over representation and issue focus in the environmental movement, see, for example, Richard Moore et al. to Jay Hair et al., SouthWest Organizing Project, March 16, 1990, https://www.ejnet.org/ej/swop.pdf; for a look back at the letter, see Marty Durlin, "The Shot Heard Round the West," *High Country News*, February 1, 2010, https://www.hcn.org/issues/42.2/the-shot-heard-round-the-west.

29. *Alan Morrison, Esquire*, 189; and Russell E. Train, "The Beginning of Wisdom," *Wilson Quarterly* 1, no. 4 (July 1, 1977): 96–104, 100–101.

30. In NRDC Records, Accession 2013-M-056, MS 1965, box 8, folder 19: John R. Quarles Jr. to Marshall Robinson, September 28, 1973; and John R. Quarles Jr., "The Environmental Movement after Five Years: An Assessment and a Proposal" (speech to the National Council on Philanthropy, December 4, 1975), *Environmental News*.

31. In NAS Papers, box B-349 (Environmental Defense Fund): William D. Ruckelshaus, "Public Policy and the Public," January 22, 1974; and William Ruckelshaus to Friend, n.d. [likely fall 1974].

32. Lewis F. Powell Jr. to Eugene B. Sydnor Jr. et al., "Confidential Memorandum: Attack on American Free Enterprise System," August 23, 1971, Wellington and Lee University School of Law, Scholarly Commons, https://scholarlycommons.law.wlu.edu/powellmemo.

33. Eugene C. Pullman, "The Federal Bureaucracy and Individual Freedom," *Pon-*

tiac Press, January 10, 1972, CCGF, box 478, folder 6; and James J. Kilpatrick, "Nader on Congress: Demons vs. Angels," *Baltimore Sun*, October 10, 1972, A19.

34. Steven M. Teles, *The Rise of the Conservative Legal Movement: The Battle for Control of the Law* (Princeton, NJ: Princeton University Press, 2010).

35. Jefferson Decker, *The Other Rights Revolution: Conservative Lawyers and the Remaking of American Government* (New York: Oxford University Press, 2016); Teles, *Rise of the Conservative Legal Movement*; and Richard B. Schmitt, "Alternative Public-Interest Law Firms Spring Up with Nader et al. as Target," *WSJ*, August 21, 1979, 13.

Chapter 8: THE CARTER ADMINISTRATION'S STRUGGLE FOR BALANCE

1. "Carter's Road Show," *Time*, August 23, 1976, 23; "Nader: Umpire or Player?" *Village Voice*, August 30, 1976, 21; Justin Martin, *Nader: Crusader, Spoiler, Icon* (Cambridge, MA: Perseus, 2002), 180; and James Fallows, "The Passionless Presidency: The Trouble with Jimmy Carter's Administration," *Atlantic Monthly*, May 1979, 33*ff.*

2. Laura Foreman, "Carter's Raiders: The Outsiders Are In," *NYT*, April 20, 1977, 50; "Carter's Road Show," *Time*, 23; and Mark Green, "Carter's Bar: Tapping a New Talent Pool," *WP*, March 22, 1977, A17.

3. Marian Burros and Warren Brown, "Nader Hits Choices," *WP*, December 8, 1976, A1; and Mark Green, "Carter's Bar."

4. Fallows, "Passionless Presidency."

5. Foreman, "Carter's Raiders"; and Juan Cameron, "Nader's Invaders Are inside the Gates," *Fortune*, October 1977, 252*ff.*

6. Foreman, "Carter's Raiders"; Green, "Carter's Bar"; and Fallows, "Passionless Presidency."

7. David S. Broder, "Citizen's Beef," *WP*, December 12, 1976, 37; and Burros and Brown, "Nader Hits Choices." See also Rachelle Patterson, "Ralph Nader Trying to Maintain Role of Adversary," *Boston Globe*, February 22, 1977, 2; "Public Affairs Groups, Now on the Outside, Expect Access to Power under Carter," *NYT*, December 1, 1976, 30; and "Consumerists Optimistic about Future," *LAT*, December 12, 1976, F1.

8. Theodore Jacqueney, "Nader Network Switches Focus to Legal Action, Congressional Lobbying," *National Journal*, June 9, 1973, 840; and Joan Claybrook, interview by the author, August 26, 2015.

9. Claybrook, interview, August 26, 2015; and Ernest Holsendolph, "Lobbyist for Nader to Head Safety Unit," *NYT*, March 19, 1977, 12.

10. Nader's concerns about the risks of delay proved prescient when the Reagan administration withdrew the airbag rule in October 1981. The Supreme Court, however, unanimously ordered the Department of Transportation to implement the requirement, or justify its refusal to do so. Secretary of Transpor-

tation Elizabeth Dole reissued the airbag ruling in 1984. Linda Greenhouse, "High Court Backs Airbags Mandate," *NYT*, June 25, 1983, 1; Holsendolph, "Lobbyist for Nader to Head Safety Unit"; and Henry Scarupa, "Joan Claybrook: The Woman in Everybody's Car," *Baltimore Sun*, June 17, 1979, SM6.

11. Scarupa, "Joan Claybrook"; and Ernest Holsendolph, "Nader Calls on Ex-colleague to Resign Safety Post," *NYT*, December 1, 1977, 18.

12. Ernest Holsendolph, "Nader-Claybrook Feud Puzzles Consumer Advocates," *NYT*, December 5, 1977, 21.

13. David Cohen, "When Government Critics Join the Government," *WP*, December 26, 1977, A17.

14. Larry Kramer, "Driving for Safety: Auto Makers, Consumer Groups Criticize Claybrook's Efforts," *WP*, June 18, 1978, K1; Stuart Eizenstat interview with Joan Claybrook, June 3, 1991, Stuart Eizenstat Papers, Manuscript Division, Library of Congress, Washington, DC, box 75, folder 9; and Ralph Nader, interview by the author, May 30, 2018.

15. "Business: Nader: Success or Excess?" *Time*, November 14, 1977, 76; "Nader: Ex-activists Work Too Cautiously in DC Jobs," *Atlanta Constitution*, December 18, 1977, 6A; Harrison Wellford, interview by the author, July 29, 2015; and Barbara Blum, "Interview: EPA Deputy Administrator Barbara Blum," *Journal (Water Pollution Control Federation)* 50, no. 5 (May 1, 1978): 815–18.

16. Wellford, interview, July 29, 2015; and John Dillin, "Environmentalists Unsure on Carter," *Christian Science Monitor*, January 17, 1978, 1.

17. Adam Clymer, "Carter's Opposition to Water Projects Linked to '73 Veto of Georgia Dam," *NYT*, June 13, 1977, 14; and Walter Pincus, "When a Campaign Vow Crashes into a Pork Barrel," *WP*, April 1, 1977, A1.

18. Stuart Eizenstat, *President Carter: The White House Years* (New York: Thomas Dunne, 2018), 254; Brock Evans, "Environmental Campaigner: From the Northwest Forests to the Halls of Congress," in *Building the Sierra Club's National Lobbying Program 1967–1981*, by Ann Lage et al. (Berkeley: Regional Oral History Office, Bancroft Library, University of California, 1985), 277–78; and Clymer, "Carter's Opposition to Water Projects."

19. Eizenstat, *President Carter*, 250, 264; Walter Pincus, "Panel Drops 9 Projects on 'Hit List,'" *WP*, July 21, 1977, A1; Evans, "Environmental Campaigner," 277–78; and Jeff Nesmith and John Reetz, "Carter: I'll Try to Stop Russell Dam," *Atlanta Constitution*, July 31, 1977, 1.

20. Eizenstat, *President Carter*, 249–50; and James W. Moorman, "Attorney for the Environment, 1966–1981: Center for Law and Social Policy, Sierra Club Legal Defense Fund, Department of Justice Division of Lands and Natural Resources" (oral history conducted in 1984 by Ted Hudson), Sierra Club History Committee, 1994, 141.

21. In NAS Papers, box B-406 (Terrible 20): Ann Graham to Stahr et al., "Water Project Update," December 5, 1977; and Ann Graham to Stahr, "Meeting with President Carter on Water Projects," November 28, 1977. Also "Environmentalists Charge Carter Shifts Water Policy," *Newsday*, March 31, 1978, 15; and

Seth King, "Win or Lose, the President Will Be Remembered for His Fight with Congress over Water Projects," *NYT*, October 14, 1980, D23.

22. Jimmy Carter, "Address to the Nation on Energy," April 18, 1977, TAPP.

23. Dick Ayres, Tom Cochran, and Tony Roisman to Center for Science in the Public Interest et al., April 22, 1977, NAS Papers, box 171 (Energy).

24. In NAS Papers, box 171 (Energy): James J. MacKenzie, Testimony before Council on Environmental Quality, December 16, 1976; and James J. MacKenzie, "Institutional Problems in Conserving Energy," 135*ff.* Also Marc H. Ross and Robert H. Williams, "Energy Efficiency: Our Most Underrated Energy Resource," *Bulletin of the Atomic Scientists*, December 1976, 30*ff*; and Amory B. Lovins, *Soft Energy Paths: Toward a Durable Peace* (San Francisco: Friends of the Earth International, 1977).

25. Ayres et al. to Center for Science in the Public Interest et al., April 22, 1977.

26. "Carter Sold Them Out, Environmentalists Say," *Newsday*, April 25, 1978, 35; and "Environmentalists Warn Carter on Synthetic Fuels," *NYT*, July 13, 1979, D3.

27. Philip Shabecoff, "Environmentalists See End to a Golden Era," *NYT*, August 6, 1979, A1; and Robert Cahn, "Jimmy Carter, Anti-environmentalist?" *Audubon* 81 (September 1979): 7*ff.*

28. Charles Warren, Gus Speth, and Marion Edey to Jimmy Carter, "Administration Policy on Domestic Nuclear Power," October 31, 1977, James Gustave Speth Papers, Manuscripts and Archives, Yale University Library, New Haven, CT, box 4, folder 6; "Carter Lie Claimed on N-Power," *Hartford Courant*, April 19, 1979, 40; and Mary McGrory, "Nader Splits with Carter on N-Power," *Boston Globe*, April 23, 1979, 15.

29. Robin Herman, "Nearly 200,000 Rally to Protest Nuclear Energy," *NYT*, September 24, 1979, A1.

30. Thomas Oliphant, "Reorganization: Carter's Newest Headache: Ending Bureaucracy Is Easier Said Than Done, He's Finding," *Boston Globe*, January 8, 1978, A3.

31. Oliphant, "Reorganization: Carter's Newest Headache."

32. For a profile of Alfred Kahn's efforts on airline deregulation, see Thomas K. McCraw, *Prophets of Regulation: Charles Francis Adams, Louis D. Brandeis, James M. Landis, Alfred E. Kahn* (Cambridge, MA: Belknap Press of Harvard University Press, 1984), 222–99. See also Laura Kalman, *Right Star Rising: A New Politics* (New York: W. W. Norton, 2010), 240–41; Bruce J. Schulman, *The Seventies: The Great Shift in American Culture, Society, and Politics* (New York: Free Press, 2001), 231; Lizabeth Cohen, *A Consumers' Republic: The Politics of Mass Consumption in Postwar America* (New York: Knopf, 2003), 390–95; Richard H. K. Vietor, *Contrived Competition: Regulation and Deregulation in America* (Cambridge, MA: Belknap Press of Harvard University Press, 1994); Jimmy Carter, Interview, November 29, 1982, Jimmy Carter Presidency, Presidential Oral Histories, Miller Center, University of Virginia, Charlottesville, https://millercenter.org/the-presidency/presidential-oral-histories/jimmy -carter-oral-history; and Stuart Eizenstat interview with Stephen Breyer,

November 30, 1992, Stuart Eizenstat Papers, Manuscript Division, Library of Congress, Washington, DC, box 70, folder 8. Also, in Exit Interview Project, Jimmy Carter Library, Atlanta, GA: "Exit Interview with David Rubenstein, Deputy Director Domestic Policy Staff, December 3, 1980," 7; and "Exit Interview with Robert (Bob) Thomson, December 10, 1980," 5. For the Nader and Kennedy quotations, see *Establishing an Agency for Consumer Protection: Hearings before a Subcommittee of the Committee on Government Operations, House of Representatives, Ninety-Fourth Congress, First Session on H.R. 7575* (Washington, DC: US Government Printing Office, 1975), 228; and Judith Stein, *Pivotal Decade: How the United States Traded Factories for Finance in the Seventies* (New Haven, CT: Yale University Press, 2010), 124.

33. "OMB Organization Study," n.d. (between June 1978 and March 1979), McIntyre Collection, box 9, chap. 1, 2. For the shift from spending programs to regulatory mandates, see R. Shep Melnick, "From Tax and Spend to Mandate and Sue," in *The Great Society and the High Tide of Liberalism*, ed. Jerome M. Mileur and Sidney M. Milkis (Amherst: University of Massachusetts Press, 2005), 387–410; Stanley S. Surrey, *Pathways to Tax Reform; the Concept of Tax Expenditures* (Cambridge, MA: Harvard University Press, 1973); Stanley S. Surrey, "The United States Income Tax System: The Need for a Full Accounting" (speech to Money Marketeers, New York City, November 15, 1967), in *Tax Policy and Tax Reform: 1961–1969* (New York: Commerce Clearing House, 1973), 575–85; and Julian E. Zelizer, *Taxing America: Wilbur D. Mills, Congress, and the State, 1945–1975* (Cambridge: Cambridge University Press, 1998), 286–99. For two early accounts of NEPA's implementation, see Richard N. L. Andrews, *Environmental Policy and Administrative Change: Implementation of the National Environmental Policy Act* (Lexington, MA: Lexington Books, 1976); and Richard A. Liroff, *A National Policy for the Environment: NEPA and Its Aftermath* (Bloomington: Indiana University Press, 1976).

34. George P. Shultz, "Memorandum for the Heads of Departments and Agencies," October 5, 1971, http://www.thecre.com/ombpapers/QualityofLife1.htm. For an account of EPA's experience with quality-of-life review during the Nixon administration, see Robert V. Percival, "Checks without Balance: Executive Office Oversight of the Environmental Protection Agency," *Law and Contemporary Problems* 54, no. 4 (October 1, 1991): 127–204, 129–38; and Joe Green Conley II, "Environmentalism Contained: A History of Corporate Responses to the New Environmentalism" (PhD diss., Princeton University, 2006), 159–65. For a key staff member's account of the pre-Reagan history of regulatory review, see Jim Tozzi, "OIRA's Formative Years: The Historical Record of Centralized Regulatory Review Preceding OIRA's Founding," *Administrative Law Review* 63 (Special Edition 2011): 37–69. For assessments of regulatory reform at the end of the Ford administration, see Domestic Council Review Group on Regulatory Reform, *The Challenge of Regulatory Reform: A Report to the President* (Washington, DC: Review Group, 1977); James C. Miller III, "Lessons of the Economic Impact Statement Program," *Regulation* 1 (1977): 14–21; George C. Eads, "Testimony before the Joint Economic Com-

mittee," August 1, 1979, McIntyre Collection, box 35 (Memoranda to James T. McIntyre from OMB Staff and Others [2/9/78–9/10/79]); Jimmy Carter, "Executive Order 12174—Federal Paperwork Reduction," November 30, 1979, TAPP; and Jimmy Carter, "Paperwork Reduction Act of 1980 Remarks on Signing H.R. 6410 into Law," December 11, 1980, TAPP. For a call for regulatory budget and paperwork budget, see Wayne Granquist to Jim McIntyre and John White, November 16, 1979, McIntyre Collection, box 4, folder "Congressional Issues, 10/6/79–12/22/79"; and "Regulatory Reform: Message from the President of the United States, March 27, 1979," 96th Cong., 1st Sess. (Washington, DC: US Government Printing Office, 1979); see also Narrative of OMB's Relationship to Regulation, October 15, 1980, McIntyre Collection, box 18 (Talking Points and Briefings [10/5/80–10/28/80]). For further discussion and documentation of debates within the Carter administration; see also Paul Sabin, "'Everything Has a Price': Jimmy Carter and the Struggle for Balance in Federal Regulatory Policy," *Journal of Policy History* 28, no. 1 (January 2016): 1–47.

35. For Drayton's activities, see "The Economy and Regulatory Reform," *EPA Journal*, January 1979, 10–12; and Richard N. L. Andrews, "The EPA at 40: An Historical Perspective," *Duke Environmental Law & Policy Forum* 21 (Spring 2011): 223–58. For a classic analysis of economic inefficiencies of the new regulation, see Eugene Bardach and Robert A. Kagan, *Going by the Book: The Problem of Regulatory Unreasonableness* (Philadelphia: Temple University Press, 1982); see also Bruce A. Ackerman and William T. Hassler, *Clean Coal/ Dirty Air: Or How the Clean Air Act Became a Multibillion-Dollar Bail-out for High-Sulfur Coal Producers and What Should Be Done about It* (New Haven, CT: Yale University Press, 1981).

36. "Ralph Nader Assesses Consumer Movement's Future," *WP*, August 5, 1979, F1; *Use of Cost-Benefit Analysis by Regulatory Agencies: Joint Hearings before the Subcommittee on Oversight and Investigations and the Subcommittee on Consumer Protection and Finance of the Committee on Interstate and Foreign Commerce, House of Representatives, Ninety-Sixth Congress, First Session, July 30, October 10, and 24, 1979* (Washington, DC: US Government Printing Office, 1980), 1, 3–4, 119, 123, 124; and Steven Rattner, "Coalition Opposes Regulatory Change," *NYT*, November 4, 1979, 46. For broader critique of cost-benefit analysis, see Mark Green, "The Faked Case against Regulation: Business Propaganda Focuses on Costs, Ignores Savings in Health and Safety Laws," *WP*, January 21, 1979, C1; and Mark J. Green and Norman Waitzman, *Business War on the Law: An Analysis of the Benefits of Federal Health/Safety Enforcement*, rev. 2nd ed. (Washington, DC: Corporate Accountability Research Group, 1981).

37. Margot Hornblower, "Muskie Criticizes White House Meddling with EPA Rules," *WP*, February 27, 1979, A2; and *Executive Branch Review of Environmental Regulations: Hearings before the Subcommittee on Environmental Pollution of the Committee on Environment and Public Works, Senate, Ninety-Sixth Congress, First Session* (Washington, DC: US Government Printing Office, 1979), 27, 29, 175. See also Edward Cowan, "Economic Advisers' New Role:

A Look at Performance," *NYT*, May 10, 1979, D1; Si Lazarus to Regulatory Process Bill File, "Meeting with Karl Braithwaite and Leon Billings," February 16, 1979, JC-CEA Collection, Charles L. Schultze's Subject Files, box 73, folder 1; and Leon G. Billings, "Cost Benefit Analysis," February 3, 1975, in Edmund S. Muskie Archives and Special Collections Library, Bates College, Lewiston, ME, Edmund S. Muskie Papers, 1826–2005, Series V: Subseries C, box 74, folder 10.

38. Margot Hornblower, "Environmentalists on Hill Confronting Economizers," *WP*, February 26, 1979, A2; and "Remarks of Senator Edmund S. Muskie," University of Michigan, February 14, 1979, JC-CEA Collection, Charles L. Schultze's Subject Files, box 73, folder 1. See also Edmund S. Muskie, "Regulation," week of April 23, 1979, JC-CEA Collection, Charles L. Schultze's Subject Files, box 73, folder 1; Hornblower, "Muskie Criticizes White House"; Edmund Muskie to Charles Schultze, January 17, 1979, http://www.thecre .com/pdf/CarterSenMuskieLet011779.PDF; and, in JC-CEA Collection, Charles L. Schultze Briefing Book Files, box 130, folder [2]: Edmund Muskie to Douglas M. Costle, March 26, 1979, and Edmund S. Muskie to Charles L. Schultze, March 12, 1979. For discussion of desirable procedures for executive branch involvement in rule making, see, in JC-CEA Collection, Charles L. Schultze's Subject Files, box 74 (Regulation: Surface Coal Mining [2]): William Nordhaus to Joan Davenport, December 6, 1978; John M. Harmon to Nina Cornell and Simon Lazarus, "Proposed Procedure for Reviewing the Economic Impact of Major Regulations," n.d. For the OMB general counsel's analysis of executive office involvement in agency rule-making, see William M. Nichols to the Deputy Director, "EOP Involvement in Agency Rulemaking," February 1, 1979, http://www.thecre.com/pdf/Carter_OMBGenCounselMemo020179 .PDF. For the Office of Legal Counsel's guidance and approval of executive office participation in the Office of Surface Mining's regulation development, see Larry A. Hammond to Cecil D. Andrus, "Consultation with Council of Economic Advisors Concerning Rulemaking under Surface Mining Control and Reclamation Act," JC-CEA Collection, Charles L. Schultze Briefing Book Files, box 130, folder [4]. For GAO's earlier assessment of economic agencies' involvement in agency rule-making, see Elmer B. Staats to Paul G. Rogers, October 4, 1978, http://www.thecre.com/pdf/Carter_GAOLet100478.PDF. See also Paul R. Verkuil, "Jawboning Administrative Agencies: Ex Parte Contacts by the White House," *Columbia Law Review* 80 (1980): 943–89.

39. Hobart Rowen, "The President's New Priorities," *WP*, November 30, 1978, A15; President's Reorganization Project, "Reorganization and Management Strategy 1979," November 3, 1978, McIntyre Collection, box 35 (Memoranda to James T. McIntyre from OMB Staff and Others, [2/9/78-9/10/79]); and James T. McIntyre Jr., "Remarks before the Business Council, Hot Springs, Virginia," October 13, 1978, McIntyre Collection, box 8, folder "McIntyre, Jim—Remarks, 10/13/78–10/28/78." And, in Michael Pertschuk Papers, Manuscript Division, Library of Congress, Washington, DC, Part I, box 76, folder 4: Jimmy Carter to Michael Pertschuk, October 3, 1978; Mike Pertschuk to

File, October 11, 1978; and Barbara Blum to Stu Eizenstat, Jim McIntyre, and Charlie Schultze, October 19, 1978.

40. Ward Sinclair, "Environmentalists Warn Carter of Backlash over Tellico Dam," *WP*, September 27, 1979, A5; Margot Hornblower, "Environment Panel Choice Is Blocked," *WP*, October 20, 1977, 4; John Yemma, "Environmentalists May Forsake Carter in 1980," *Christian Science Monitor*, September 28, 1979, 3; Richard J. Cattani, "If Not Carter, Who Can Environmentalists Back?" *Christian Science Monitor*, December 28, 1979, 4; Philip Shabecoff, "Carter, at Meeting with Environmental Leaders, Asks Their Support," *NYT*, November 8, 1979, 30; and McGrory, "Nader Splits with Carter on N-Power." For the Tellico Dam story, see Zygmunt J. B. Plater, *The Snail Darter and the Dam: How Pork-Barrel Politics Endangered a Little Fish and Killed a River* (New Haven, CT: Yale University Press, 2013).

41. David S. Broder, "Nader Says Time Nears for New Political Party," *WP*, May 8, 1979, A2; and Rogers Worthington, "Nader Still the Watchdog to Watch," *Chicago Tribune*, August 22, 1979, A1.

42. Stuart Eizenstat interview with Joan Claybrook, June 3, 1991. For an account of the struggle for the consumer agency, see Lizabeth Cohen, *Consumers' Republic*, 361–63; Joseph Lelyveld, "Nader Undaunted by Setbacks to Consumer Drive in the Congress, Press, Universities and White House," *NYT*, November 24, 1975, 73; Larry Kramer and John M. Berry, "Ralph Nader Assesses Consumer Movement's Future," *WP*, August 5, 1979, F1; and Eleanor Randolph, "Carter Chooses Prominent Capital Lawyer as Counsel," *LAT*, August 18, 1979, 1.

43. Worthington, "Nader Still the Watchdog to Watch"; and Martha Shirk, "Commoner on Campaign Trail," *St. Louis Post-Dispatch*, February 22, 1980, 3B.

44. For Commoner's larger story, see Michael Egan, *Barry Commoner and the Science of Survival: The Remaking of American Environmentalism* (Cambridge, MA: MIT Press, 2007). See also Worthington, "Nader Still the Watchdog to Watch"; Ernest Furgurson, "Kennedy, Anderson, Carter 1-2-3 in Grading on Environmental Issues," *Baltimore Sun*, May 10, 1980, A5; Philip Shabecoff, "Major Environment Leaders Back Carter Re-election Bid," *NYT*, September 28, 1980, 36; B. Drummond Ayres Jr., "Liberal Group Announces New Party and Plan for Presidential Race," *NYT*, August 2, 1979, D17; and Robert Benjamin, "Commoner Carries Flag of New Party," *Chicago Tribune*, October 8, 1980, 1. For Nader and Commoner as the two primary candidates considered by the Citizens Party, see Stanley Weiss, "The Shocking Campaign Ad That Put a Third-Party Candidate on the Political Map," *Time*, December 2, 2016, https://time.com/4584919/barry-commoner-shocking-ad; Shirk, "Commoner on Campaign Trail"; Robert L. Turner, "A Third Party in the Ring," *Boston Globe*, January 29, 1980, 23; Robert Scheer, "Heading 'Fourth-Party' Campaign: Candidate Commoner Wants to Reorder U.S. Priorities," *LAT*, October 26, 1980, D1; "Third Party Hopes Time Is Right," *Hartford Courant*, October 12, 1980, B9; Philip Shabecoff, "Commoner Says Victory Is Not Object of His Drive," *NYT*, October 30, 1980, B19; and Joseph Pulitzer IV, "Citizens' Party Sets High Goal: 5 Percent of the Vote," *St. Louis Post-Dispatch*, November 2, 1980, 3B.

45. For Anderson, see, for example, John Harte, interview by the author, March 14, 2010; Jon Ward, *Camelot's End: Kennedy vs. Carter and the Fight That Broke the Democratic Party* (New York: Twelve, 2019); and Stuart Eizenstat interview with Joan Claybrook, June 3, 1991.

46. "Campaign Report: Nader Finds Carter Best of 3 on Consumer Issues," *NYT*, September 19, 1980, B4; "Barry Commoner Calls on Carter to Give Up Bid for Re-election," *NYT*, April 30, 1980, A24; "Nader Gives Carter a Nod," *Newsday*, September 19, 1980, 15; and Matthew Jeffrey, "Reagan or Carter? Wrong Questions for Blacks," *Philadelphia Tribune*, October 31, 1980, 9.

47. Gus Speth, Jane Yarn, and Bob Harris to President Jimmy Carter, "Major Environmental Accomplishments of Your Administration," December 15, 1980, in James Gustave Speth Papers, Manuscripts and Archives, Yale University Library, New Haven, CT, box 4, folder 5. For private praise of an "outstanding list of great accomplishments," see Brock Evans to Gus Speth, January 26, 1981, in Speth Papers, box 4, folder 10. See also "Carter-Appointed 'Outside Agitators' Mostly Happy with Their Records," *Baltimore Sun*, January 5, 1981, A10; and Caroline E. Mayer, "Nader's Empire Is 10 Years Old—and Showing Signs of Age," *Boston Globe*, September 19, 1981, 2.

Chapter 9: STALEMATE: THE 1980 ELECTION AND ITS LEGACY

1. Margot Hornblower, "Conservative Winds Reshaping Public Interest Law," *WP*, January 14, 1980, A3. James Moorman expressed similar sentiments in a 2012 interview: Environmental Law Institute, "James Moorman," YouTube, January 4, 2016, https://www.youtube.com/watch?time_continue=12&v=sad7dL8ISxY.

2. Karen Aptakin, ed., *Good Works: A Guide to Social Change Careers* (Washington, DC: Center for Study of Responsive Law, 1980), vii; and Joan Anzalone, ed., *Good Works: A Guide to Careers in Social Change*, 3rd ed. (New York: Dembner, 1985), ix–x.

3. Aptakin, *Good Works*; James T. Yenckel, "Careers: Guide to Good Works," *WP*, May 20, 1980, B5; Anzalone, *Good Works*, ix–x; and Charles A. Reich, *The Greening of America: How the Youth Revolution Is Trying to Make America Livable* (New York: Random House, 1970), 18.

4. "Nader Resigns as Chief of Public Citizen Inc," *NYT*, November 2, 1980, 75; Alan Morrison, email to the author, June 18, 2020.

5. Warren Weaver Jr., "Gardner Organizing a Lobby of Citizens," *NYT*, July 31, 1970, A1.

6. Mark J. Green, James M. Fallows, and David Zwick, *Who Runs Congress?* (Toronto: Bantam, 1972), 1.

7. For a recent discussion of the diverse political origins of the deregulation movement, see Eduardo Federico Canedo, "The Rise of the Deregulation Movement in Modern America, 1957–1980" (PhD diss., Columbia University, 2008). See also Richard H. K. Vietor, *Contrived Competition: Regulation and*

Deregulation in America (Cambridge, MA: Belknap Press of Harvard University Press, 1994); Judith Stein, *Pivotal Decade: How the United States Traded Factories for Finance in the Seventies* (New Haven, CT: Yale University Press, 2010), 124; Eileen Shanahan, "Reformer: Urging Business Change: Nader Interview," *NYT*, January 24, 1971, F1; Mark Green, ed., *The Monopoly Makers: Ralph Nader's Study Group Report on Regulation and Competition* (New York: Grossman, 1973), ix; Ted Kennedy, "1980 Democratic National Concession Address" (speech at the Democratic National Convention, Madison Square Garden, New York, August 12, 1980), American Rhetoric, https://www.americanrhetoric.com/speeches/tedkennedy1980dnc.htm; and Jimmy Carter, "White House Conference on Regulatory Reform Remarks at a Meeting of the Conference," January 11, 1980, TAPP.

8. Green et al., *Who Runs Congress?*, 250; and Ronald Reagan, "Announcement for Presidential Candidacy," November 20, 1975, Ronald Reagan Presidential Library & Museum, https://www.reaganlibrary.gov/archives/speech/ronald-reagan-announcement-presidential-candidacy. For the rightward turn against government and toward private and market-based solutions, see Daniel T. Rodgers, *Age of Fracture* (Cambridge, MA: Belknap Press of Harvard University Press, 2011); and Sean Wilentz, *The Age of Reagan: A History, 1974–2008* (New York: Harper, 2008).

9. Ronald Reagan, "Inaugural Address," January 20, 1981, TAPP.

10. Ronald Reagan, "Official Announcement" (Reagan for President, New York, November 13, 1979).

11. Donella H. Meadows, Dennis L. Meadows, Jørgen Randers, and William W. Behrens III, *The Limits to Growth: A Report for the Club of Rome's Project on the Predicament of Mankind* (New York: Universe Books, 1972); and Ronald Reagan, "Government & Business in the '80s," *WSJ*, January 9, 1981, 18.

12. C. Brant Short, *Ronald Reagan and the Public Lands: America's Conservation Debate, 1979–1984* (College Station: Texas A&M University Press, 1989), 41–46.

13. Jimmy Carter, "Comprehensive Environmental Response, Compensation, and Liability Act of 1980 Remarks on Signing H.R. 7020 into Law," December 11, 1980, TAPP; and Jimmy Carter, "Paperwork Reduction Act of 1980 Remarks on Signing H.R. 6410 into Law," December 11, 1980, TAPP.

14. Richard Nixon, "Remarks on Signing the National Environmental Policy Act of 1969," January 1, 1970, TAPP.

15. *Paperwork Reduction Act of 1980: Hearings before a Subcommittee of the Committee on Government Operations, Ninety-Sixth Congress, Second Session on H.R. 6410 . . . February 7, 21, and 28* (Washington, DC: US Government Printing Office, 1980), 96.

16. Carter, "Comprehensive Environmental Response"; Carter, "White House Conference on Regulatory Reform"; Carter, "Paperwork Reduction Act of 1980"; E. Stanly Godbold Jr., *Jimmy and Rosalynn Carter: The Georgia Years, 1924–1974* (Oxford: Oxford University Press, 2010), 189, 268. For Carter's enthusiasm for government reorganization, see Carl P. Leubsdorf, "Political

Problems Delay Bureaucratic Streamlining: Analysis," *Baltimore Sun*, February 4, 1979, A1; and Thomas Oliphant, "Reorganization: Carter's Newest Headache: Ending Bureaucracy Is Easier Said Than Done, He's Finding," *Boston Globe*, January 8, 1978, A3.

17. "Douglas M. Costle: Oral History Interview," interview conducted by Dr. Dennis Williams on August 4–5, 1996, US Environmental Protection Agency, EPA 202-K-01-002, January 2001, https://archive.epa.gov/epa/aboutepa/douglas-m-costle-oral-history-interview.html; and Charles Halvorson, "Deflated Dreams: The EPA's Bubble Policy and the Politics of Uncertainty in Regulatory Reform," *Business History Review* 93, no. 1 (2019): 25–49. For Carter administration assessments of the Reagan campaign's rhetoric on deregulation, see, in JC-CEA Collection, Charles L. Schultze's Subject Files, box 72: "Talking Points: Reagan Economic Announcement," September 9, 1980; Ronald Reagan, "A Strategy for Growth: The American Economy in the 1980s" (speech to the International Business Council, Chicago, September 9, 1980); and Charlie Schultze to Jimmy Carter, "Major Economic Themes for the Debate," October 23, 1980. See also James McIntyre, Interview, October 28–29, 1981, Jimmy Carter Presidency, Presidential Oral Histories, Miller Center, University of Virginia, Charlottesville, https://millercenter.org/the-presidency/presidential-oral-histories/james-mcintyre-oral-history.

18. Reagan, "Strategy for Growth"; Reagan, "Government & Business in the '80s"; Reagan, "Inaugural Address," January 20, 1981; David Stockman and Jack Kemp, "Memo to Reagan—'Avoiding an Economic Dunkirk,'" *NYT*, December 14, 1980, F19; and Peter Behr, "Reagan's Regulation Relief Beckons to Business like a Jellybean Jar," *WP*, February 8, 1981, A3.

19. Ronald Reagan, "Postponement of Pending Regulations" (memorandum to the cabinet), January 29, 1981, http://www.thecre.com/pdf/ReaganMemo.PDF; and Exec. Order No. 12291, 46 Fed. Reg. 13193, 3 C.F.R. 127 (1981). James Miller, who headed the Office of Information and Regulatory Affairs during Reagan's first year in office and then led OMB during Reagan's second term, recalled in a 2001 interview that he and C. Boyden Gray had pushed Executive Order 12291 through very quickly in the administration's first weeks, taking the regulatory agencies "completely by surprise," before their political appointees were fully established. The order was presented to agency general counsels as a finalized document already signed by the president. James Miller, Interview, November 4, 2001, Ronald Reagan Presidency, Presidential Oral Histories, Miller Center, University of Virginia, Charlottesville, https://millercenter.org/the-presidency/presidential-oral-histories/james-miller-oral-history.

20. For "next logical steps," and "completely different," see William Nordhaus, interview by the author, May 7, 2014. For "eviscerate . . . ," see Christopher DeMuth, interview by the author, November 19, 2012. To the OMB staff members actually trying to implement regulatory reform in the Reagan administration, some of whom had simply moved over from the Council on Wage and Price Stability, the heated rhetoric and political polarization were "endlessly infuriating," DeMuth said. For a related account of how the Reagan

administration's regulatory relief rhetoric "posed problems for the progress of benefit-cost analysis," see also Thomas Hopkins, interview by the author, January 5, 2015. See also "Douglas M. Costle, Oral History Interview." For a similar argument that Reagan's "antiregulation approach ... dissipated much of the political momentum for regulatory reform," see W. Kip Viscusi, "The Misspecified Agenda: The 1980s Reforms of Health, Safety and Environmental Regulation," in *American Economic Policy in the 1980s*, ed. Martin Feldstein (Chicago: University of Chicago Press, 1994), 453–504, 501; see also Susan Rose-Ackerman, *Rethinking the Progressive Agenda: The Reform of the American Regulatory State* (New York: Free Press, 1993), 9; Robert V. Percival, "Checks without Balance: Executive Office Oversight of the Environmental Protection Agency," *Law and Contemporary Problems* 54, no. 4 (October 1, 1991): 127–204, 174. Carter economic advisor George Eads called Reagan's abandoned relief effort a "long, expensive detour," in George C. Eads and Michael Fix, *Relief or Reform?: Reagan's Regulatory Dilemma* (Washington, DC: Urban Institute Press, 1984), 6, 11. Reagan economic advisor Murray Weidenbaum largely blamed the "strong language and public stands" of James Watt and Anne Gorsuch for arousing environmental opposition, but conceded that the concept of "regulatory relief" rather than "reform" may "have set the wrong tone." Murray L. Weidenbaum, "Regulatory Reform under the Reagan Administration," in *The Reagan Regulatory Strategy: An Assessment*, ed. George C. Eads and Michael Fix (Washington, DC: Urban Institute Press, 1984), 17–18. Efforts to pass regulatory reform legislation, for example, which would have explicitly extended regulatory analysis requirements to independent agencies, met strident opposition and failed to proceed. For recent continuing efforts to extend regulatory analysis requirements to independent regulatory agencies, see S.1173, "Independent Agency Regulatory Analysis Act of 2013," 113th Congress, 1st Session, June 18, 2013; and Administrative Conference of the United States, "Benefit-Cost Analysis at Independent Regulatory Agencies," Recommendation 2013-2, June 13, 2013, https://www.acus.gov/recommendation/benefit-cost-analysis-independent-regulatory-agencies. For the assertion that independent agencies should already be subject to regulatory review requirements, see Peter L. Strauss and Cass R. Sunstein, "The Role of the President and OMB in Informal Rulemaking," *Administrative Law Review* 38, no. 2 (April 1, 1986): 181–207.

21. Morton Rosenberg, *Presidential Control of Agency Rulemaking: An Analysis of Constitutional Issues That May Be Raised by Executive Order 12291* (Washington, DC: US Government Printing Office, 1981), https://www.google.com/books/edition/Presidential_Control_of_Agency_Rulemakin/PLG0xgEACAAJ?hl=en, 69–70, 73. For an attack on OMB's intrusion on EPA authority, drawing on the Dingell committee's oversight activities, see Jim Sibbison, "Whose Agency Is It, Anyway? How OMB Runs EPA," *Washington Monthly*, December 1985, 19*ff*; Felicity Barringer, "Keeping Track of Budgeteers: OMB Watch Monitors Government for the Monitors of Government," *WP*, December 21, 1984, A21; and Gary D. Bass, "Testimony before the Subcommittee on

Intergovernmental Relations on OMB's Regulatory Powers," in *Oversight of the Office of Management and Budget Regulatory Review and Planning Process: Hearing before the Subcommittee on Intergovernmental Relations of the Committee on Governmental Affairs, United States Senate, Ninety-Ninth Congress, Second Session, January 28, 1986* (Washington, DC: US Government Printing Office, 1986), 299.

22. Peter Behr and Merrill Brown, "1-Year Moratorium Recommended on New Regulations: A One-Year Moratorium Urged on New Regulation," *WP*, November 9, 1980, G1.

23. "#1 Mtg w/Pres. 1/15 - P.M.," 1981 budget meeting prep materials, Glenn Schleede Records, US National Archives and Records Administration, Washington, DC; and Joanne Omang, "Costle Says Successor Must Teach Reagan to Resist 'Pillage' Crowd," *WP*, December 14, 1980, A2.

24. "Seveso Disaster," *NYT*, August 19, 1976, 34; Donald V. Feliciano, "The U.S. Environmental Protection Agency: An Analysis of Its Controversies," Congressional Research Service, Report 83-114 ENR, June 1, 1983, 9; and Joanne Omang, "Denver Lawyer Reagan's Choice to Head EPA," *WP*, February 21, 1981, A4.

25. Russell E. Train, "The Destruction of the EPA," *WP*, February 2, 1982, A15; Stuart Auerbach, "Consumer Opposition Group Formed," *WP*, March 8, 1983, D7; and Robert SanGeorge, "Group to Watch Health-Safety Policy," March 7, 1983, UPI Archives, https://www.upi.com/Archives/1983/03/07/Group-to-watch-health-safety-policy/4654415861200.

26. Mountain States Legal Foundation, *Second Annual Report*, 1978–1979, James G. Watt Papers, Politics and Public Affairs Collections, American Heritage Center, University of Wyoming, Laramie, Accession 7667, box 7, folder 4; James G. Watt, Excerpts from Speech in Dallas, Texas, May 8, 1978, reprinted in *Briefing by the Secretary of the Interior: Oversight Hearing before the Committee on Interior and Insular Affairs, House of Representatives, Ninety-Seventh Congress, First Session, on Briefing by the Secretary of the Interior, Hearing Held in Washington, D.C., February 5, 1981* (Washington, DC: US Government Printing Office, 1981), 58–68; and Short, *Ronald Reagan and the Public Lands*, 52–53.

27. James G. Watt to Edwin Meese III, James A. Baker III, and David A Stockman, "1983 Budget Appeals," December 3, 1981, in James G. Watt Papers, Politics and Public Affairs Collections, American Heritage Center, University of Wyoming, Laramie, Accession 7667, box 10, folder 6; Short, *Ronald Reagan and the Public Lands*, 51; and Seth S. King, "Interior Secretary Says He Won't Try to Drop Any Park Lands Now," *NYT*, April 27, 1981, 1.

28. George Cameron Coggins and Doris K. Nagel, "'Nothing beside Remains': The Legal Legacy of James G. Watt's Tenure as Secretary of the Interior on Federal Land and Law Policy," *Boston College Environmental Affairs Law Review* 17, no. 3 (Spring 1990): 473–550.

29. Carolyn E. Mayer, "Nader's Empire Is 10 Years Old—and Showing Signs of Age," *Boston Globe*, September 19, 1981, 2.

30. Mark J. Green, *Winning Back America* (New York: Bantam, 1982), ix–xi.

31. Philip Shabecoff, "Environmentalists, Seeing Threat in White House Policy, Plan Fight," April 19, 1981, 1; Robert Gottlieb, *Forcing the Spring: The Transformation of the American Environmental Movement*, rev. and updated ed. (Washington, DC: Island Press, 2005), 167–75; and J. Michael McCloskey, *In the Thick of It: My Life in the Sierra Club* (Washington, DC: Island Press, 2005), 214.

32. "Consumerists Look to Cover Grass Roots," *WP*, January 11, 1981, L4; Gottlieb, *Forcing the Spring*; Shabecoff, "Environmentalists, Seeing Threat"; and James W. Moorman, "Attorney for the Environment, 1966–1981: Center for Law and Social Policy, Sierra Club Legal Defense Fund, Department of Justice Division of Lands and Natural Resources" (oral history conducted in 1984 by Ted Hudson), Sierra Club History Committee, 1994, 125.

33. Green, *Winning Back America*, 330–31.

34. Green, *Winning Back America*, 329–30.

35. Debra Whitefield, "Environmental Groups Refocus on Local Action," *LAT*, November 18, 1980, 1.

36. Mayer, "Nader's Empire Is 10 Years Old"; Ellen L. James, "Reaganism and Ralph Nader: Consumer Advocate Changes Tactics for Administration," *LAT*, July 17, 1981, G6; Peter H. Stone, "A Rejuvenated Nader Is Setting His Course for the 1990s," *Hartford Courant*, March 19, 1989, A1; Juan Williams, "Return from the Nadir," *WP*, May 23, 1982, SM6; and Hornblower, "Conservative Winds Reshaping." See also, for example, Paul Blustein and Toni Locy, "To Gadfly of the Right, Clinton Administration Is Unsafe at Any Speed," *WP*, November 17, 1996, A17; Steven M. Teles, *The Rise of the Conservative Legal Movement: The Battle for Control of the Law* (Princeton, NJ: Princeton University Press, 2010); and Joe Klein, "Ralph Nader: The Man in the Class Action Suit," *Rolling Stone*, November 20, 1975.

37. Philip Shabecoff, "Rita Lavelle Gets 6-Month Term and Is Fined $10,000 for Perjury," *NYT*, January 10, 1984, A1; and William P. Clark, Interview, August 17, 2003, Ronald Reagan Presidency, Presidential Oral Histories, Miller Center, University of Virginia, Charlottesville, https://millercenter.org/the-presidency/presidential-oral-histories/william-p-clark-oral-history. For a critical account of Reagan's first-term environmental policies, see Norman J. Vig and Michael E. Kraft, eds., *Environmental Policy in the 1980s: Reagan's New Agenda* (Washington, DC: CQ Press, 1984).

38. The urban historian Michael Katz articulated how he personally wrestled with this dilemma in his 2010 essay: Michael B. Katz, "Was Government the Solution or the Problem? The Role of the State in the History of American Social Policy," *Theory and Society* 39, no. 3/4 (May 1, 2010): 487–502.

Epilogue

1. Colin McEnroe, "First Couple Revisits Spirit of Yale Law '73," *Hartford Courant*, October 9, 1993, A1.

2. Laura G. Holland, "Invading the Ivory Tower: The History of Clinical Edu-

cation at Yale Law School," *Journal of Legal Education* 49, no. 4 (1999): 504–34; Stephen Wizner and Dennis Curtis, "Here's What We Do": Some Notes about Clinical Legal Education, *Cleveland State Law Review* 29, no. 4 (1980): 673–84; Laura Kalman, *Yale Law School and the Sixties: Revolt and Reverberations* (Chapel Hill: University of North Carolina Press, 2005); and Hillary Rodham, "Children under the Law," *Harvard Educational Review* 43, no. 4 (December 1973): 487–514. Hillary Rodham Clinton worked during the summer of 1970 for Marian Wright Edelman's Washington Research Project, which later evolved into the Children's Defense Fund.

3.   Jimmy Carter, "Alternative Approaches to Regulation: Memorandum from the President," June 13, 1980, TAPP.

4.   William J. Clinton, "Address before a Joint Session of Congress on Administration Goals," February 17, 1993, TAPP; and William J. Clinton, "Remarks Announcing the National Performance Review," March 3, 1993, TAPP.

5.   Clinton, "Remarks Announcing the National Performance Review"; and Al Gore, *From Red Tape to Results: Creating a Government That Works Better & Costs Less. Report of the National Performance Review* (Washington, DC: US Government Printing Office, 1993), 7.

6.   Gore, *From Red Tape to Results*, i, iv, 13, 18. Public interest advocates responded with skepticism to many of these initiatives. Instead of stopping White House review of agency regulations, as Nader and other critics hoped, Clinton's Office of Management and Budget restored Carter's more balanced approach to regulatory review. "The American people deserve a regulatory system that works for them, not against them," Clinton declared in a 1993 executive order that continued to require agencies to do extensive cost-benefit analysis of proposed regulations. White House, "Executive Order #12866: Regulatory Planning and Review," September 30, 1993, http://www.archives.gov/federal-register /executive-orders/pdf/12866.pdf. Clinton's executive order revoked Ronald Reagan's Executive Order #12291 and aimed to open the review process to greater public scrutiny and to "reaffirm the primacy of Federal agencies in the regulatory decision-making process." For a defense of Clinton's approach, see Elena Kagan, "Presidential Administration," *Harvard Law Review* 114, no. 8 (June 2001): 2245–85.

7.   Cindy Skrzycki, "Rule Reinvention: Wrenching Change or Minor Tinkering: A Clinton-Gore Report Card," *WP*, September 20, 1996, F1; "For a Greater Good, EPA Lets Companies Break the Rules," *Christian Science Monitor*, August 16, 1996, 4; Gary Lee, "Regulatory Reform Effort Helps Industry Hit Targets: EPA," *WP*, April 4, 1996, A29; Cindy Skrzycki, "The Perils of Reinventing: Critics See a Playground for Polluters in EPA's XL Plan," *WP*, January 24, 1997, D1; and Cindy Skrzycki, "Putting a Little Formality behind EPA's Free-Style Rulemaking," *WP*, November 7, 1997, D1. In 1997, Browner folded these programs into a new EPA "Office of Reinvention." "Browner Announces New EPA Offices to Support Children's Health, Regulatory Reinvention and Right to Know," Environmental Protection Agency, February 27, 1997, https:// archive.epa.gov/epa/aboutepa/browner-announces-new-epa-offices-support

-childrens-health-regulatory-reinvention-and-right.html. See also "Reinventing Environmental Protection—EPA's Approach," Environmental Protection Agency, Office of Reinvention, EPA100F-98-010, May 1998. For a recent call to expand flexibility, collaboration, and performance-based regulation, see Daniel J. Fiorino, *The New Environmental Regulation* (Cambridge: MIT Press, 2006); "Government Performance Results Act of 1993," Office of Management and Budget, https://obamawhitehouse.archives.gov/omb/mgmt-gpra /gplaw2m; Gore, *From Red Tape to Results*, 73; Cindy Skrzycki, "Slowing the Flow of Federal Rules: New Conservative Climate Chills Agencies' Activism," *WP*, February 18, 1996, A1; and Michael B. Katz, "Was Government the Solution or the Problem? The Role of the State in the History of American Social Policy," *Theory and Society* 39, no. 3/4 (May 1, 2010): 487–502.

8.   William J. Clinton, "Address before a Joint Session of the Congress on the State of the Union," January 23, 1996, TAPP.

9.   Tish Durkin, "The Un-candidate: Ralph Nader May Be the Presidential Nominee for the Green Party, but He's Not a Member of the Party, Won't Take Contributions and Has No Campaign Manager. Just What Is He Doing?" *NYT Magazine*, October 20, 1996, 48; Ralph Nader and Theodore Jacobs, "Do Third Parties Have a Chance? Ballot Access and Minority Parties," *Harvard Law Record* 27, no. 3 (October 9, 1958): 1; B. Drummond Ayres Jr., "Ralph Nader Is Nominated for President, but Vows He Will Ignore His Party's Platform," *NYT*, August 20, 1996, A16; and "Nader Raps President on Safety," *WP*, September 22, 1996, A18.

10. *An Unreasonable Man*, directed by Henriette Mantel and Steve Skrovan (IFC Films, 2006); and PBS *NewsHour*, "Newsmaker: Ralph Nader," Public Broadcasting Service, June 30, 2000.

11. "Nader Assails Major Parties," CBS News, April 6, 2000, https://www .cbsnews.com/news/nader-assails-major-parties. The "Tweedledum and Tweedledee" line had been used by Nader since the 1970s, and his father used it in an op-ed in the *Hartford Courant* on the political parties in 1978. Nathra Nader, "People, Not Parties, Rule a Democracy," *Hartford Courant*, July 23, 1978, 39A. "My father used to say, 'What the Democrats say about the Republicans is true. And what the Republicans say about the Democrats is true.'" "Laura Nader: A Life of Teaching, Investigation, Scholarship and Scope," interview transcript, 2013, Regional Oral History Office, Bancroft Library, University of California, Berkeley (Regents of the University of California, 2014), 101; and Dana Calvo, "Nader Refuses to Cease Fire on Gore, Bush," *LAT*, October 21, 2000, B1. See also "Mr. Nader's Electoral Mischief," *NYT*, October 26, 2000, A34; Robert F. Kennedy, "Nader's Threat to the Environment," *NYT*, August 10, 2000, A21; and "Mr. Nader's Misguided Crusade," *NYT*, June 30, 2000, A24. Nader's campaign later claimed he didn't mean that Bush was better than Gore, but in other statements Nader had said that James Watt energized the environmental movement. Melinda Henneberger, "Nader Sees a Bright Side to a Bush Victory," *NYT*, November 1, 2000, A29.

12. Calvo, "Nader Refuses to Cease Fire"; and Wes Boyd to Friend of MoveOn,

"Nader Ushers in Bush Presidency," October 27, 2000, in People for the American Way Papers, Manuscript Division, Library of Congress, Washington, DC, box 178, folder 17.

13. Steven Greenhouse, "Nader, in Harlem, Attacks Gore and Bush with Gusto," *NYT*, November 7, 2000, A24. See also Alexander Lane, "Nader Almost Said Gore=Bush, but Not Quite," Politifact, June 30, 2008, http://www.politifact .com/truth-o-meter/statements/2008/jun/30/ralph-nader/nader-almost-said -gore-bush-but-not-quite/#; and Lenora Todaro, "Ralph Nader Lashes Back," *Village Voice*, December 19, 2000, 29.

14. James Fallows, "I Love You, Ralph (Nader), But . . . ," *Atlantic*, September 19, 2011,   http://www.theatlantic.com/politics/archive/2011/09/i-love-you-ralph -nader-but/245349.

Index

later careers, 89–90
Nader as individual crusader and, 164
Nader's management style and, 88–89
popularity of, 87–88
on regulatory capture, 86–87
reports by, 87
water pollution campaign, 83–86
National Air Pollution Control Administration, 78
National Association of Manufacturers, 173
National Audubon Society, 43, 65, 125, 179
National Council on Philanthropy, 129–30
National Environmental Policy Act (NEPA) (1970), 103–4, 124, 152, 170
National Federation of Independent Business, 173
National Highway and Transportation Safety Administration, 136, 139
National Highway Traffic Safety Administration (NHTSA), 31
National Industrial Recovery Act, 94
National Labor Relations Act (1935), 8
National Performance Review, 187–88
National Safety Council, 28
National Welfare Rights Organization, 107
Natural Gas Pipeline Safety Act (1968), 60
Natural Resources Defense Council (NRDC)
attitudes toward government, 47, 91–92
Carter administration and, 137, 147, 148
conservative legal organizations and, 132
elite demographics and, 47
elite establishment and, 53–54
energy policy and, 147, 148
Ford Foundation funding for, 45, 53–54
founding of, 44–45, 91, 97–98
institutionalization of, 123, 127
membership program, 67–68, 105
New Deal trust in government agencies and, 99
Nixon administration attacks on, 55
organizational entrepreneurs and, 56
Reagan administration and, 180
regulatory reform and, 154
Nelson, Gaylord, 79
Neustadt, Richard, 52
New Deal, 4–6, 94, 99, 101, 151
See also New Deal Order
New Deal Order
as balance of countervailing powers, 7–8, 41
Clintons on, 186
flaws of, xiii, xiv, xv–xvii, xviii
growth of, 3–4
infrastructure and, 8–9, 9, 102–3, 144

infrastructure in, 8–9, 144
institutional control and, 12–13
institutional corruption and, 59–60, 167
Kennedy administration and, 3
New Deal origins of, 4–6
New Left challenge to, 13
power of, 14
public interest exclusion from, 8, 11, 41–42, 46, 76
public interest movement attacks on, xiv–xv, xvi, 165–66
Reagan Revolution as end of, 165
science and technology in, xv, 14, 16–17
urban redevelopment in, 15, 17
See also regulatory agencies
New Left, 13
1980 presidential election, 158–60
1996 presidential election, 189, 190
Nixon, Richard, and administration
Burger and, 95
Cox and, 38
election of, 73, 118, 139
environmental issues and, 84, 85, 99–100, 170
Nader's attacks on, 79, 114
Public Citizen Litigation Group lawsuit against, 119
public interest law and, 54–55
Watergate scandal and, 120, 135
Nixon, Tricia, 38
nongovernmental organizations (NGOs), 13
Nonprofit Economy (Weisbrod), 67
nonprofit sector
growth of, xiii, 65–68, 114
lobbying limitations on, 124
Reagan administration and, 178
NRDC. See Natural Resources Defense Council
nuclear power, 148–49

Oakes, John B., 91
Obama, Barack, and administration, xvii
Occupational Safety and Health Act (1970), 60
Occupational Safety and Health Administration (OSHA), 129, 171
Office of Management and Budget (OMB), 136, 150, 153, 170, 173, 174, 175
ombudsman proposals, 26–27, 126, 133, 167
OMB Watch, 174
Operation Phoenix, 50

Pacific Legal Foundation, 132
Paperwork Reduction Act (1980), 170, 171, 172